P9-AOY-067

SMITH'S REVIEW SERIES

Wills, Trusts, Probate, Administration and the Fiduciary
THIRD EDITION

LIZABETH A. MOODY
Professor of Law
Cleveland-Marshall
College of Law,
Cleveland State University,
Member of Ohio,
Connecticut and
U.S. Supreme Court Bars

HOWARD M. ROSSEN
Director, Ohio Bar Review and
Writing Seminar
Member of Ohio,
District of Columbia,
Florida, Pennsylvania and
U.S. Supreme Court Bars

WILTON S. SOGG
Adjunct Professor of Law,
Cleveland-Marshall
College of Law,
Cleveland State University
Lecturer on Law,
Harvard Law School
Member of Ohio,
District of Columbia,
Florida, U.S. Tax Court and
U.S. Supreme Court Bars

SMITH'S REVIEW SERIES

Wills, Trusts, Probate, Administration and the Fiduciary
Third Edition

for Law School, Bar and College Examinations, Trust Officers and Life Underwriters

WEST PUBLISHING COMPANY
St. Paul, Minnesota © 1982

Copyright © 1958, 1973 by **WEST PUBLISHING COMPANY**

Copyright © 1982 By **WEST PUBLISHING COMPANY**

50 W. Kellogg Boulevard
P.O. Box 3526
St. Paul, Minnesota 55165

All Rights Reserved.

Printed in The United States of America.

Library of Congress Cataloging in Publication Data

Moody, Lizabeth R.
    Will, trust, probate, administration, and the fiduciary.

    (Smith's review series)
    Combines the revised and updated texts of Smith's review of trusts and Smith's review of wills and administration.
        Includes index.
        1. Inheritance and succession—United States—Examinations, questions, etc. 2. Trust and trustees—United States—Examinations, questions, etc. I. Rossen, Howard M., 1936–   . II. Sogg, Wilton S., 1935–   . III. Smith, Chester Howard, 1893–1964.
    IV. Title. V. Series.
    KF753.Z9M62   1982   346.7305'2   81-21873
    ISBN 0-314-61793-0   347.30652   AACR2

1st Reprint—1983

For Alan Paul Buchmann

PREFACE

This Review constitutes a newly revised and updated edition of this volume in the Smith's Review Series. In this Third Edition the authors have attempted not only to include all important developments in these subject areas, but also to reflect the most current approach to the study of the subject matter, as well as the important case law in the field. This Review has also been designed as a quick reference for the probate attorney, trust officer and life underwriter.

To these ends, much of the text has been restructured and the case material completely revised. Chapter XIII, Life Cycle of Estate Administration, through the use of both a chart and text provides the reader with an overview of the administration of estates. Special attention has been given to the advent of the Uniform Probate Code and its likely effect on the development of the law in the near future. A Table of Statutory References keys in text citations to the Uniform Probate Code, the Restatement of Trusts, Second, and other statutory materials.

The authors have made use of the CAVEAT and NOTE throughout, to alert the reader to important areas of change and development.

Apart from the cases cited, the citations in this Review are as follows: "Atkinson" refers to Thomas E. Atkinson, Handbook of the Law of Wills, Second Edition, 1953 by West Publishing Co.; "Bogert" refers to George G. Bogert and George T. Bogert, Handbook of the Law of Trusts Fifth Edition, 1973 by West Publishing Co.; "Clark" refers to Elias Clark, Cases and Materials on Gratuitous Transfers, Second Edition, 1977 by West Publishing Co.; "Dukeminer" refers to Jesse Dukeminer and Stanley M. Johnson, Family Wealth Transactions: Wills, Trusts and Estates, Second Edition, 1978, by Little Brown and Co. "Palmer" refers to George E. Palmer, Cases and Materials on Trusts and Succession, Second Edition, 1968, by the Foundation Press; "Restatement of Conflict of Laws" refers to Restatement of the Law Second, Conflict of Laws 2d, as Adopted and Promulgated by the American Law Institute 1969 and published by American Law Institute Publishers, 1971; "Restatement of Property" refers to Restatement of the Law Second, Property, Tentative Draft No. 2, Submitted by the Council to the Members of the American Law Institute 1979 and published by American Law Institute Publishers, 1979; "Rest." refers to Restatement of the Law Second, Trusts 2d, As Adopted and Promulgated by the American Law Institute 1957 and published by American Law Institute Publishers, 1959; "Rheinstein" refers to Max Rheinstein and Mary Ann Glendon, The Law of Decedents' Estates, 1971, by The Foundation Press; "Ritchie" refers to John Ritchie,

Neill H. Alford Jr. and Richard W. Effland, Cases and Materials on Decedents' Estates and Trusts, Fifth Edition, 1977, by The Foundation Press; "Scoles" refers to Eugene F. Scoles and Edward C. Halbach Jr., Problems and Materials on Decedents'; Estates and Trusts, Second Edition, 1973 by Little Brown and Co.; "Scott" refers to Austin Wakeman Scott, Abridgement of the Law of Trusts, 1960 by Little Brown and Co.; "Simes" refers to Lewis M. Simes, Handbook of the Law of Future Interests, Second Edition, 1966 by West Publishing Co.; "UPC" refers to Uniform Probate Code approved by the National Conference of Commissioners on Uniform State Laws and the American Bar Association, 1969, as Amended 1975, Official Text with comments, by West Publishing Co.

This volume would not be complete without thanks to Geraldine Hall Urbanic, Research Assistant at Cleveland State College of Law for her support and assistance in the preparation of these materials on probate administration and the fiduciary.

Lizabeth A. Moody
Howard M. Rossen
Wilton A. Sogg

Cleveland, Ohio
March, 1982

SUMMARY
OF CONTENTS

TABLE OF CONTENTS

STUDY OUTLINE

I.   **FREEDOM OF TESTATION AND INTESTATE SUCCESSION**

    A.   Death transfers are a property right based on
        1.   natural rights, or
        2.   a right granted by the state

    B.   Special rules govern estates depending on whether one dies
        1.   intestate (without leaving a will)
        2.   testate (leaving a valid will)

    C.   Early English law distinguished between the rules for
        1.   real property which passed directly to the heir under the doctrine of primogeniture
        2.   personal property which went to the decedent's personal representative for administration and distribution to the next of kin

    D.   Modern laws have abolished early English distinctions but continue to use the nomenclature.

    E.   Statutes of descent and distribution determine the order in which person succeed to an intestate estate by
        1.   seeking to carry out the distribution which most intestates would have provided had they made wills
        2.   establishing an order of preference among named relatives of the deceased or if none to the next of kin, determined by the blood relationship (consanguinity) to the deceased by either
            a.   the civil law method counting the generations from the decedent up to the common ancestor and down to the claimant, or
            b.   the common law method, counting the generations to the common ancestor and down to the claimant taking only the larger figure of the steps to the ancestor

    F.   Special relationships which may affect the right to inherit are
        1.   half-bloods who may:
            a.   inherit equally with whole bloods
            b.   be excluded where there are whole bloods
            c.   inherit equally except with respect to ancestral property
        2.
            a.   at common law had no right to inherit from either parent
            b.   under modern law are treated as the child of the mother
            c.   generally are not treated as a child of the father unless legitimated either by
                i.   the subsequent marriage of the parents
               ii.   the subsequent marriage and acknowledgment by the father, or
              iii.   adjudication of paternity before the father's death
            d.   may be denied equal protection under the U.S. constitution in cases where discrimination is based on illegitimacy

      3. adopted children who
        a. at common law have no right to inherit
        b. under modern law generally inherit from and through the adoptive parents
        c. under some statutes may inherit from both the natural and adoptive parents

G. Various approaches are taken to the problem of which relations inherit from and through the adopted child:
    1. only the natural relatives inherit
    2. only adoptive relatives inherit
    3. both natural and adoptive relatives share equally; or
    4. adoptive relatives take property which came from the adoptive family with natural relatives taking the remainder

H. Some jurisdictions permit a person to designate another person as his heir at law in the event of his death

I. Gifts by the deceased prior to his death to a prospective heir may be intended as
    1. a loan,
    2. an absolute gift, or
    3. an advancement, which is a gift made by an intestate during his life to certain designated relatives with the intent that it be applied against any share to which such person may be entitled in the intestate's estate

J. Qualifications which have developed with respect to the right to inherit include
    1. being alive or in embryo at the time of intestate's death
    2. presumptions with respect to
        a. simultaneous death, or
        b. failure to survive for a fixed period after decedent's death

K. Disqualifications which may bar persons from inheriting from the intestate include
    1. fraud, undue influence or duress practiced on decedent
    2. abandonment of a child or spouse
    3. adultery of a spouse
    4. status as a non-resident alien

II. PROTECTION OF THE FAMILY

A. Legal issues concerning protection of the spouse of a decedent concern
    1. the portion of the decedent's estate to which a surviving spouse is entitled
    2. the extent to which such rights may be defeated by lifetime transfers, and
    3. the extent to which a spouse may take priority over creditor's claims

B. A surviving spouse may be protected against disinheritance by
    1. community property statutes which generally treat husband and wife as co-owners of property acquired by either during the marriage so that on death the survivor is entitled to one-half the property
    2. dower (or curtesy) which gives a fixed interest to one spouse in the land owned during the marriage; and/or
    3. an elective share which allows a surviving spouse to elect a specified share or the provision made in the deceased's will

C. Intervivos transfers of property by one spouse during marriage may deprive the surviving spouse of statutory protections depending upon whether
   1. the transfer was made with intent to defeat the election
   2. the transfer was real or illusury, or
   3. the spouse has waived or released statutory rights by an agreement which is fair and made with full disclosure of relevant facts

D. Children may be completely disinherited by their parents except where
   1. pretermitted heir provisions give children born or adopted after the execution of a will an intestate share
   2. there is a legal duty upon the deceased parent to support a minor child

E. Protections for the family of a deceased include
   1. homestead
   2. family allowance
   3. exemption of certain property from creditor's claims against the estates
   4. mortmain statutes which limit gifts to charity by a deceased by
      a. limiting the amount of the gift to a certain proportion of the estate
      b. invalidating gifts made within a specified period preceding death, *e.g.* within six months

III. EXECUTION AND VALIDITY OF WILLS

A. A will is a legal declaration of intention to dispose of property after death
   1. at common law
      a. personal property was disposed of by a testament
      b. real property was disposed of by a will
   2. Modern usage has eliminated distinctions between real and personal property

B. The right to make a will is statutory; there was no common law right to make a will
   1. State statutes derive from the English statutes of wills and the Statute of Frauds
   2. There is no will without compliance with the statute

C. A person who dies leaving a valid will dies testate and is called a testator

D. Persons who administer the estate include
   1. a personal representative authorized by the court,
   2. an executor named in the will
   3. an administrator authorized by the court for the estate of an intestate

E. A valid will requires three essential elements
   1. a competent testator of sound mind and the requisite age
   2. physical compliance with the statute, and
   3. intent that the instrument be a will

F. Sound mind means that a testator must be able to understand
   1. the nature and extent of his property
   2. the natural objects of his bounty
   3. the nature of making a will and
   4. the foregoing elements in relation to each other

G. A testator may not be of sound mind if he suffers from
1. mental deficiency, or
2. mental derangement

H. A will is invalid if executed under
1. undue influence which is the substitution of another's will for that of the testator, or
2. fraud
   a. in the execution, or
   b. in the inducement

I. Mistake in the execution of a will
1. as to the nature of the document voids the will
2. as to legal effect of the language does not void the will
3. in omitting a provision has no effect on the will
4. in including a provision may be omitted if
   a. the deletion will not substantially alter the rest of the will
   b. the intention of the testator will be best effectuated thereby

J. Parol evidence
1. may be admitted to explain an ambiguity in a will
2. may not be used to alter the terms of a will

K. Classification of will based on the form of execution include
1. holygraphic wills completely written and signed in the handwriting of the testator
2. nuncupative wills made orally
   a. during the last illness, or
   b. to witnesses who the testator requests to witness
3. written and witnessed will subject to statutory requirements relating to
   a. writing
   b. signing
   c. publication
   d. presence
   e. witnessing or attestation

L. Witnesses are required to be credible or competent to testify
1. at common law beneficiaries were not competent to testify
2. modern law looks to competency under the rules of evidence at the time the will is executed
3. many states have purging statutes which eliminate the beneficial interest so the witness can testify

M. A joint will is written on a single piece of paper and executed by two testators as the wills of both

N. Mutual wills have reciprocal provisions and may include contracts not to revoke

O. Contracts to bequeath or devise property must be tested by contract law and not by enjoining the probate of the last will

P. A will may involve another document or action
1. integration means the determination of the papers which constitute the will
2. incorporation by reference occurs when the testator has by a provision in his will included other existing material such as a book or record which
   a. must be in existence at the time of making the will
   b. is referred to by the will as in existence
   c. is intended to be incorporated, and
   d. is identical to the material described in the will
3. a will may dispose of property by reference to the occurrence of another act of independent legal significance

4. a testamentary gift to a trust in existence at the time of the testator's death is valid if
   a. incorporated by reference, or
   b. the creation of the trust is held to be an act of independent significance

IV. **REVOCATION, REVIVAL AND CONSTRUCTION OF WILLS**

A. Revocation may be effected
   1. by subsequent instrument which may be
      a. a later will,
      b. a codicil, or
      c. a revocatory instrument which disposes of no property
   2. by physical act designated by statute, or
   3. by operation of law where there is a change in the family situation or property holdings of the testator
B. Conditional revocation occurs where a revocation is expressly conditional
C. Dependent relative revocation occurs where a testator revokes his will and the revocation is included by a mistake of law or fact resulting in a conditional revocation.
D. Lost wills
   1. last known to be in the testator's possession are presumed to be revoked
   2. last known to be in the possession of a third person are presumed unrevoked
E. Codicils operate to make a specific change in a will without changing the will entirely
F. Republication describes
   1. the validating of an invalid will, and
   2. the reaffirmation of an earlier will by a later or codicil
G. Revival occurs by
   1. re-execution
   2. re-acknowledgment, or
   3. execution of a codicil
H. Dispositions under a will are classified as
   1. specific
   2. demonstrative
   3. general, or
   4. residuary
I. Ademption invalidates gifts
   1. by extinction where the gift property either is no longer in the estate or has been substantially changed in character
   2. by satisfaction where the testator had already given the legatee all or part of his share under the will
J. Abatement determines the order of distribution of property absent any expressed intent by the testator; the usual order is
   1. intestate property
   2. residuary gifts
   3. general bequests
   4. demonstrative bequests
   5. specific bequests and devises
K. If the beneficiary predeceases the testator
   1. the gift will lapse, or
   2. an anti-lapse statute may apply
L. Rules of construction apply only when the intent of the testator is unclear.

V. TRUSTS—INTRODUCTION AND ANALYSIS

A. Analysis of trust problems involves
1. classifying the trust on the basis of intent
   a. express
   b. implied
2. determining if any rule of law will operate to make the trust invalid or unenforceable
3. examining the relationship of the various parties
   a. to each other, and
   b. to the trust property
4. identifying the intent of the creator as to the rights and duties of each party
5. determining the effect of the invalidity of any interest on the trust property
6. considering the effect of a breach of trust
7. determining the ability of the parties to change or modify the intent of the creator
B. Definitions relating to trust law include
1. A trust is a fiduciary relationship wherein one or more persons hold property for the benefit of another person
2. A trust involves the concept of split title
   a. legal title in the trustee
   b. equitable title in the beneficiary
3. A trust is
   a. a means of holding and disposing of property
   b. a mode of reasoning on which to fashion a remedy against persons who are holding title to property
C. Trust elements include
1. a settlor
2. trust property (corpus, res or subject matter)
3. a trustee
4. a beneficiary (cestui que trust), and
5. terms of the trust
   a. duties and powers of the trustee
   b. rights of the beneficiary
D. Trusts are to be distinguished from other relationships including
1. bailment
2. executorship and administratorship
3. guardianship
4. agency
5. debt
6. lien and pledge
7. mortgage
8. third party beneficiary contract
9. equitable charge
10. corporate directorship

VI. BASICS OF TRUSTS

A. Trusts are classified on the basis of
1. the intent manifested by the creator
   a. express
      i. private
      ii. charitable

          b.   implied
              i.   resulting
             ii.   constructive
    2.   the duties imposed upon the trustee:
          a.   active trusts in which the trustee has some affirmative duty to perform
          b.   passive units in which the trustee holds title without any other duty with respect to the trust res

B.   The intention to create an express trust may be manifested by words, conduct or both
    1.   precatory words used by the settlor create a trust only when the settlor intended to impose enforceable obligations
          a.   under the earlier view this intent could be expressed through mere statement of a desire
          b.   under the modern view, this intent exists only when the entire language of the instrument, considered in the light of the situation of the settlor, describes clearly every element required for a trust
    2.   deposits made in a bank by one person "in trust" for another may create
          a.   a revocable trust called a tentative or totten trust which
              i.   may be revoked by
                  A.   withdrawal of the deposit prior to the depositor's death
                  B.   death of the beneficiary prior to the death of the depositor, or
                  C.   any manifestation of intention to revoke by the depositor
              ii.   are subject to the rights of
                  A.   the depositor's creditors
                  B.   the surviving spouse
          b.   an irrevocable trust
          c.   no trust
    3.   an intention to create a trust in the future does not create a trust
    4.   a trust is invalid as illusory where the settlor, either by the terms of the trust or by dealing with the trust property manifests no intention to relinquish any rights in the trust property
          a.   the mere reservation of income for life or income plus a right to revoke will not render a trust illusory
          b.   a reservation of income plus the right to revoke and other retained rights may render a trust illusory depending upon the degree of control retained and exercised by the settlor.

C.   The subject matter of the trust must be
    1.   in existence
    2.   definite or definitely ascertainable
    3.   voluntarily transferable by the settlor, and
    4.   may consist of
          a.   equitable interests
          b.   contingent interests
          c.   a policy of insurance on the life of the settlor by which
              i.   the policy is payable to a designated person as trustee
             ii.   the policy is payable to a designated beneficiary

who in turn agrees to hold the proceeds in trust

      iii.   the policy is assigned to a third person as trustee

D.   The trustee may be a person who has the capacity to sue; however, limitations exist with respect to the ability of certain persons to be trustees including

   1.   infants

   2.   insane persons

   3.   non-residents of the state

   4.   aliens

   5.   corporations

   6.   governmental bodies

   7.   partnerships

   8.   a trust will not fail for want of a trustee; a successor trustee will be appointed

      a.   if the trustee dies, resigns or fails to qualify

      b.   unless the creator conditioned the creation on the acceptance of a particular person

   9.   a court may remove a trustee in its discretion

E.   settlors and beneficiaries may also be trustees except that the sole beneficiary cannot be the sole trustee

F.   a private trust must have a named or ascertainable beneficiary who may be

   1.   a natural person

   2.   a corporation if it is empowered to take title to property

   3.   an alien

   4.   a class of persons who are definite or definitely ascertainable

   5.   a partnership

   6.   an unborn child

      a.   if there is another beneficiary in existence at the time of creating the trust who can enforce the trust

      b.   if there is no beneficiary in existence at the time of the creation but the trust is created by a transfer in trust

   7.   the settlor

G.   Dispositions to the heirs of the settlor or of a third party may not result in the heirs' obtaining an interest under the

   1.   Doctrine of Worthier Title

   2.   Rule in Shelley's Case

VII.   CREATION, MODIFICATION AND TERMINATION OF TRUSTS

A.   A trust may be created by

   1.   a declaration of trust where the owner of property declares that he holds it as trustee for the benefit of another

   2.   a transfer in trust where the owner of property transfers it to a third person for the benefit of another or of the transferor

      a.   by deed in which case it is an inter vivos or living trust, or

      b.   by will in which case it is called a testamentary trust

   3.   the exercise of a power of appointment

      a.   a person holding a general power of appointment may appoint a person as trustee for himself or for others

      b.   a person holding a special power of appointment can only appoint among particular persons or classes of persons and can create a trust by appointing to a trustee for the benefit of such persons

   4.   contractual arrangements wherein a promisee of an enforce-

able promise holds or directs a beneficiary to hold the promise in trust

5. statutes which provide for the creation of trusts for designated persons or purposes

B. In order to create a trust the settlor must have the capacity to
transfer the property which is the subject matter of the trust

1. In the case of an inter vivos trust, the settlor must have the
capacity to transfer the legal title to the property

2. In the case of a testamentary trust, the settlor must have
testamentary capacity

C. Consideration is not necessary to the creation of a trust

D. Notice to the beneficiary is not necessary in the creation of a
trust

E. A beneficiary need not accept a trust but he may disclaim if he
has not by words or conduct manifested acceptance of the trust

F. The parol evidence rule applied to trusts operates

1. to exclude evidence that the transferee was intended to hold
the property in trust where the writing provides that the
transferee is to take the property for his own benefit

2. to exclude evidence that the transferee was intended not to
hold the property in trust or to hold the property on a different
trust where the writing provides that the transferee is to
hold the property in trust for a particular purpose

3. to exclude evidence that the settlor intended to hold free of
trust or for a different trust where the owner of property by
a writing has stated that he holds property upon a trust

4. not to exlude evidence to show that the transferee was intended to hold the property in trust either for the transferor
or for a third party where the writing does not provide either
that the transferee is to hold the property in trust for a particular person or that the transferee is to take the property
for his own benefit.

G. An enforceable trust can be created without a writing unless a
statute requires a writing.   Such statutes

1. do not apply to oral trusts of personalty

2. do require that an express trust of real property be evidenced by a writing

3. are usually based on the English Statute of Frauds

H. The Statute of Frauds

1. applies to both declarations of trust and transfers in trust

2. makes oral trusts in land only voidable and not void

3. can be raised only by the trustee who may perform the trust
if he chooses to do so

4. can be satisfied by a memorandum which

a. contains the essential terms of the trust

b. is signed

i. in a declaration of trust by the owner prior to, at
the time of, or subsequent to the declaration of trust

ii. in a transfer of trust

A. by the transferor prior to or at the time of transfer

B. by the transferee prior to, at the time of or subsequent to the transfer

5. may be satisfied by part performance which may consist of

a. the trustee's delivering possession of the land to the
beneficiary

b. the trustee's permitting the beneficiary to make improvement on the land

       c. any act to the beneficiary in reliance on the trust with the trustee's consent

I. Testamentary trusts must comply with the Statute of Wills which requires that all of the elements of the testamentary trust must be ascertainable
1. from the face of the will
2. from the face of the will and from an existing document incorporated by reference, and/or
3. from facts which have independent significance apart from the intended testamentary disposition

J. A trust may not be created for the unlawful purpose including
1. the commission of a crime
2. the commission of a tort
3. a violation of public policy
4. defrauding creditors or other third parties
5. trusts for which the consideration is illegal

K. A settlor may only revoke or modify a trust if he has expressly reserved the right to do so. Factors which will show that a power to revoke is reserved include
1. the improvidence of setting up the trust without such power
2. the relationship between the settlor and beneficiary
3. the purposes for creating the trust
4. the nature of the trust property
5. the impact of federal taxes on the provisions as drafted.

L. A trust may be terminated regardless of a reserved power to revoke where
    a. the period expires for which the trust was created
    b. the condition upon which the trust is to terminate is satisfied
    c. the purposes for which the trust was created become impossible or illegal
    d. the continuance of the trust would defeat the purposes for which the trust was created
    e. the settlor, if he is also the sole beneficiary of the trust, consents
    f. the trustee conveys legal title to the trust property to the beneficiaries
    g. all of the beneficiaries and the settlor consent to the termination
    h. all of the beneficiaries consent to the termination unless the trust is an active trust and its material purposes have not been accomplished.

VIII. CHARITABLE TRUSTS

A. Charitable trusts developed in England as a way of avoiding restrictions on direct gifts to certain persons or for certain purposes
1. initially charitable trusts were unenforceable in the courts
2. later charitable trusts were enforced by the Chancellor

B. The elements required for a charitable trust are
1. an intention of the settlor to create a trust
2. a trustee to administer the trust
3. a res or subject matter
4. a charitable purpose
5. a definite class to be benefitted, and

6. indefinite beneficiaries within the definite class
C. A charitable trust is created in the same manner as a private express trust
D. The difference between a charitable trust and a private trust is that
   1. a private express trust must have definite beneficiaries which can enforce it, and
   2. a charitable trust has indefinite beneficiaries and must be for a charitable purpose enforceable by the attorney general
E. Charitable purposes which will support a trust are
   1. relief of poverty
   2. improvement of government
   3. advancement of religion
   4. advancement of education
   5. advancement of health
   6. generally purposes which will benefit the community
F. Trusts for "benevolent" purposes which are not limited to "charitable" purposes are not valid as charitable trusts
G. Trust for named persons or for profit cannot be charitable trusts
H. Trusts for both charitable and non-charitable purposes are not valid unless
   1. the charitable and non-charitable purposes are charitable
   2. the primary purpose of the trust is charitable and the whole of the corpus may be applied to such charitable purposes
I. Charitable trusts should be distinguished from honorary trusts in that honorary trusts are not for charitable purposes
J. Charitable trusts may last indefinitely
K. Charitable trusts may be enforced by
   1. the attorney general
   2. particular persons entitled to receive a benefit under the trust
   3. members of an unincorporated association or a small class for whose benefit the trust is created
   4. co-trustees, and
   5. potential beneficiaries
L. Statutes of Mortman limit charitable trusts.
M. If the trustee named in a charitable trust is unable or unwilling to serve.
   1. the court will appoint a successor
   2. if the duties are personal to a particular person, the trust will fail
N. If it is impossible to carry out the terms of a charitable trust, a court may
   1. allow the trustee to deviate from a term of the trust in order to accomplish the purposes of the trust
   2. apply the doctrine of cy pres and devote the trust property to a different purpose "as near as may be" to that designated by the settlor where it is found that the settlor had
      a. a general charitable intent
      b. a specific charitable intent which is impossible or impractical to accomplish
O. Cy pres may be ordered when
   1. the amount of property is insufficient
   2. the specific purpose has been accomplished
   3. a third person whose consent is necessary refuses to give such consent
   4. the purpose is useless

5. the purpose is illegal
6. the beneficiary may not be capable of holding as a beneficiary
7. a specific site is impracticable, and
8. changed circumstances have rendered the purpose impractical

IX. **LIMITATIONS ON CREATION AND DURATION OF INTERESTS IN TRUSTS**

A. The Rule Against Perpetuities
1. applies to both legal and equitable interests in trusts
2. is a rule against remoteness of vesting
3. invalidates any interest which may remain contingent beyond twenty-one years after lives in being at the date of the creation of the interest
4. applies only to interests in transferees
5. does not apply to interests in transferors
6. applies to charitable interests except gifts over from a first charity to a second charity on a condition precedent
7. is qualified in some states by the doctrine of
   a. Wait and see
   b. Cy pres
B. The Rule Against the Suspension of the Power of Alienation invalidates any attempt to suspend the power to alienate property for more than a specified period
C. Statutes may limit the duration of
1. all private trusts
2. certain types of trusts
   a. voting trusts
   b. honorary trusts
D. Statutes may limit the duration of provisions for accumulations in private trusts to
1. the period of the Rule against Perpetuities
2. the life of the donor
3. twenty-one years after the donor's death
4. the minorities of persons living at the donor's death, or
5. the minorities of persons entitled to income in the absence of a provision for accumulation

X. **RESULTING TRUSTS**

A. Resulting trusts arise in situations in which
1. property is disposed of
2. under circumstances which raise an unrebutted inference
3. that the transferor does not intend that transferor have the beneficial interests therein, and
4. such beneficial interest is not disposed otherwise
B. The elements of a resulting trust are
1. an inferred intention to create the trust
2. a trustee
3. a trust res, and
4. a beneficiary
C. A resulting trust arises in the following situations
1. where an express trust fails

2. where an express trust does not use or exhaust the trust property
3. where property is purchased and paid for by one person and title is taken in the name of another

D. A resulting trust
   1. is a passive trust in which the trustee must transfer the legal title to the beneficiary
   2. is not subject to the Statute of Frauds with respect to its creation
   3. may be extinguished by parol

E. The inference of a resulting trust will not arise when
   1. the doctrine of cy pres is applied to a charitable trust
   2. the express trust fails for an illegal purpose
   3. there is an intention proved to the contrary
   4. a grantor has been paid for the trust property
   5. the title holder is the natural object to the payor's bounty

F. Purchase money resulting trusts
   1. arise proportionately to the amount of the contribution to the purchase price
      a. if there is no agreement as to the amount of the share
      b. if there is an oral agreement that the payor will take a greater share
   2. to the lesser amount agreed upon if there is an oral agreement by the payor to take a smaller share
   3. in a specified interest agreed upon if there is an oral agreement to that effect

G. Some jurisdictions
   1. recognize a resulting trust only if the purchase price represents an aliquot share
   2. have abolished purchase money resulting trust

XI. **CONSTRUCTIVE TRUSTS**

A. A constructive trust is a remedy created by courts of equity to obtain title from one person and place it in another to whom it belongs

B. Common instances of constructive trusts include fact situations where
   1. title to property is obtained by fraud, duress, mistake or undue influence
   2. a person murders another and succeeds to the victim's property
   3. one takes property from a trustee with notice of the trust
   4. a grantee obtains property by absolute deed on an oral promise he will hold in trust if
      a. the grantee obtained the property by misrepresentation
      b. there is a confidential relationship between the grantor and grantee
      c. in a minority of jurisdictions the grantee would be unjustly enriched
   5. a person obtains a gift by will or by intestacy in an oral promise to hold for another if
      a. there is an express or implied promise to hold in trust, or
      b. there is reliance by one decedent

XII.   **PROBATE-DOMICILE AND JURISDICTION**

A.   Jurisdiction over probate of wills is vested in special state courts usually called probate courts
    1.   an administrator may be appointed in any state where
        a.   the decedent was domiciled at the time of death
        b.   any state where the decedent left property

B.   A person's domicile is his home or if he has more than one residence it is usually the residence where he spends the most time
    1.   at common law a person always had just one domicile
    2.   modern law may recognize more than one domicile
    3.   there are three types of domicile:
        a.   domicile of origin which is a person's place of birth
        b.   domicile of choice which requires
            i.   physical presence at the new home and,
            ii.   the intent to presently make the new location his home
        c.   domicile by operation of law occurs when domicile is assigned because of legal status
    4.   A finding of domicile by one state is not binding on other states

C.   An executor or administrator has power only in the state where he is appointed
    1.   primary or domiciliary administration is administration in the state of the decedent's domicile
    2.   ancillary administration is administration of the decedent's affairs in another state
    3.   An ancillary administrator
        a.   collects the decedent's local assets
        b.   pays the local creditors, and
        c.   turns over the remaining assets to the domiciliary personal representative

D.   Title
    1.   to personal property vests in the personal representative as of the time of death and after payment of debts is transferred to the legatees or heirs
    2.   to real property vests in the devisee's or heirs subject to the right of the personal representative to use to pay debts

E.   State law determines which court will have jurisdiction over trusts
    1.   some states give jurisdiction over testamentary trusts to the probate court
    2.   other states give jurisdiction over all trusts to the court of general jurisdiction
    3.   absent a statute to the contrary, the court of equity jurisdiction will also have plenary jurisdiction of trusts
    4.   the validity of a trust concerning real property is determined by the laws of the state where the land is located
    5.   the validity of a trust of chattels is determined by the laws of the state where the testator was domiciled unless it would defeat his intent in which case the law of the state where the chattels are situated applies
    6.   the validity of an inter vivos trust is governed by the law of the state where the chattels are situated when the trust was created
    7.   the administration of a trust of chattels is governed by the

law of the state where the settlor designates the trust is to be administered

XIII. LIFE CYCLE OF ESTATE ADMINISTRATION

A. Estate administration is necessary in order to achieve
  1. the orderly transfer of assets on the death of their owner
  2. the protection of creditors and
  3. the identification of successors
B. The nature of probate proceedings is determined by whether a person dies
  1. intestate in which case they involve the appointment of a personal representative, or
  2. testate, in which case they involve the appointment of a personal representative and the probate of the will
C. The probate of a will means the proving thereof in court; the proceeding is concerned with
  1. genuineness
  2. due execution
  3. capacity, and
  4. chronology as the last expression of the testator's intent
D. A personal representative is the public official whose duty it is to wind up the affairs of the decedent
E. Steps in the probate process include:
  1. filing the will in court with a petition to admit to probate and to grant letters testamentary
  2. a proceeding to prove the will, in either
     a. common form—proved by proponent and testimony of witnesses without notice to interested parties
     b. solemn form—notice to interest parties and hearing
  3. proof of
     a. the death of the testator
     b. domicile
     c. genuineness of the will
     d. compliance with statutory requirements for the execution of wills, and
     e. testamentary capacity
F. Lost or destroyed wills may be admitted to probate in the same manner as those extant upon proof of
     a. contents and
     b. due execution
G. Proceeding by which the grant or denial of probate may be questioned include
  1. contest or caveat
  2. appeal from the order granting or denying probate and/or
  3. separate actions to set aside the order granting or denying probate
H. Will contest proceedings
  1. are proceedings in rem
  2. concern only external validity issues, and
  3. may be brought by "interested persons" including
     a. next-of-kin
     b. beneficiaries under prior wills
     c. purchasers of property from heirs
     d. administrators or executors under prior wills, or
     e. the state

I.   A person may be estopped to contest a will if
    a. he has accepted benefits under the will
    b. failed to object to probate proceedings, or
    c. he has taken action relative to the will relied on by a third party

J.   The burden of proof in a will contest case is on
    1. the person seeking to establish the validity with respect to
      a. due execution and
      b. mental capacity
    2. the contestant with respect to
      a. undue influence
      b. fraud, or
      c. revocation

K.   The decree of probate
    1. may not be collaterally attacked on matters of external validity
    2. may be set aside on grounds of
      a. fraud
      b. failure to comply with statutory provisions, such as the Soldiers' and Sailors' Relief Act, or
      c. new evidence

L.   Later wills may be probated after a decree of probate or intestacy in the same manner as if no other proceeding were had

M.   Conditions in a will that a gift shall be void if the beneficiary disputes the will
    1. are of no effect if the will is declared invalid
    2. if the contest is without probable cause will be upheld
    3. if the contest with probable cause will be enforced in some but not other jurisdictions
    4. are strictly construed on the grounds of disfavoring forfeitures

N.   Agreements not to contest a will between the testator and his heir at law or beneficiaries, are valid if
    1. supported by consideration, and
    2. otherwise a valid agreement

O.   Settlements of will contests are generally held to be valid even though it will defeat the intention of the testator

P.   A personal representative is the public official whose duty it is to wind up the affairs of the decedent, including
    1. an executor
    2. an administrator
    3. an administrator with the will annexed (c.t.a.)
    4. an administrator De bonis non (d.b.a), or
    5. a special administrator

Q.   When a personal representative has met the statutory qualifications the court issues
    1. in the case of a will, letters testamentary
    2. in the case of intestacy, letters of administration

R.   Letters of appointment of the personal representative may be revoked when
    1. the supposed decedent is not dead
    2. a will is found naming an executor after an administrator is appointed
    3. a later will is found
    4. the appointment was obtained by fraud
    5. the decedent was not domiciled in the state nor had any property there
    6. another person had priority for appointment

      7. lack of qualification at the time of appointment

      8. the personal representative becomes incapacitated

      9. the personal representative fails to properly administer the estate

S. A newly qualified personal representative

    1. cannot undo the acts of his predecessor with respect to

      a. bona fide purchasers

      b. debts paid

    2. can compel the return of property distributed to the next of kin or legatees

T. Claims against the estate must be presented within the statutory period of limitations

U. Types of claims which may be presented are determined by statutes which, depending upon the jurisdiction, provide

    1. enumerated causes of action survive in addition to those which survived at common law

    2. all causes of action survive except enumerated actions, or

    3. all causes of action survive

V. Non-claim statutes provided that all claims must be presented to the personal representative by a certain time or be "forever barred"

W. Contingent claims are treated differently in various jurisdictions

    1. Some require the personal representative to provide for their payment

    2. Others allow the creditor to proceed once the claim has become absolute

X. The rule of exoneration provides that one who receives mortgaged property is entitled to have the personal representative pay the debt out of the general assets of the estate unless the will indicates otherwise.   This is subject to statutory variations including considerations of

    1. the source of the mortgage

    2. the nature of the property, and

    3. the particular statute

Y. The usual order of priority with respect to insolvent estates is:

    1. family allowances

    2. funeral expenses

    3. cost of administration

    4. federal taxes

    5. state taxes

    6. wages, rents and judgment debts, and

    7. all other debts

Z. A personal representative can reject claims in which case the creditor must sue within a specified time or be forever barred

AA. Overpayments made by a personal representative may generally be recovered on the grounds of mistake

BB. Additional steps in one process of administration include:

    1. filing the inventory of the assets of the estate

    2. filing an appraisal valuing the estate

    3. the collection and preservation of the assets of the estate by the personal representative who may

      a. marshall the assets of the estate

      b. pay creditors and hold the remainder for distribution

      c. commence actions and compromise claims

      d. be reimbursed from the assets for reasonable expenditures

      e. file all required federal and state tax returns and pay the taxes thereon

    4. management of the estate including

      a. performing impersonal contracts of the decedent

      b. winding up the business conducted by the decedent unless given authority to continue it by

        i. the court

        ii. the testator's will

        iii. consent of all interested parties

      c. selling property to satisfy obligations of the estate

    5. will construction proceedings

      a. are usually brought after the will has been admitted to probate

        i. by the personal representative in order to carry out his duties without incurring personal liability

        ii. by parties to an action at law where the outcome may be affected by the interpretation of a will, or

        iii. by parties who oppose the personal representative's plan of distribution

      b. are usually necessary to

        i. clear up ambiguities in the will

        ii. provide for situations which the testator did not foresee

        iii. determine the meaning of words used by the testator, or

        iv. determine which is controlling where two or more terms of a will are contradictory

    6. periodic accountings which

      a. require the personal representative to show receipts and expenditures during the administration

      b. on note to interested parties with an opportunity to object, constitute a conclusive adjudication of their correctness and propriety

    7. a decree of final distribution which is

      a. conclusive of the rights of the legatees, devisees and heirs

      b. res judicata both as to person to take and the shares

      c. not subject to collateral attack

    8. the actual distribution

      a. to specific legatees by the delivery of the chattel

      b. to pecuniary legatees by payment in cash

      c. to residuary legatees and intestate distributees in cash or in kind depending on statute

  CC. Informal administration provisions allow the administration of an estate with minimum court supervision. These include

    1. non-intervention administration which allows the executor to administer the estate without court supervision if

      a. the will so provides, or

      b. the residuary legatees and the executor consent

    2. summary procedures for releasing small estates from administration if

      a. an application is filed setting forth the assets

      b. notice is given by publication or otherwise

    3. provisions allowing the payment of bank accounts, wages and insurance without administration

  DD. The Uniform Probate Code

    1. adopts a flexible system of administering decedent's estates

2. requires neither the probate of a will nor the appointment of a personal representative
3. provides two methods for probating wills
    a. informal
    b. formal
4. provides two methods for appointing a personal representative
    a. informal by a non-judicial officer without notice
    b. formal by a judicial officer with notice
5. allows estate settlement to be
    a. fully supervised
    b. "in and out" supervision
6. protects
    a. purchasers from personal representatives and distributes without adjudication of the propriety of the sale
    b. personal representatives who distribute without a formal adjudication
7. provides statutes of limitation which
    a. make informal probate final within the period
    b. make intestate status final within the period
    c. bar all claims not presented within the period

XIV. THE FIDUCIARY

A. Sources of appointment for fiduciaries are
    1. the trust document for trustee of an inter vivos trust
    2. a court of appropriate jurisdiction for
        a. executor
        b. administrator
        c. testamentary trustee
B. Special state provisions relating to the appointments
    1. may set priorities among individuals who may seek appointment
    2. provide special rules for non-residents or aliens
    3. generally require a bond prior to qualification
C. The duties of the fiduciary include
    1. marshalling the assets of the estate and maintaining control of the property
    2. administering the property solely in the interest of the beneficiary, who may not
        a. engage in self dealing between himself and the trust or estate
        b. enter into competition with the beneficiary
        c. disclose confidential information
        d. deal with the beneficiary unless there is full disclosure
        e. delegate his duties to another except for ministerial acts
        f. commingle the trust property and his own property
    3. using due care to preserve the property
    4. supervise act and conduct of agents and co-fiduciaries
    5. keep clear and accurate accounts and file them with the court if required
    6. furnish complete information on the beneficiary
    7. take reasonable action to enforce claims of and claims against one estate
    8. invest trust property and make it productive bound by

      a. directions of the settlor or testator
      b. statutes governing investment by fiduciaries, or
      c. the standards which would govern a prudent person in making investments of his own property having in mind the presider of the estate and the income to be earned
  9. acting impartially and with due regard for the respective interest of successive beneficiaries
  10. distributing income and principal in accordance with
      a. the direction in the document
      b. if the document if silent
          i. income is the return derived from the principal
          ii. principal is the property received as a change in form of the original corpus
  11. allocating dividends, depending on the jurisdiction, in accordance with the
      a. Kentucky Rule
      b. Pennsylvania Rule, or
      c. Massachusetts Rule
  12. allocating expenses, in accordance with
      a. the document, or
      b. ordinary expenses out of income, extraordinary expenses out of principal
      c. special rules apply to
          i. wasting assets
          ii. delayed sale of unproductive property
          iii. undistributed income on death of a life beneficiary

D. the powers of the fiduciary include
  1. express powers
  2. implied powers
      a. necessary to the accomplishment of the trust purposes such as the power to
          i. incur reasonable expenses
          ii. lease trust property
          iii. sell property
          iv. compromise, abandon or arbitrate claims
          v. vote and exercise other rights of shareholders
      b. except those prohibited by the terms of the instrument

E. The fiduciary's liabilities include
  1. personal liability on all contracts made in the administration of the trust
  2. personal liability for all torts committed in the administration of the trust
  3. liability for breach of trust including
      a. any loss resulting from the breach of trust
      b. any profit resulting from the breach of trust
      c. any profit the trust would have made in the absence of the breach of trust
  4. liability for a loss caused by the breach of trust of a co-trustee, and
  5. liability for profits arising out of transaction involving the trust property

F. A fiduciary may be relieved from liability for breach of trust
  1. by express exculpatory clauses except
      a. with respect to willful wrongdoing or gross negligence

b. if the clause resulted from the breach of a fiduciary or confidential relationship

G. A fiduciary is entitled to reasonable compensation for his services in an amount
1. stipulated in the document
2. fixed by a court, or
3. fixed by statute or court rule

H. A fiduciary is entitled to indemnity out of the property for
1. expenses
2. liabilities incurred in the administration of the property

I. If a trustee wrongfully disposes of trust property, the beneficiary can
1. trace either the property or its product into the hands of third parties, or
2. enforce an equitable lien upon the product in the hands of the trustee
3. not enforce a constructive trustee against a bona fide purchaser who takes without notice

PART ONE

WILLS

I FREEDOM OF TESTATION AND INTESTATE SUCCESSION

Summary Outline

1. The ability to transfer property at death is one of the bundle of rights which is included in the concept of private property.

2. Two major theories exist as to the nature of the right to make death transfers at death:

   (a) That it is a natural right inherent in the people. Nunnemacher v. State, 129 Wis. 190, 108 N.W. 627 (1906);

   (b) That it is a right granted by the state and as such can be taken away or regulated by the state. Blackstone, *Commentaries*, Vol. 2, pp. 9–12 (21st Edition 1844). This is the more widely held view.

3. Different results in succession cases may be dictated depending upon which view (a or b above) is accepted. If (a) is accepted that the right to inherit and make death transfers is a natural right, the state is restricted in placing limitations on such right. If (b) is accepted the state has the absolute power to grant or deny such rights, or to place such limitations thereon as it sees fit. See CASE 14, below. See also Rheinstein, pp. 55–80.

4. Policy arguments as to the wisdom of a system which allows wide latitude in disposing of one's property at death are frequently made in connection with the enactment or construction of legislation in this field.

5. Policy Arguments for and against freedom of inheritance are:

   (a) Against:

      (i) Inheritance violates the basic democratic ideal of equality of opportunity.

      (ii) The dead cannot wisely dictate the best uses of property for long periods of time after their death.

      (iii) Persons who inherit large amounts of wealth may not be prepared to use it in the best interests of society.

      (iv) Inheritance causes indulgence and encourages the recipient to be unproductive.

   (b) For:

      (i) Inheritance provides an incentive for productive activity toward accumulating wealth while one is alive.

      (ii) Inherited wealth is necessary to the economy as an important source of capital.

      (iii) Inheritance provides a source of support for dependents of the deceased.

      (iv) Philanthropy is principally supported by inherited wealth.

(v)   The usual recipients of inheritance have contributed indirectly to its production.

(vi) Abolition of inheritance results in state socialism.

See Clark, pp. 3–4.

INTESTATE SUCCESSION— TERMINOLOGY

1. *Intestate* means that one dies without leaving a will.

2. *Testate* means that one dies leaving a valid will.

3. In early English law there were distinctions made between real and personal property as to succession at the death of the owner.

(a) One could not dispose of real property at death because of the Doctrine of Primogeniture which held that property must pass to the eldest son.

(b) One could make a *testament* whereby the church courts, which had jurisdiction over testamentry matters involving chattels, would distribute the personal property as the decedent wished or name a personal representative to distribute the property.

(i)   Real property passed directly to the taker rather than through the estate. In England all land passed by intestacy until 1540 when Parliament passed the Statute of Wills permitting a devise of land. 32 Hen. VIII, c. 1 (1540).

(ii) Personal property went to the decedent's personal representative for administration and distribution to the next of kin. See CASE 102, below. See also Atkinson, pp. 11–23.

4. Traditionally, intestate real property passes by "descent" which originally meant that property passed down the lineal line from parent to child, but it now generally refers to those relatives named in a state statute providing for intestate succession.

5. One who takes realty by descent is an *heir* or an *heir at law*.

6. The word *distribution* refers to the historic power of the personal representative to distribute the personal property as he saw fit.

7. One who takes personalty through distribution is a *distributee*, or *next of kin*.

8. Modern legislation, for the most part, has abolished these distinctions, though the terminology is still in use.

    e.g. The Uniform Probate Code makes no distinction between real and personal property: an intestate's property, whether real or personal, passes by intestate succession to the heirs.

9. *Consanguinity* means blood relationship and is either lineal or collateral.

    (a) *Lineal* means that relationship between persons when one is directly related to the other, in either a descending or ascending line; e.g. grandfather, father, son.

    (b) Collateral means that persons are related who have a common ancestor:

        (i)   brothers (if A and B are brothers they have the same father or mother which is the common ancestor);

        (ii) cousins (if C and D are first cousins they have a common grandparent);

        (iii) uncles and aunts to nephews and nieces (if E is F's uncle, E's grandparent is F's parent—the common ancestor).

    See generally Palmer, pp. 1–7; Ritchie, pp. 5–10, and Scoles, pp. 1–8.

    Compare, Definitions of Will Terms, Chapter III, below.

STATUTES OF DESCENT AND DISTRIBUTION

1. Statutes in every state set out the order in which persons succeed to an intestate's property.   See UPC 2–101.

2. These statutes provide for an orderly administration by identifying successors to an intestate's estate.   They seek to carry out the distribution which most intestates would have provided had they made wills on the theory that most persons prefer their nearest relatives to more remote relatives.

3. Such statutes generally establish an order of preference among certain named relatives of the deceased.   A typical pattern provides for a line of succession much as follows: wife, children, parents, brothers and sisters and their lineal descents, grandparents and their lineal descendants, etc.; if none, then to next-of-kin; if no next-of-kin, then escheat to the state. Some more modern statutes eliminate takers more remote than issue of grandparents and thus the need to determine next-of-kin.   See Wyo.Stats.Ann. 2–3–101 (1977).   See also UPC 2–103, 2–105.

4. A person's next-of-kin are all those living persons standing on the lowest degree (which is the closest degree) of consanguinity (blood relationship) to the person.

5. Two methods have developed for computing degrees of consanguinity (to determine next-of-kin):

(a) the civil law method, and

(b) the common law method.

In the U.S. the civil law method is used almost exclusively.

6. In the civil law method the degree of blood relationship is computed for collateral relatives by counting the generations from the decedent up to the common ancestor and down to the claimant.   In the lineal line it is not necessary to find the common ancestor; it is only necessary to count generations, either in the descending or ascending line.

e.g. Great grandfather and a great grandson are related in the third degree by counting down as follows: grandfather, father and son; or by counting up as follows: father, grandfather, great grandfather.   See CHART 1, below.

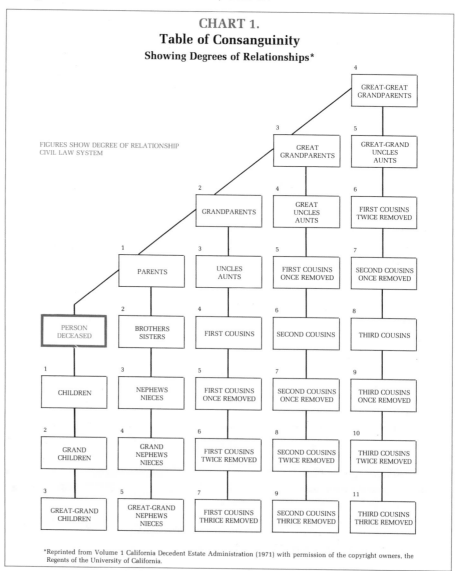

CHART 1.
Table of Consanguinity
Showing Degrees of Relationships*

FIGURES SHOW DEGREE OF RELATIONSHIP
CIVIL LAW SYSTEM

*Reprinted from Volume 1 California Decedent Estate Administration (1971) with permission of the copyright owners, the Regents of the University of California.

7. The canon law method (also known as the common-law rule) computes the degree of relationship by counting the generations to the nearest common ancestor (as in the civil law method), but instead of taking the sum of the steps to the ancestor and down to the claimant, taking only the larger figure of the steps to the ancestor.

e.g. A nephew is related to his uncle in the second degree. Count up from the uncle to the parent of uncle resulting in one step and down from the uncle's parent (nephew's grandparent) to the nephew's parent to the nephew (two steps).

NOTE—Some states do not use the designations found in CHART I as to cousins. Instead they use simplified nomenclature as found in CHART IA on page 8.

(a) In CHART II, using the *civil* law method of counting C is the parent of X, Y and Z. X and Y are related in the second degree, computed by counting C as first degree and Y the second; or by counting from Y to X, C is the first degree and X is the second. D and N are related in the fourth degree counting X as one, C as two, Z as three and N as four. E and S are related in the fifth degree counting X as one, C as two, Y as three, G as four and S as five with C the common ancestor. L is related to K in the second degree counting Z as one and K as two with Z the common ancestor and L and K being brothers or sisters, or brother and sister. H and R are related in the third degree counting Y as first, G as second, and R as third, with Y as the common ancestor being the father of H and grandfather of R.

(b) Using the *canon* law method, X and Y are related in the first degree computed by counting from X to C and from Y to C and getting one in each instance. D and N are related in the second degree counting from D–X as one, C as two and counting from N, Z is one, C is two. E and S are related in the third degree counting from E, X is one, C is two and counting from S, G is one, Y is two, C is three and taking the higher number (3). L is related to K in the first degree counting one either from L to Z or from K to Z. H and R are related in the second degree, counting from R, G is one, Y is two and counting from H, Y is one and taking the higher number (2).

8. A third system of determining takers is one which does not involve the computation of degrees. It is the *parentelic system* in which all descendants of the nearest ancestor are preferred over descendants of more remote ancestors, e.g. all descendants of a descendent's parents would take to the exclusion of descendants of decedent's grandparents even though in a closer degree of

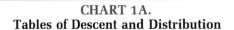

CHART 1A.
Tables of Descent and Distribution

COMPUTATION OF DEGREES OF KINDRED

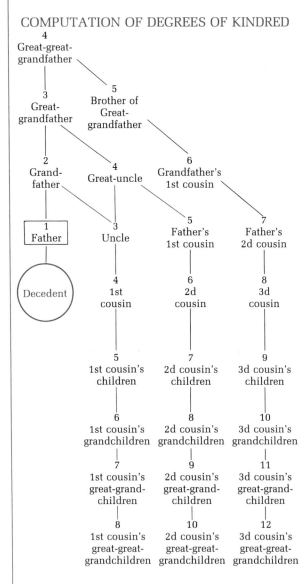

4
Great-great-
grandfather

3
Great-
grandfather

5
Brother of
Great-
grandfather

2
Grand-
father

4
Great-uncle

6
Grandfather's
1st cousin

1
Father

3
Uncle

5
Father's
1st cousin

7
Father's
2d cousin

Decedent

4
1st
cousin

6
2d
cousin

8
3d
cousin

5
1st cousin's
children

7
2d cousin's
children

9
3d cousin's
children

6
1st cousin's
grandchildren

8
2d cousin's
grandchildren

10
3d cousin's
grandchildren

7
1st cousin's
great-grand-
children

9
2d cousin's
great-grand-
children

11
3d cousin's
great-grand-
children

8
1st cousin's
great-great-
grandchildren

10
2d cousin's
great-great-
grandchildren

12
3d cousin's
great-great-
grandchildren

ORDER OF PRIORITY AMONG KINDRED

Order of Priority	Relationship to Decedent	Degree to Kindred
First:—	Grandparents	2d
Second:—*	Uncles and aunts	3d
Third:—*	Great-grandparents	3d
Fourth:—*	First Cousins	4th
Fifth:—*	Great-uncles and great-aunts	4th
Sixth:—*	Great-great-grandparents	4th
Seventh:—	Children of first cousins	5th
Eighth:—	First cousins of parent	5th
Ninth:—	Brothers and sisters of great-grandparents	5th
Tenth:—	Grandchildren of first cousin	6th
Eleventh:—	Second cousins	6th
Twelfth:—	First cousins of grandparent (i. e. children in ninth class)	6th
Thirteenth:—	Great-grandchildren of first cousin	7th
Fourteenth:—	Children of second cousin	7th
Fifteenth:—	Children of first cousin of grandparent (i.e. second cousin of parent) ..	7th
Sixteenth:—	Great-great-grandchildren of first cousin	8th
Seventeenth:—	Grandchildren of second cousin ..	8th
Eighteenth:—	Third cousins (i.e. children of fifteenth)	8th
Nineteenth:—	Great-grandchildren of second cousin	9th
Twentieth:—	Children of third cousin	9th
Twenty-first:—	Great-great-grandchildren of second cousin	10th
Twenty-second:—	Grandchildren of third cousin	10th
Twenty-third:—	Great-grandchildren of third cousin	11th
Twenty-fourth:—	Great-great-grandchildren of third cousin	12th

*There is some doubt as to Second and Third. It is possible that members of these two classes would all share equally. The Massachusetts statute says that if there are two or more collateral kindred claiming through different ancestors those claiming through the nearest ancestor are preferred. Uncles and aunts claim through a nearer ancestor than great-grandparents. On the other hand, the latter are not strictly collateral kindred. So perhaps, both groups being of the third degree, they would share together, without priority. The same question would arise as to Sixth compared with either Fourth or Fifth. The actual likelihood of the question ever arising in either case is obviously very remote.

Taken from Newhall, Settlement of Estates and Fiduciary Law in Massachusetts (4th ed.)

kinship. A number of states retain this principle in their statutes of descent and distribution. See Clark, p. 81.

9. At common law realty descended to the eldest son through the Doctrine of Primogeniture which gave preference to the eldest male lineal descendants. This Doctrine never existed in the U.S. See Intestate Succession—Terminology, above.

CHART II. Kinship—Civil and Canon Law Methods Compared

The following example demonstrates the method of determining kinship under the civil and canon law systems:

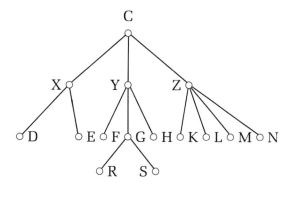

10. The doctrine of escheat provides that if there can be located no individuals who are next-of-kin under the provisions of the applicable statute, the intestate estate passes to the state.

11. At common law one could not renounce an intestate share. Modern statutes permit such renunciation. This is important with respect to tax planning. See UPC 2-801.

   See generally Atkinson, pp. 37–59; Palmer, pp. 6–7; Ritchie, pp. 53–67; and Scoles, pp. 41, 43.

PER CAPITA AND PER STIRPES, REPRESENTATION

1. The terms *per capita* and *per stirpes* are frequently used in statutes and in dispositive documents to indicate the generation level at which the initial division into shares is established.

2. Taking *per capita* means taking equally based on the number of takers.

   e.g. C dies leaving six grandchildren as his only heirs, three are children of his son X, two are children of his daughter Y and one is the child of his son Z. They are all related in the second degree and each takes one-sixth of the property, per capita.

3. Taking *per stirpes* (or by right of representation) means taking by the root or by right to represent a deceased ancestor.

   e.g. C dies leaving two children X and Y and grandchildren M and N, the children of C's deceased child Z. In such case C's property is divided into three parts, one going to X, one to Y, and the other third is divided between N and M taking per stirpes, i.e. through their father whom they represent.

4. Some confusion exists as to which level is used as the root level in a *per stirpes* distribution. The choice is between:

(a) the level nearest the decedent, or

(b) the first level where there is a survivor.

The confusion is caused by statutes and rules of construction which apply both *per capita* and *per stirpes* principles.

5. Under the minority approach the estate is first divided into a number of shares equal to the number of persons in the closest degree of kinship to the decedent who survive or leave issue who survive.

e.g. D dies leaving as his only heirs: M, the child of D's deceased child X; N and O, the children of D's deceased child Y; and Q and R, the grandchildren of D's deceased child Z, who had one child P also deceased. Under this approch M would take one-third, N and O would divide one-third each taking one-sixth and Q and R would divide one-third, each taking one-sixth.

6. The more commonly accepted method is to divide the estate into a number of shares equal to the number of persons who survive or who have issue who survive in the closest degree where there is at least one survivor. Using this system in the example in number 5, above, M would take one-fourth, N one-fourth, O one-fourth and Q and R would divide one-fourth or take one-eighth. See CHART III, below.

NOTE—The Uniform Probate Code adopts this construction. It provides "If representation is called for by this Code, the estate is divided into as many shares as there are surviving heirs in the nearest degree of kinship and deceased persons in the same degree who left issue who survive the decedent, each surviving heir in the nearest degree receiving one share and the share of each deceased person in the same degree being divided among his issue in the same manner. UPC 2–106.

See generally Atkinson, pp. 42–43, 71, 72; Clark, pp. 86–89; Ritchie, pp. 11–17; and Scoles, pp. 45–46.

Case 1 *Per stirpes distribution uses ancestor nearest decedent to determine distributive shares*

D died leaving a trust to be divided upon the death of the last of his seven children. The trust agreement stated that the property should be distributed at the death of the surviving child to D's descendants as they would have been entitled as his heirs at law if D had died at

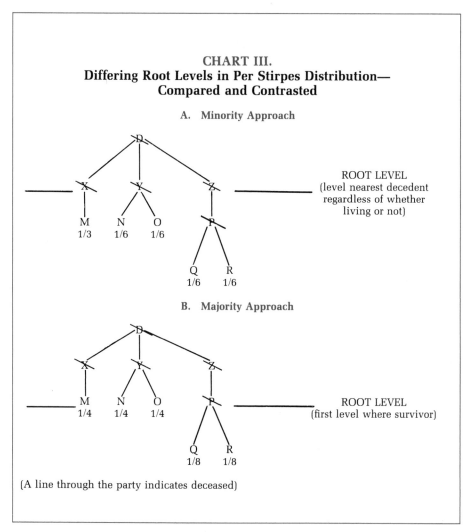

CHART III.
**Differing Root Levels in Per Stirpes Distribution—
Compared and Contrasted**

A. Minority Approach

ROOT LEVEL
(level nearest decedent
regardless of whether
living or not)

M 1/3   N 1/6   O 1/6   Q 1/6   R 1/6

B. Majority Approach

ROOT LEVEL
(first level where survivor)

M 1/4   N 1/4   O 1/4   Q 1/8   R 1/8

(A line through the party indicates deceased)

the time of distribution.   D was survived by four grandchildren and
two great-grandchildren, as shown in the chart, below. The applicable
statute provided that all of the descendants of the same degree take
per capita otherwise they take per stirpes.   How should the property
be distributed?

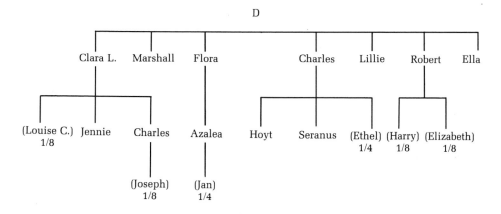

D

Clara L.   Marshall   Flora   Charles   Lillie   Robert   Ella

(Louise C.) Jennie   Charles   Azalea   Hoyt   Seranus   (Ethel) (Harry) (Elizabeth)
1/8   1/4   1/8   1/8

(Joseph)   (Jan)
1/8   1/4

Answer. Louise and Joseph take one-eighth each, dividing the one-fourth share of Clara, Jan takes the one-fourth share of Flora, Ethel takes the one-fourth share of Charles, Harry and Elizabeth take one-eighth each, dividing the one-fourth share of Robert. To take per capita all descendants should be in the same class or degree. Since the surviving descendants in the case are of unequal degree they will take per stirpes. The estate will be divided at the level nearest the decedent as these are persons in such levels who have descendants living at the time of distribution. Per stirpes means taking the share of an immediate ancestor who takes the share of his immediate ancestor until a common ancestor is reached. If there is more than one descendant the interest of the person at the level nearest the descendant is divided among the descendants in fractional parts.

See Maud v. Catherwood, 67 Cal.App.2d 636, 155 P.2d 111 (1945).

NOTE—Under the alternate approach the number of shares would have been determined at the level of grandchildren (i.e. the first level where there are survivors. The result would be that each would have taken one-sixth: Louise, Harry and Elizabeth taking in their own right; Joseph taking the share of Charles and Jan taking the share of Azalea. See number 3(b) above.

Case 2 *Per capita distribution when all heirs are equally related to decedent*

D died intestate leaving three grandchildren A, B and C as next of kin. A is the daughter of D's deceased son M; B and C are the sons of D's deceased son O. See chart, below. The relevant statute provides that the property is to pass, "in equal shares to the children of said deceased person or the legal representatives of deceased children." A claims that she is entitled to take one-half of the estate in that the grandchildren are representatives of the deceased children and therefore take per stirpes. B and C claim that all three take directly as heirs per capita. How should the estate be distributed?

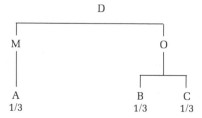

Answer. The estate should be divided one-third to each A, B and C. Most American statutes providing for descent and distribution are derived from the English Statute of Distributions under which it became established at an early date that the doctrine of representation

*applied only when the claimants are related to the decedent in un-
equal degrees.   When they are equally related to the intestate in the
same degree they took directly and per capita.   The same construction has followed in American jurisdictions which have adopted the
English statute.   The rule is manifestly just and in harmony with
other provisions which provide that father and mother share equally,
brothers and sisters share equally and next-of-kin share equally.
Such a construction is therefore to be given preference over the al-
ternative interpretation.*

See in re Martin's Estate, 96 Vt. 455, 120 A. 862 (1923).

Per stirpes distribution based on statutory definition   Case 3

The deceased, D, died intestate leaving surviving the following relatives only: (a) two nephews, A and B, sons of D's deceased brother,
James, (b) four nieces, E, F, G and H, daughters of D's deceased sister,
Mary, and (c) five grand-nephews, K, L, M, N and P, sons of D's
deceased sister Mary's deceased daughter, Julia.   The relationships
are diagrammed below.   The applicable statute provided that the
relatives of the deceased intestate standing in the same degree shall
take per capita and when some in such same degree are dead leaving
issue, then the issue shall take per stirpes.   How should D's property
be distributed?

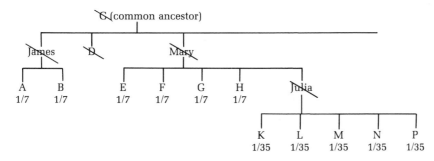

(A line through the party indicates deceased)

Answer.   A, B, E, F, G and H take per capita from D.   Each takes
one seventh of his property.   K, L, M, N and P take per stirpes from
D through their deceased mother, Julia.   Each of these five persons
takes one thirty fifth of D's property.   The reasons are these: The
approach to distribution set out in number 5 above is the one adopted
by the applicable statute. James and Mary are in the second degree
of relationship to the deceased D, but neither of those in this second
degree of consanguinity is alive.   So we look to that living person
or persons who are in the closest degree of relationship to decedent.
That group includes the nephews and nieces who are all in the third
degree.   Each living nephew or niece therefore takes per capita.
Where some in that degree are dead (Julia in this case), then their

issue (in this case Julia's five children) take by right of representations. So the one-seventh share that would have come to Julia is divided equally among her five children—¹⁄₃₅th to each.

See Kincaid v. Cronin, 61 Ohio App. 300, 22 N.E.2d 576 (1939).

Case 4   *Where taker is entitled to take in more than one capacity*

H and W are husband and wife. They have two children, A and B. B dies leaving two children, C and D. H and W adopt C and D. W dies testate giving her property to H. H then dies intestate and the statute provides that adopted children shall have the same rights as children born in lawful wedlock and that property of an intestate shall pass to his children and their desendants. How shall H's property descend?

Answer. A should receive one-fourth, C one-fourth as a child of H, D one-fourth as a child of H, and C and D shall take per stirpes the share of their deceased father, B, which would be an additional one-eighth to each. The reason for such distribution is this: C and D are both children of H and grandchildren of H. As children they take per capita with A. As grandchildren they take per stirpes throuh their father, B, as the root or the stirpes. So A gets one-fourth, C gets three-eighths and D gets three-eighths, which shares make up the total estate left by H.

See In re Benner's Estate, 109 Utah 172, 166 P.2d 257 (1946). Contra: Mississippi Valley Trust Co. v. Palms, 360 Mo. 610, 229 S.W.2d 675 (1950). See also Clark, p. 105.

NOTE—The trend of modern statutes on adoption is to treat the child as a member of his adoptive family not of the natural family. See *The Effect of Adoption on the Right to Inherit*, below. See also, Clark, pp. 101–107.

SPECIAL RELATIONSHIPS WHICH AFFECT THE RIGHT TO INHERIT

1. At common law the Doctrine of Ancestral Property provided that an heir to real property must be a blood relative of the first purchaser. This doctrine required that the property go only to persons of the blood of the ancestor from whom it was inherited; e.g. B inherits property from his father A. On B's death, his only heirs are two brothers: C who is a full brother and X who is the son of B's mother and H whom B's mother married after A's death. Under the Doctrine of Ancestral Property only C could inherit the property B derived from A. The only vestiges of the doctrine in this country are in special rules for half-bloods, (i.e. brothers or sisters who have only one parent in common rather than two and the descendants of such half-bloods) adopted children, and stat-

utes altering intestate succession with respect to property which an intestate surviving spouse derived from a spouse who predeceased.   See West's Ann.Cal.Prob.Code §§ 228, 229.   See also Atkinson, pp. 77–81.

2. Statutory intestate schemes take a number of approaches to the ability of the half-blood to inherit.

   (a) The most common scheme is for relatives of the half-blood to inherit equally with whole bloods.   This is also the general rule if there is no statutory provision.   See UPC 2–107.

   (b) A few states exclude half-bloods unless there are no whole bloods of his same degree of kinship.   See Conn.G.S.A. § 45–276.

   (c) Some statutes provide special rules for "ancestral" property.

      e.g. Relatives of the half blood inherit equally with whole bloods except with respect to certain "ancestral" property which the intestate decedent derived from an ancestor not of the blood of the half-blood.   See In re Estate of Robbs, 504 P.2d 1228 (Okl. 1972).

INTESTATE RIGHTS OF ILLEGITIMATE CHILDREN

1. At common law, an illegitimate child, is a child of no one and has no right to inherit.   Similarily none other than his own issue has the right to inherit from him.   This has been changed universally by statutes which vary from state to state.

2. The most common rule is that an illegitimate child is treated as the child of the mother and may inherit from her and from her relatives and they from him.

3. The general rule is that an illegitimate child is not treated as a child of the father unless legitimated or acknowledged by the father.

4. In some jurisdictions the illegitimate child is treated as the child of both its natural parents.   See Ore.Rev.Stats. 109.060.

5. A legitimated child is treated the same for inheritance purposes as any other child of the parent.

6. When a man has children by a woman and afterward married her, such issue will be legitimated either:

   (a) by their subsequent marriage, or

   (b) by the subsequent marriage and acknowledgement of the father.

7. The issue of parents whose marriage is null in law nevertheless are legitimate.

e.g. H marries W_1 by whom he has children A and B and then contracts a bigamous marriage with W_2 by whom he has children C and D. A, B, C and D are all legitimate even though the marriage to W_2 is void. See UPC 2–109; Ark.Stat. 61–141; 83 Okla.Stat.Ann. § 215.

8. The trend is toward liberalizing the rights of illegitimates to inherit from their fathers.

   e.g. The Uniform Probate Code allows a child to inherit from the father if the paternity is established before the father's death by adjudication or thereafter by clear and convincing proof. See UPC 2–109.

9. Recent U.S. Supreme Court cases, by reason of the Equal Protection Clause of the 14th Amendment have raised serious questions as to the ability of the states to enact classifications which discriminate on the basis of illegitimacy. Such classifications have been held unconstitutional despite the following argument for their validity:

   (a) that they promote legitimate family relationships,

   (b) that difficulties in proving paternity justify total disinheritance of illegitimates, or

   (c) that the father could have provided for the child by will.

   See CASE 5–7, below.

Case 5 *Discrimination against illegitimate children as denial of equal protection*

A state statute provides a right of recovery for wrongful death of a deceased parent in favor of the surviving children of the deceased. Deceased mother left surviving five illegitimate children. The State Supreme Court has held that a surviving "child" under the statute does not include an illegitimate child. On appeal to the United States Supreme Court the children contend the statute denies them equal protection under the Fourteenth Amendment of the U. S. Constitution. Are they correct in their contention?

Answer. *Yes. Illegitimate children are "persons" within the meaning of the equal protection clause of the Fourteenth Amendment, and as such the State Supreme Court's interpretation of the statute is an invidious classification denying without reason rights which other citizens enjoy. "Legitimacy or illegitimacy of birth has no relation to the nature of the wrong allegedly inflicted on the mother. These children though illegitimate were dependent on her; she cared for them and nurtured them; they were indeed hers in the biological and spiritual sense; in her death they suffered wrong in the sense* *any dependent would."* Thus the statute, as construed by the State Supreme Court, is unconstitutional in that there is no rational basis for the difference in classification of legitimate and illegitimate children.

See Levy v. Louisiana, 391 U.S. 68, 88 S.Ct. 1509, 20 L.Ed.2d 436 (1967).

Discrimination against illegitimate children in state's intestate scheme does not violate equal protection

Case 6

Intestate was survived only by collateral relations and an illegitimate daughter, who had been acknowledged but not legitimated by the intestate. The jurisdiction in which the intestate died has a statute which provides, "Illegitimate children though duly acknowledged cannot claim the rights of legitimate children"; and one which reads: "Natural children are called to the inheritance of their natural father, who has duly acknowledged them . . . to the exclusion only of the state." The father could have left the child property by will. The child claims that the intestate succession laws which bar an illegitimate child from sharing equally with legitimate children constitute a violation of the equal protection and due process clauses of the U. S. Constitution. Is the illegitimate child entitled to inherit equally with legitimate children?

Answer. No. The statutory scheme is valid. It is within the state's power to establish rules for the protection and strengthening of family life and for the disposition of property. The rule in question is reasonable in achieving such results within the requirement of equal protection. The case is to be distinguished from the situation in CASE 5, above, where the state creates a statutory tort and provides for the survival of a decedent's cause of action so that a large class of persons injured by the tort could recover damages in compensation for their injury and excludes from the class potential plaintiffs. In this case the father by will could have left property to the illegitimate child. The state, therefore, has not prevented the child from inheriting. Rules of intestate succession attempt to reflect the intent of a decedent, and such schemes as the state allows which do not constitute an insurmountable barrier are constitutional.

See Labine v. Vincent, 401 U.S. 522, 91 S.Ct. 1017, 28 L.Ed.2d 288 (1971).

Statute discriminating against acknowledged child from inheriting from father unconstitutional

Case 7

D died intestate survived by his parents B and C and an illegitimate daughter X. D had been under a court order to support X. The state statute relative to inheritance provides that an illegitimate child is the heir of its mother. Only if the parents marry and the father acknowledges the child is an illegitimate child treated as legitimate and able to inherit under the statute of descent and distribution. X claims the state statute is unconstitutional in that it discriminates between legitimate and illegitimate children.

Answer. D should receive the property. The statute violates the equal protection clause of the Fourteenth Amendment. Imposing sanctions on children does not bear a rational relationship to promoting a legitimate family relationship. Since D was ordered to support X, paternity had already been established and for this class of child there was little danger of spurious claims to upset the orderly settlement of estates.

See Trimble v. Gordon, 430 U.S. 762, 97 S.Ct. 1459, 52 L.Ed.2d 31 (1977). See also NOTE following CASE 8, below.

Case 8   *State statute conditioning inheritance on establishing paternity prior to father's death does not violate equal protection*

D died intestate domiciled in State A. He was survived by B and S his illegitimate children. A has a statute which provides: "An illegitimate child is the legitimate child of his father so that he and his issue inherit from his father if a court of competent jurisdiction has, during the lifetime of the father, made an order of filiation declaring paternity in a proceeding instituted during the pregnancy of the mother or within two years from the birth of the child." No such order of filiation was made during D's life; however D openly referred to B and S as his children. After D's death, B and S claim they are entitled to inherit from D's children. They claim that A's statute conditioning inheritance by illegitimates on a judicial determination of paternity during the father's life violates the Equal Protection clause of the U.S. Constitution. Are B and S entitled to share in D's estate?

Answer. No. The issue involved here is whether A's statute unreasonably discriminates against B and S on the basis of their illegitimate birth. Classifications based on illegitimacy are invalid under the Fourteenth Amendment to the U.S. Constitution if they are not substantially related to permissible state interests. The primary goal of the state statute in question here is the just and orderly disposition of a decedent's property. Inheritance from the father by illegitimates involves difficult problems of proof. The state legislature's judgment that paternity disputes are to be settled in a judicial forum during the father's lifetime prevents fraudulent assertions of paternity and allows a man to defend his reputation. Estate administration is also facilitated when the determination is made prior to death. *The statute is aimed at justifiable state objectives and is a reasonable means for attaining them; therefore, it is constitutional. This situation is unlike that in CASE 7, above where illegitimate children whose parent did not subsequently intermarry were completely excluded from inheriting. In such a case it was held that the orderly settlement of estates goal could be achieved by other means and that the statute in question was unconstitutional.*

See *Lalli v. Lalli*, 439 U.S. 259, 99 S.Ct. 518, 58 L.Ed.2d 503 (1978).

NOTE—Only three justices joined in the opinion of the court in the case above. Two other justices concurred in the result: one on the basis of Labine v. Vincent case above suggesting that Trimble v. Gordon, case above, should be overruled; the other on the basis of his dissent in Trimble in which he contended that legislative classifications based on illegitimacy need only have a fair and substantial relation to the object of the legislation and should be upheld unless "mindless and patently irrational."

THE EFFECT OF ADOPTION AND DESIGNATED HEIRSHIP ON THE RIGHT TO INHERIT

1. Adoption was unknown at common law and any rights of adopted children to inherit from adoptive parents must be conferred by statute.

2. Statutes generally give the adopted child the right to inherit from the adoptive parent.

3. State statutes do not follow a uniform scheme as to whether the adopted child may inherit from and through the natural parents.

4. The modern trend is to treat the adopted child solely as a member of the adoptive family and to cut off all inheritance rights between the adopted child and his natural family.

5. Where a child is adopted by the spouse of the natural parent, many modern statutes provide that a child adopted by the spouse of the natural parent retains the right to inherit from his other parent. This is the approach of the Uniform Probate Code.

    e.g. C is the child of H_1 and W who are divorced. W marries H_2 who adopts C. C's inheritance rights from W and H, are not cut off. See UPC 2–109.

6. Other approaches taken to the problem of which relatives inherit from and through the adopted child are:

    (a) Only natural relatives inherit;

    (b) Only adopted relatives inherit;

    (c) Both natural and adopted relatives share equally;

(d) Adopted relatives take property which came from the adopted family with natural relatives taking the remainder.

NOTE—State provisions requiring the sealing of adoption records might present an obstacle to identification of heirs in states where natural relations may inherit from the adoptee; however the typical statute provides for release of information on a showing of good cause.   See N.Y.Dom.Rel.Law § 114.   See also Alma Soc'y, Inc. v. Mellon, 601 F.2d 1225 (2d Cir. 1979), cert. denied 444 U.S. 995, 100 S.Ct. 531, 62 L.Ed.2d 426.

7. Some jurisdictions permit a person to designate another person as his heir at law in the event of his death.   The designated person stands thereafter to the declarant (and to the declarant's blood relations) as a legitimate child born to declarant.   See Ohio R.C. § 2105.15.

e.g. H designates his wife W as his heir at law.   H is the only child of F.   F dies intestate predeceased by H and the applicable statute gives all of F's property to his lineal descendants per stirpes.   W inherits all of F's property as H's heir not as his surviving spouse.   See generally Atkinson, pp. 86–92;   Clark, pp. 96, 101–107;   Ritchie, pp. 69–70;   and Scoles, pp. 58–59.

Case 9   *Construction of state statute making adopted child a family member of adopted parents—cuts off any rights from natural grandparents.*

T died leaving as his only blood relative a granddaughter, the issue of T's son who had predeceased T.   Three months prior to T's death, T had executed a will leaving all of his estate to charitable institutions.   Three months before the death of T his granddaughter M was adopted by her stepfather who had married T's daughter-in-law after the death of M's father.   A state Mortmain statute provided: "If a testator dies leaving issue   .   .   .   or the lineal descendants of [lineal descendants], and the will of such testator gives, devises or bequeaths such testator's estate or any part thereof to a benevolent, religious, educational or charitable purpose,   .   .   .   such will as to such gift, devise, or bequest such be invalid unless it was executed at least one year prior to the death of the testator."   Another statute of the same state provides "for the purpose of inheritance to, through and from a legally adopted child, such child shall be treated the same as if he were the natural child of his adopting parents, and shall cease to be treated as the child of his natural parents for the purposes of intestate succession."   M's guardian brings an action for construction of the will claiming that the gifts to charity are void by reason of the Mortmain statute.   T's executor claims that the gifts are valid in that M by reason of the adoption statute is no longer to be considered a lineal descendant or her natural father. Are the charitable gifts valid?

Answer. Yes. If M is considered a lineal descendant of her natural father after her adoption, then the Mortmain statute quoted above would invalidate the charitable bequest in question. The provisions of the statute creating the rights of inheritance between the parties to an adoption and the provisions of the law of descent and distribution of intestate estates are in pari materia and should be construed together. The legislature has the power to declare the legal status of an adopted child and make her capable of inheriting from the adopting parent. It, likewise, has the power to cut off inheritance rights from natural parents. Under the state statutory scheme the adopted child ceased to be the child of her natural parent for the purpose of inheritance under the Statute of Descent and Distribution; the blood line was completely severed for these purposes, and the child is precluded from inheriting from its natural grandfather's estate. Further, considering the Mortmain statute and the Adoption statute in pari materia the conclusion must be drawn that T died without issue or the lineal descendant of issue and therefore the charitable bequests are valid as set forth in the will.

See *Campbell v. Musart Soc'y of Cleveland Museum of Art*, 131 N.E.2d 279, 2 Ohio Op. 517 (Cuy.Prob.Ct.1956).

NOTE—in 1975 the Uniform Probate Code was amended to provide " . . . an adopted person is the child of an adopting parent and not of the natural parents except that adoption of a child by the spouse of a natural parent has no effect on the relationship between the child and *either* natural parent." This change would dictate a different result in CASE 16, above.

Interpretation of statutes re adoption   Case 10

Testatrix left a gift by will to named nephews and nieces with the proviso that if any of the nephews and nieces predecease her the gift goes to the child of his or her body. The state has a statute which provides that after an order of adoption is entered the relationship of parent and child between the adopted person and his natural parents shall be completely altered and all the rights, duties, and other legal consequences or the relationship shall cease to exist. Can the children of testatrix' deceased nephew who were adopted by their mother's second husband after her divorce from the nephew before his death take from their aunt's will?

Answer. Yes. The children will inherit. The intent of the testatrix is not affected by this legal effect of the statute in this instance.

The use of the term "children of the body" is to identify recipients. It does not incorporate the state's law of adoption or that of descent and distribution.

See In re Estate of Zastrow, 42 Wis.2d 390, 166 N.W.2d 251 (1969).

ADVANCEMENTS

1. An advancement is a gift made by an intestate during his life to certain designated relatives with the intent that it be applied against any share to which such person may be entitled in the intestate's estate.

   CAVEAT—It is important to compare Advancement with Ademption by Satisfaction in the law of wills. See *Ademption*, Chapter IV, below.

2. An advancement is computed as part of the total value of the estate and the taker who receives the advancement has the amount credited against his share of the amount to be distributed. If the amount of the advancement is greater than the intestate share of its recipient the excess need not be refunded.

   e.g. T died intestate leaving three children, A, B and C as his sole statutory heirs and a net estate of $1400. During his lifetime he gave A $300 and B $100 and there is no evidence of T's intention with respect to these gifts. Under the doctrine of advancements the net estate would be calculated to be $1800. Out of the $1400 estate A would receive $300, B would receive $500 and C would receive $600.

3. Whether the gift is intended to be absolute or an advancement is a question of the intention of the intestate. A gift to a prospective heir may be intended as

   (a) a loan,

   (b) an absolute gift, or

   (c) an advancement.

4. Evidence of intention may include such things as declarations made at the time of the gift, books of account, surrounding circumstances, and the purpose for which the transfer was made. Gifts to children for maintenance, education and support are usually not considered advancements.

5. The Uniform Probate Code and other modern statutes require written evidence of the intent that an inter vivos gift be an advancement before a gift will be so treated. See UPC 2–110; McKinney's, N.Y.E.P.T.L. § 2–1.5.

6. Under the general rule the advancement is valued at the date of the transfer rather than at the date of death. See UPC 2–110.

See generally Atkinson, pp. 716–725. Palmer, pp. 175–176, Ritchie, pp. 81–84, and Scoles, pp. 67–70.

Advancements in excess of statutory share   Case 11

T dies intestate leaving three sons, A, B and C, as his sole statutory heirs. T leaves no debts and his total estate consists of $200 in cash. During his lifetime he gave to A, $300, to B, $100 and to C nothing. How should the administrator distribute the estate?

Answer. B should get $50 and C should get $150. The gifts made to A and B are presumed to be advancements. But such presumption is rebuttable and may be shown to have been a gift absolute by evidence of the intestate's contrary intention at the time of the gift. Since there is no evidence of such contrary intention the advancements must be added into the estate. By adding A's $300 to B's $100 and to the $200 left by T would make $600 of which A, B and C each should take only a one-third share or $200. Every advancement is a gift which cannot be taken away from the donee. Hence, A will not share in the distribution, but he will not have to repay $100 to the estate. B and C will share pro rata in the remainder including B's advancement with B's $100 being credited against his share. So the administrator simply distributed to B $50 which, added to his $100 advancement, makes his total $150. C having received no advancement receives the remaining $150 of his parent's $200 estate.

See *Gaylord v. Hope Natural Gas Co.*, 122 W.Va. 205, 8 S.E.2d 189 (1940).

NOTE—It should be kept in mind that advancements apply only in case of total intestacy and should be compared with the doctrine of ademption in case of testacy.

QUALIFICATIONS ON THE RIGHT TO INHERIT

1. A person must be in being (either alive or in embryo) at the time of death of an intestate in order to inherit.

2. Persons conceived at the time of death of the intestate and born alive thereafter inherit as if they had been born in the intestate's lifetime. See Clark, pp. 117–119.

3. Many states provide that if there is no evidence of the order of death of two or more persons neither shall be presumed to have died first and the estate of each shall pass and descend as though he had survived the others. See Uniform Simultaneous Death Act (U.L.A.) § 1.

4. Many modern statutes provide that any person who fails to survive the decedent by a fixed period is deemed to have predeceased for purposes of intestate succession.   See UPC 2–601.

5. Many states have enacted statutes barring a person who feloniously and intentionally kills the decedent from sharing in the estate of his victim.   Some statutes require an adjudication of guilt in order to bar a taker; others allow a court to so determine by a preponderance of the evidence for such purpose.   See UPC 2–803.   See also CASE 12, below.

6. A person may be deprived of his share of an estate if he has practiced fraud, undue influence or duress upon the decedent.   See CASE 13, below.   See also Chapter XI, Constructive Trusts.

7. In many states a parent may not share in the estate of a child whom he has abandoned, or neglected.   Likewise it is often provided that a husband may not take from the estate of a wife he has failed to support.

8. In many states abandonment or adultery will bar a guilty husband or wife from participating in the spouse's estate.

See generally Atkinson, pp. 147–158; Clark, pp. 119–120; Ritchie pp. 101–108; and Scoles, p. 62.

Case 12   *One who intentionally kills another and inherits from him holds the estate in constructive trust for the next of kin*

D died intestate of gun shot wounds inflicted by his wife W who was later convicted of manslaughter.   Under the state statute of descent and distribution W is entitled to the whole of D's estate.   Having been convicted of manslaughter in connection with D's death is W entitled to his estate?

Answer. *No.   A person convicted of manslaughter in connection with the death of intestate may not inherit from his estate.   Many states have enacted statutes which prevent persons who kill another from taking by descent or distribution from the person who is killed. Where no statute exists three approaches have been taken by the court: (1) The legal title passes to the slayer and may be retained by him in spite of his crime.   (2) The legal title will not pass to the slayer because of the equitable principle that no one should be permitted to profit by his own fraud, or take advantage and profit as a result of his own wrong or crime.   (3) The legal title passes to the slayer but equity holds him to be a constructive trustee for the heirs or next of kin of the decedent.   The third approach is the better approach in that it avoids a judicial engrafting on the statutory laws of Descent and Distribution for title passes to the slayer, but equity treats the slayer as a constructive trustee and compels a conveyance to the heirs or the next of kin of the property held in the constructive* *trust. The principle that one should not profit by his own wrong should not be extended to every case where a slayer acquires property from a victim. It is only applicable to cases involving intentional and unlawful killing and therefore, generally does not apply to involuntary manslaughter which is not accompanied by an intention to take life. The determination must be made by an equity court which must determine upon proof that the slayer willfully killed the decedent before charging W as a constructive trustee. The fact that he is convicted in a criminal case does not dispense with the necessity of proof of murder in an equitable proceeding.*

See Estate of Mahoney, 126 Vt. 31, 220 A.2d 475 (1966).

NOTE—Contra *Bird* v. *Plunckett*, 139 Conn. 491, 95 A.2d 71 (1953) which held that a murderer is not barred from inheriting from a victim except where such limitation is imposed by statute. See also Chapter XI Constructive Trusts, below.

1. At common law aliens could not inherit real property but alien **ALIENS** friends could take personalty.

2. The trend is away from restrictions on an alien's right to inherit and in many states aliens may succeed to and transmit property as fully as any citizen. Some states, however, have retained some of the common law disabilities especially as to land.

3. Many states have statutes which place conditions on a non-resident alien's right to inherit:

(a) Some condition the right of a non-resident alien to inherit upon the right of a citizen of the state to inherit in the country of the non-resident alien (reciprocity statutes);

(b) Others condition the non-resident's right to inherit on his proof that if he receives the property in his country he will be entitled to its full use and benefit (retention statutes).

4. Many statutes limiting the rights of non-resident aliens to inherit are considered unconstitutional as an intrusion by the state into the field of foreign affairs which the Constitution entrusts exclusively to the President and Congress. See CASE 13, below.

See generally Atkinson, pp. 93–94; Clark, pp. 39–41; Ritchie, pp. 108–116; and Scoles, p. 59.

Statute providing for escheat where non-resident alien claims **Case 13**
personalty unconstitutional as invasion of area of foreign affairs

A state statute provides for escheat where a non-resident alien claims personalty unless: (1) there is a reciprocal right of a U.S. citizen to inherit property in the country of the non-resident alien on the same terms as the citizen of the foreign nation may inherit; (2) U.S. citizens have the right to receive payment here of funds from estates in the foreign country; and (3) foreign heirs have the right to receive the proceeds of estates without confiscation. Intestate's only heirs are residents of East Germany. The State petitions for escheat. The State statute required proof by the foreign heirs that they would receive the benefit, use and control of the money. Is the State statute unconstitutional?

Answer. Yes. The statute is unconstitutional in that it involves the state in foreign affairs and international relations, which are entrusted to the U.S. Congress and the President. Under the statute, the State court was mandated to make inquiries concerning the administration of foreign law and the credibility of foreign officers. Where state courts seek to ascertain if the rights protected by foreign law are the "same" rights enjoyed by citizens of the state it makes, "unavoidable judicial criticism of nations established on a more authoritarian basis." The case is to be distinguished from the situation where on the face of the statute the only thing required by the state or local court is that it make a routine reading of foreign law to ascertain if the foreign country concerned has a general reciprocity provision. The reciprocity type of provision has only a remote possibility of disturbing a foreign nation in that no inquiry is made into the administration of the law. It is where the court must make detailed inquiries into the administration of the foreign country's law that the foreign relations power of the federal government is infringed.

See *Zschering v. Miller*, 389 U.S. 429, 88 S.Ct. 664, 19 L.Ed.2d 683 (1968).

NOTE—In CASE 13, above, the opinion of the court was concurred in by only four justices; no majority of the court supported any one view. There were eight justices sitting with four opinions being written. Some justices would have held all reciprocal state statutes invalid as an intrusion into foreign relations. It, therefore, must be concluded that this area is still unsettled since no subsequent case has reached the court at this date. See Comment, The Demise of the "Iron Curtain" Statute, 18 Vill.L.Rev. 49 (1972).

Case 14 *Special rules for non-resident aliens not a denial of equal protection*

D died intestate, domiciled in the State of California. D's intestate successors are citizens of the USSR and residents in various parts of that country. A state statute provides that all non-resident aliens must demand their interests within five years from the date of succession or such interests will escheat. The statutory provision governing other heirs provides that they need only demand their interest within five years from the date of a decree of distribution. Claimants *who are non-resident aliens did not demand their interest within five years after D's death but did appear prior to the expiration of five years after the decree of distribution. The state brings an action for escheat and claimants contend that the statute is unconstitutional on the basis of lack of due process, denial of equal protection and state interference with foreign relations. Is the state entitled to escheat of claimants' interest in D's estate?*

Answer. *Yes. The state statute applying different rules to non-resident aliens from those applied to others does not constitute a denial of equal protection or due process, nor does it infringe the federal government's exclusive power over foreign relations. Assuming that the equal protection clause of the Fourteenth Amendment to the U.S. Constitution applies to non-resident aliens, the statutory scheme does not constitute an unreasonable classification in that the state has a legitimate interest in fixing title to property within its boundaries within a reasonable period of time and to prefer itself over non-resident-aliens as successors if they do not claim their inheritance within a fixed time. The classification is reasonably related to such purposes in that it is reasonable that, "Citizens and resident aliens are likely to have contacts and relationships within the state that non-resident aliens lack," and in recognition of such relationships to indulge these persons in a longer period of time before escheat. As to due process, the state (subject to the Federal Government's treaty making power, equal protection and privileges and immunity) has full power to regulate the descent and distribution of decedents' estate and may, if it sees fit, vest in non-resident aliens a conditional interest only in a decedent's estate. Since the state has full power to prohibit any succession, it may grant succession subject to any conditions it determines and there is no violation of a vested property right involved. The foreign relations power of the Federal Government is not infringed by the statutory provision in that the Code applies to all non-resident aliens regardless of country and does not involve a state court in any inquiry as to foreign law or administration.*

See In re Estate of Herman, 5 Cal.3d 62, 485 P.2d 785 (1971).

II | PROTECTION OF THE FAMILY

Summary Outline

A. Protection of the Spouse

B. Community Property

C. Dower, Curtesy and Elective Share
1. definitions
2. inter vivos transfers of property

D. Protection of Children
1. after borns
2. deceased parent's duty to support

E. Homestead, Family Allowance, and Exemptions

F. Gifts to Charity-Mortmain Statutes
1. limitations on amount
2. invalidation

PROTECTION OF THE SPOUSE

1. The balance between allowing freedom of testation and imposing certain limits on the objects of the disposition is reflected in the rules relating to mandatory shares of the estate provided for the surviving spouse and children. See *Transfers on Death—Introduction*, above.

2. The provision for the spouse and children of a decedent is a major reason both for allowing testamentary disposition of property and for placing limitations upon the freedom of testation. See *Protection of Children*, below.

3. The legal issues in this area usually concern:

   (a) the portion of the decedent's estate to which a surviving spouse is entitled;

   (b) the extent to which such rights may be defeated by lifetime transfers or other actions of decedent;

   (c) the extent to which a spouse may take priority over creditor's claims.

4. Three basic statutory approaches have developed to protect the surviving spouse against disinheritance. These are often available either in combinations (the election of some to the exclusion of others) or independently. They are:

   (a) the elective share;

   (b) community property; and

   (c) dower (or curtesy).

   NOTE—Homestead, exempt property and family allowances also protect the spouse, but are really directed to protection of the entire family unit against creditors. See *Homestead, Family Allowance and Exemptions*, below.

COMMUNITY PROPERTY

1. A community property system generally treats the husband and wife as co-owners of property acquired by either during the marriage. On the death of one, the survivor is entitled to one-half the property and the remainder (along with property not part of the community) goes according to the will of the decedent or under the relevant statute, if he dies intestate.

2. Property acquired by gift, bequest, descent or devise and property acquired by the decedent prior to the marriage is not part of the community.

3. Eight states have some form of community property. There are substantial differences among them with respect to the right to manage, control and alienate the property.

e.g. Under recent California legislation both spouses have equal management and control over the marital property. As a result each spouse is able to alienate for a valuable consideration the community personal property, without the consent of the other spouse.

See generally Atkinson, pp. 63–64; Clark, pp. 137–140; and Ritchies, pp. 77–78, 131–132.

1. At common law the wife was entitled to *dower,* a life interest in *one-third* of the land owned by her husband in fee simple or fee tail during the marriage.

2. *Curtesy* was the right of a husband, if there were issue born of the marriage, to a life interest in *all* of his wife's lands held in fee simple or fee tail.

3. Dower or curtesy gives a fixed interest to one spouse in all land owned during the marriage. Unless released by the holder thereof, a dower or curtesy interest cannot be defeated by transfer to a bona fide purchaser and is not subject to creditors' claims.

4. The dower interest in lands of a spouse is "inchoate" during the life of that spouse, i.e. the dower holder must survive his or her spouse to take a possessory interest. On survival the inchoate interest becomes "consummate", i.e. vested in possession.

5. Most states have abolished common law dower and curtesy. Many have established similar statutory schemes, usually treating husband and wife identically. Some statutes subject dower to debts of the decedent and some extend such rights to personalty as well as to land. Some allow dower in addition to testamentary provisions; others in lieu of testamentary provisions. See Rheinstein, pp. 89–92.

6. Most states have statutes allowing a surviving spouse to elect either a forced share (usually one-third or what would have gone to such spouse by intestacy) or the provision made in the spouse's will. This election must be exercised in the manner and within the time provided in the statute. In some states such provision is in lieu of dower. In others dower still attaches to property transferred by a decedent during life without consent or waiver, and in others one may choose between several alternatives. Election provisions usually attach to the net probate estate and the statutory interests are therefore subject to creditors' claims.

7. Whether an inter vivos transfer during marriage is effective to deprive a surviving spouse of an elective share depends on whether:

DOWER, CURTESY AND ELECTIVE SHARE

(a) it was made with intent to deter the election; or

(b) the transfer is real or illusory.

See *Illusory Trusts*, Chapter VI, below.   See also CASE 42, below.

8. The Uniform Probate Code provisions abolish all rights of the spouse except an elective share in one-half of the decedent's estate which is adjusted to include certain lifetime transfers and which credits against the survivor's share benefits received during the decedent's lifetime.   See UPC, PART 2, *General Comment;* UPC 2–201–2–207.   See also McKinney's N.Y.E.P.T.L. 5–11.

9. Some states have statutes which protect a spouse against unintentional disinheritance by giving the spouse a share of the estate where a will was executed by decedent prior to the marriage and where it does not appear that the omission was intentional.   See UPC 2–301.

10. A spouse may usually waive, release or contract away dower or other statutory rights by either ante-nuptial or post-nuptial agreement if the agreement is fair and made with knowledge of all the relevant facts.

See generally Atkinson, pp. 104–126; Clark, pp. 140–144; Rheinstein, pp. 87–102; Ritchie pp. 117–130; and Scoles, pp. 74–81.

Case 15   *Right of surviving spouse to invalidate Totten trust*

D died intestate leaving H as her surviving spouse.   During her lifetime she placed funds in a savings account in which she was named as trustee and the accounts were for the benefit for her two children by a prior marriage.   She retained control over this account during her lifetime and made deposits in and withdrawals from it.   The account specifically provided that it was to be paid to the children named therein on her death.   H as administrator and as surviving spouse has filed an action claiming that the trust is a fraud on his marital rights and is illusory and if sustained will defeat his right to one-third of the decedent's estate and to a widower's award.   He asks that the bank account be turned over to him as the administrator of the estate.   Is he correct?

Answer. *Yes, to the extent of his statutory share.   The general rule is that a savings account trust is no different from any other revocable inter vivos trust even though the enjoyment of the interest is postponed and the interest may be destroyed by the settlor prior to death.   The question remains, however, whether such a trust is valid to defeat the surviving spouse's statutory share in the estate of* *the deceased spouse and the right to a widower's award. Some cases have suggested that the result should depend upon whether or not the deceased intended to defraud the surviving spouse of a statutory share. This approach is undesirable in view of the difficulties of determining whether such intent is tainted with fraud. The better approach is to consider the trust illusory as to the surviving spouse. The expressed statutory policy is to protect him since, during her life, D retained absolute control over the bank account. The enjoyment of the proceeds by the beneficiaries was, therefore, dependent upon the account remaining intact at her death.*

See Montgomery v. Michaels, 54 Ill.2d 532, 301 N.E.2d 465 (1973).

NOTE—Arrangements for bypassing Probate such as a trust, insurance, and jointly-held property with the right of survivorship are increasingly major forms of wealth transmission. Many of the statutory devices for protecting the family are ineffective to protect family members against such transfers. A modern trend in other countries is to authorize the court to make such allowances for the spouse and children as are appropriate from these assets. Under these arrangements, if a dependent of a decedent is of the opinion that the will does not make an adequate provision for support and maintenance, the dependent may apply to a court which will order such reasonable provision as the court thinks fit out of the decedent's property. This is the approach of the British system. See Inheritance (Family Provision) Act, 1938, 1 and 2 Geo. VI, page 45 and subsequent amendments thereto. See also Clark, pp. 208–210.

Survivor of parties who cohabit not entitled to share in estate in absence of agreement or will Case 16

D and M although unmarried, lived together as husband and wife for thirteen years prior to D's death. D died intestate. M filed a claim against the estate claiming $30,000 or a one-half interest in the real property in D's estate. M claims that she is entitled to a portion of D's property on the ground that during the period of cohabitation they had shared their earnings and resources and had purchased property with their combined earnings which were placed in D's name. Is M entitled to share in D's estate?

Answer. *No. M cannot obtain an interest in D's property unless she can establish a contract to that effect between herself and D. M's only evidence on which to base a claim for a one-half interest in D's estate is that she rendered services to him during life, including housework and assisting in heavy work in constructing walls and rockeries. It is presumed that these services were rendered gratuitously in the absence of an agreement that since D neither made a will or married M, he must be presumed to have intended to keep the real property and to pass it to his heirs at death.*

See *Green v. Richmond, 369 Mass. 47, 337 N.E.2d 691 (1975).*

NOTE—Other cases have allowed recovery in similar situations on finding that a contract was established or on the basis of quantum meruit.

PROTECTION OF CHILDREN

1. The general rule is that children may be completely disinherited by their parents.

2. Many states have *pretermitted heir* provisions which give children born or adopted after the execution of a will an intestate share unless it appears that the omission was intentional. Such provisions also extend to children thought dead, but who were in fact alive, at the time of the execution of the will. See UPC 2–302.

3. Where there is a legal duty upon the parent to support a minor child, it is thought that an action may be maintained against the deceased parent's estate for support payments.

   See generally Atkinson, pp. 138–146; Clark, pp. 194–196; and Ritchie, 143–144.

HOMESTEAD, FAMILY ALLOWANCE, AND EXEMPTIONS

1. Statutes providing for family allowance, homestead and exempt properties give a measure of protection to a family by providing additional property for them and exempting property from creditors' claims. These provisions vary from state to state.

2. Homestead allows the continuation of residence free from creditors' claims in the family home usually during the minority of the children and/or life of the widow.

3. The family allowance (usually not available to a widower) allows a certain amount for the support of the widow and children during the administration process.

4. Exempt property usually allows specified chattels, such as wearing apparel, furniture and personal effects, to pass to the family of the decedent not subject to general creditors' claims.

   See generally Atkinson, pp. 126–138; Rheinstein, pp. 102–104; Ritchie, pp. 78–80; and Scoles, pp. 73–74.

GIFTS TO CHARITY— MORTMAIN STATUTES

1. At common law various statutes were enacted which restricted or forbade charitable and religious societies or corporations from holding property. These statutes were known as Statutes of Mortmain (literally "Dead Hand") and were intended to prevent

land from becoming perpetually controlled by one dead hand, that of the charitable entity.

2. Many states have "mortmain" type statutes which limit the power of a testator to make charitable gifts. Modern mortmain statutes are usually for the purpose of protecting the family of a decedent from disinheritance by death-bed gifts to charity. Such limitations are usually operative only where near relatives (usually children, grandchildren, parents and surviving spouse) survive.

3. Such statutes limit charitable gifts in one or both of the following ways:

   (a) limit the amount of the gift to a certain proportion of the estate;

   (b) invalidate gifts made within a specified period preceding death, e.g. within six months.

   See generally Atkinson, pp. 135–138; Clark, pp. 196–199; Ritchie, p. 150; and Scoles, p. 91

Disinheritance by express inclusion not effective　　　　Case 17

One month prior to her death testatrix executed a will leaving all of her property to charity and contained in the will was the following provision: "I have knowingly and intentionally failed to make any provision herein for my granddaughter, Susan, who has shown me no affection over the years and it is my express desire that she in no way share in my estate." The will contained no other clause which would be operable if the gifts to charities should fail. Susan was heir at law of testatrix. The gifts to charities were void under the provision of the state's mortmain statute and thus Susan would take as an heir at law. Can Susan inherit the decedent's estate?

Answer. *Yes. A testator can disinherit his heirs and next of kin only by leaving the property to others. Mere words of disinheritance will not suffice when property is not otherwise disposed of by will. Upon failure of the gift to charity it descends and is distributed under the state's statute of descent and distribution.*

See Balytat v. Morris, 28 Ohio App.2d 191, 276 N.E.2d 258 (1971). See also Atkinson, p. 145.

Pretermitted heir takes where will does not show intent to disinherit them　　　　Case 18

Testator died leaving as his heirs at law one daughter and ten grandchildren who are children of a deceased daughter, Myrtle. Eight of

Myrtle's children were not mentioned in the will, five being born after its execution.   The only mention of the deceased daughter in testator's will was in a disposition giving property to a grandchild to wit;   To "my granddaughter, Myrtle, daughter of my daughter, Myrtle."   A state statute provides "when any testator omits to provide in his will for any of his children or for the issue of any deceased child unless it appears that such omission was intentional, such child, or the issue of such child must have the same share in the estate of testator as if he had died intestate.   .   .   ."   Are the omitted grandchildren entitled to a share of the decedent's estate?

Answer.   Yes.   It is not clear from the four corners of the will that the testator intended to disinherit either his daughter or his grandchildren.   The mention of the name of the daughter was only a descriptive name to properly identify a granddaughter and was consistent with the manner in which testator uniformly identified other takers under the will.   The statute is directed to an 'omission to provide' rather than an 'omission to name' the testator's child or child of a deceased child.   Therefore, the omitted grandchildren are entitled to take a share of the estate under the terms of the statute.

See Atkinson, pp. 141–146.

III EXECUTION AND VALIDITY OF WILLS

Summary Outline

1. A will is a *legal* declaration of one's intention to dispose of his property after death.

2. At common law an instrument disposing of *personal* property was called a "testament"; one disposing of *real* property, a "will". This distinction has been eliminated in modern times and an instrument conveying real and/or personal property is called a "will" or a "last will and testament".

3. Every will is ambulatory, which means that it can be changed or revoked at any moment before death by a competent testator. See *Contracts to Devise or Bequeath Property*, below.

4. There is no common law right to make a will; such right is wholly statutory.

5. There is no will without compliance with the statutory requirements.

6. One who dies leaving a will dies *testate*, and is called a *testator*.

7. Gifts made by will are called:

    (a) if of land, a *devise*,

    (b) if of money, a *legacy*, and

    (c) if of personalty, a *bequest*.

8. The *personal representative* is the person authorized by the Court to administer the estate.

9. An *executor* is a person named in a will to administer the estate.

10. An *administrator* is a person appointed by the court to administer the estate of an intestate.

11. When an executor cannot serve or will not serve, or when the will fails to appoint such, the Court will appoint an *administrator with the will annexed* (or administrator cum testamento annexo) to administer the will. See *The Appointment of the Personal Representative*, Chapter XIII, below.

    Compare *Intestate Succession—Terminology*, Chapter I, above.

**WHO MAY MAKE
A WILL**

1. All states have statutes enabling persons to make wills and prescribing the formalities for executing wills. These derive from the English Statute of Wills (1540) and the Statute of Frauds (1676). See UPC 2–501, 2–502. See also *Written and Witnessed Wills*, below.

2. A valid will requires the co-existence of three essential elements:

    (a) a competent testator;

(b) physical compliance with the requirements of the statute; and

(c) animus testandi, the testator's intent that this instrument shall be a will.

3. A competent testator is one who is of sound mind and of a requisite age at the time of making the will.

4. All states have a minimum age (usually 18) below which a person lacks capacity to make a will. A person under the minimum age must necessarily die intestate.

5. At common law, married women were unable to make wills. This rule has been abolished generally. See *e.g.* Ohio R.C. § 2107.02.

6. One has testamentary capacity, or sound mind, if he has sufficient mind:

(a) to understand:

   (i) the nature and extent of his property,

   (ii) the natural objects of his bounty,

   (iii) the nature of the testamentary act, and

   (iv) the foregoing elements in relation to each other; and

(b) to form an orderly desire as to the disposition of his property. See Atkinson, p. 232.

7. A testator may be incapacitated mentally because of:

(a) mental deficiency (idiocy, imbecility); or

(b) mental derangement (having insane delusions such as those found in paranoia paresis, senile dementia). See Ritchie, p. 311.

8. An insane delusion is the belief in a state of facts when there is no evidence to support it and all evidence demonstrates the contrary. For an insane delusion to invalidate a will, there must be the delusion, *and* the will must be the product of such delusion.

e.g. A man believes contrary to facts known to him, that his wife is unfaithful to him. He makes a will disinheriting her. This is an insane delusion and the will is a product of the delusion.

9. A person who suffers from mental derangement may have *lucid intervals* during which he may execute a valid will.

10. There can be no insane delusion unless the belief is subject to disproof by demonstrative evidence.

e.g.   A religious belief in the hereafter, the truth of which can neither be proved nor disproved, cannot be an insane delusion.

11. Moral depravity, illiteracy, extreme old age, great weakness, being deaf and dumb, blindness and severe illness do not disqualify a testator although they may be elements in determining mental capacity.   See Atkinson, p. 249.

12. Mere eccentricities or prejudices or unusual religious beliefs do not by themselves constitute insane delusions.   See generally Atkinson, pp. 228–252; Clark, pp. 225–230; and Ritchie, pp. 319–321.

Case 19   *Issue of whether will is a product of testator's insane delusion is a question for the jury*

T executed a will one month before his death.   By its terms he cut off his wife, leaving her the minimum statutory share and left the remainder of his estate to certain named relatives.   When the will was offered for probate, the widow filed objections claiming that the purported will was invalid in that testator was not of sound and disposing mind and memory.   At the trial evidence was adduced which showed that testator and W had had a long and happy marriage until shortly before testator's death when he became obsessed with the idea that his wife was unfaithful to him.   He told friends and strangers alike using obscene and abusive language, about his wife's infidelity; otherwise, he was normal and rational in all respects. The executor based his contention that there was a reasonable basis for T's belief on several incidents concerning the receipt of an anniversary card addressed to the wife alone, some reference to a letter whose contents was not established, the fact that W answered the telephone whenever it rang and that W had once asked T when he was leaving the house what time she might expect him to return. The jury decided that the testator was not of sound and disposing mind and memory at the time he made the purported will.   T's executor has appealed.   What Result?

Answer.   The jury's verdict should be upheld.   The issue to be resolved is not whether W was unfaithful but whether R had any reasonable basis for believing that she was.   The test is, "If a person persistently believes supposed facts, which have no real existence except in his perverted imagination, and against all evidence and probability, and conducts himself, however logically, upon the assumption of their existence, he has so far as they are concerned under a morbid delusion; and delusion in that sense is insanity."   When the contestant has produced evidence reflecting the operation of the testator's mind, it is the proponent of the will's duty to provide a basis for the alleged delusion.   When in the light of a long and happy marriage a husband expresses suspicions of his wife's unfaithfulness and the proponent has produced only trivia to support such irrational and unwarranted beliefs, the court cannot conclude as a matter of law that there was a basis for the alleged delusion. In such case the issue of sanity is one of fact for the jury to determine. Moreover, if T was laboring under an insane delusion the existence of other reasons for his disposition such as the size of W's independent fortune and the need for his actual legatees, are not enough to support the validity of the instrument. A will is invalid when its depositive provisions were or might have been caused or affected by the delusion.

See In re Honingman's Will, 8 N.Y.2d 244, 203 N.Y.S.2d 859, 168 N.E.2d 676 (1960).

Dominant intention of testatrix gathered from the instrument as a whole determines if a will is conditional

Case 20

T executed an instrument containing the following language: "I am going on a journey and may not ever return. If I do not, this is my last request. The mortgage on the King house is to go to the Methodist Church. All the rest of my property both real and personal to my adopted son." T subsequently went on her journey returned to her home and resumed her occupation and died several months later. When offered for probate, probate was denied on the ground that the will was conditioned upon an event which did not come to pass. Should the will have been admitted to probate?

Answer. Yes. The question presented is whether the instrument is void because of the return of the deceased from her contemplated journey. On the one hand the literal language of the document indicates that decedent's failure to return from the journey is a condition of the bequest. On the other hand, however, the primary intent of T may be gathered from the instrument as a whole. "Courts do not incline to regard a will as conditional where it can be reasonably held that the testator was merely expressing his inducement to make it, however inaccurate his use of language might be, if strictly construed." It was natural for T to express the general contingency of death in the concrete form in which she just then imagined it. Moreover, the nature of the two gifts was of a kind that indicates an abiding and unconditioned intent, one to a church the other to a person whom she called her son. It is unlikely that such a condition would be attached to such gifts. If her failure to return from the journey had been in fact a condition of her bounty, it is more likely that she would have explained the contingency rather than giving the reason which on the face of it has a reference to an unconditioned gift.

See Eaton v. Brown, 193 U.S. 411, 24 S.Ct. 487, 48 L.Ed. 730 (1904).

FRAUD AND UNDUE INFLUENCE

1. A will executed through either undue influence or fraud is invalid. The test of undue influence is the *substitution of another's will* for that of the testator. The elements of undue influence are:

   (a) a susceptible testator,

   (b) another's opportunity to influence the testator,

   (c) improper influence in fact either exerted or attempted, and

   (d) the result showing the effect of such influence.

2. Mere advice, persuasion, affection, or kindness does not alone constitute undue influence.

3. The existence of a confidential relationship between a testator and a beneficiary may raise a presumption of undue influence, especially if combined with some other factor such as an unnatural disposition.

   e.g. A lawyer-draftsman of a will who is given the estate to the exclusion of testator's family, will be presumed to have exerted undue influence on the client.

4. Fraud is distinguishable from undue influence in that fraud involves an element of deceit.

5. Fraud consists of either:

   (a) fraud in the *execution*,

   i.e., the testator is deceived as to the character or contents of the document he is signing; or

   (b) fraud in the *inducement*,

   i.e., when the testator makes the will or provision relying upon a false representation of a material fact made to him by one who knows it to be false.

6. Innocent misrepresentations will not invalidate a will.

   See generally Atkinson, pp. 255–269; Ritchie, pp. 337–342, 349–352; and Scoles, pp. 482–487.

Case 21   *Bequest is void if it is the fruit of a fraud perpetrated on testatrix*

T died leaving a duly executed will in which she left the bulk of her estate to "my husband J." T's heirs contested the validity of the will on the ground that T mistakenly believed that J was her husband when she made the will. T had gone through a marriage ceremony with J a year before her death. They were not legally married because J was already married to another woman. The trial court refused revocation of probate as a matter of law. T's heirs have appealed. What result?

Answer. *The issue should have been sent to the jury.* *Evidence that T's marriage to J was induced by his misrepresentation that he was free to marry her, she made the will shortly thereafter in the belief that he was her lawful husband and that she was never undeceived on that point is sufficient to have sustained a possible verdict by the jury invalidating the will.* *There can be no question that the testatrix was a victim of a fraud perpetrated by J and that if the bequest to J were the direct fruit of such fraud it is void.* *The question is one of fact for a jury to have determined.* *Even though the contestants offered no direct evidence that the inducing reasons in T's mind for her bequest to J was her belief that he was her legal husband and offered only evidence that T had been tricked into the marriage, it is not an unreasonable inference from the fact that they were recently married when the will was made and that the bulk of the estate was left to the husband that she would not have left the property to him if she had not believed they were married.* *Even in the absence of proof of other circumstances the inference is not an unreasonable one from the fact of the bigamous marriage alone, and a jury may on such evidence determine that the will was a result of the fraud.*

See In re Carson's Estate, 184 Cal. 437, 194 P. 5 (1920).

MISTAKE IN THE EXECUTION OF A WILL

1. If a testator signs the wrong document in the mistaken, belief that it is his will, there is no will.

2. If a testator *omits* to include some provision in his will there can be no relief because a will cannot be reformed and the deceased testator cannot comply with the statute of wills.

3. If the testator is mistaken as to the legal effect of the language he uses in his will there cannot be any relief for it would be making a will for a decedent.

4. A provision *included* in a will by mistake may be omitted by the probate court when the will is admitted to probate. This will usually depend upon whether or not the inclusion is separable. This rests upon two considerations:

   (a) Will the deletion substantially alter other provisions in the instrument, and

   (b) If a substantial alteration will occur, will the intention of the testator be effectuated best by probating the will as written or by deleting the materials mistakenly included and the provision affected by the deletion? See Ritchie, p. 341.

5. If there is an ambiguity in describing either the person to take or the property to pass, then parol evidence is admissible to explain the person or property intended.

6. If the words used by the testator describe a particular person or property exactly and none other, then no parol evidence is available to show he intended some other person or property. See *Case 22,* below.

7. A will generally is not invalid where testator makes a will on the basis of a mistake in a material fact, *mistake in the inducement.*

   e.g. Where testator makes no provision for his niece believing her to have married a wealthy man and in fact he is a pauper, the will is valid.

8. Some statutes give relief where a testator has made a will mistakenly believing that an absent child is dead. Such statutes usually give the child the share he would have taken, had testator died intestate. See *Protection of Children,* Chapter II, above.

9. If both the mistake and the testator's desires, but for the mistake, appear on the face of the will a court may give some remedy to effectuate the intent of the testator. Such cases are extremely rare. To do so is consistent with cases of dependent relative revocation.

   See Gifford v. Dyer, 2 R.I. 99 (1852). See also Conditional Revocation and Dependent Relative Revocation, Chapter IV, below. See generally Atkinson, pp. 273–288; Ritchie, pp. 359–361 and Scoles, pp. 133–134.

Case 22 *Evidence admitted to clarify latent ambiguity*

T died leaving a validly executed will which contained a clause as follows: "To Robert J. Crouse, now of 4708 North 46th Street, Milwaukee, Wisconsin, if he survives me, one percent (1%)." T had never had any contact with said Robert J. Crouse, however T had employed a person named Robert W. Crouse for many years who lives near but not at 4708 North 46th Street. In addition the legacy appeared in a sequence of similar legacies to former employees of T. Robert W. brought an action for construction of the will on the basis that T had meant to give the legacy to him rather than to the Robert J. Crouse who lived at the address indicated in the will. At the trial the court took judicial notice of the fact that the telephone directory of Milwaukee and Vicinity listed 14 subscribers by the name of Robert Crouse with varying middle initials, among them Robert J. at 4708 North 46th Street. Who is entitled to the legacy?

   Answer. *Robert W. Upon consideration of the evidence the court could come to no other conclusion than that T intended to designate Robert W. as his legatee. The issue, however, is whether or not the* *court could properly consider such evidence in determining testi-mentary intent. The general rule is that unless there is ambiguity in the text of a will read in the light of surrounding circumstances extrinsic evidence is inadmissible for the purposes of determining intent. A latent ambiguity exists where the language of a will though clear on its face is susceptible of more than one meaning when applied to the extrinsic facts to which it referred. In the will in question there is no ambiguity in that the terms of the bequest exactly fit Robert J. and no one else. Under the traditional rule wills may not be reformed even in the case of demonstrable mistake. Even though courts may subscribe to an inflexible rule against reformation, they have often used construction to identify property or beneficiaries. Courts may also in probating the will deny probate to a provision which was included by mistake. In the present case the details of identification, particularly middle initials and street addresses in a metropolitan area, should not be allowed to frustrate an otherwise clearly demonstrable intent. Therefore, it is proper to disregard the middle initial and street address and determine that Robert W. Crouse is the person to whom the legacy was made.*

Admissibility of parol evidence to explain latent ambiguities   Case 23

T's will provided, "I give my house on 8th Street to the son of George Gord." Upon T's death it was discovered that T had two houses on 8th Street and that George Gord had two sons, John and James. Parol evidence was offered to show that John Gord was a barber and that one house on 8th Street known as number 14 was peculiarly fitted to be used as a barbershop and that T had told several friends that he wanted John to have number 14 when T died. Was the evidence admissible?

Answer. Yes. From the face of the will it is evident that T intended not either house on 8th Street, but a specific house for he says "my house". Likewise it is apparent that he intended not either son of Gord but "the son". Had it been either house or either son, then the devise should fail for indefiniteness, and no parol evidence would be admissible to make valid a devise which is invalid because too vague. But there being ambiguity in the description of the house to pass and the son to take it is not a violation of the parol evidence rule to permit parol evidence to explain but not to alter the terms actually used in an instrument. The offered evidence that son John was a barber, that house number 14 was well fitted as a barbershop and that T had actually declared that John was to have the house, makes quite clear that which was before ambiguous. The words of the will are not changed but rather explained.

See *Doe v. Needs,* Ct. of Exch. 1836, 2 M. & W. 129; Ch. Div. 1916, 1 Ch. 461. See also Atkinson, p. 281.

REMEDIES FOR FRAUD, UNDUE INFLUENCE OR MISTAKE

1. The general rule is that persons deprived of benefitting under a will because of fraud or duress can obtain relief only by invalidation of the will.

2. When only a part of a will is affected by undue influence, fraud, mistake or insane delusions only the affected part will be invalidated.   See Atkinson, pp. 289–290.

3. Where a testator has been prevented from executing or revoking a will by fraud, duress or undue influence there is a trend to impose a constructive trust against the wrongdoer in favor of the person who otherwise would have benefitted.

   See Case 24, below.   See generally Atkinson, pp. 270–271; Palmey, p. 598; and Ritchie, pp. 367–372.

Case 24   *Duress preventing revocation of a will*

Testatrix died leaving a will giving her whole estate to the leader of a religious cult and one of his followers.   After executing this will testatrix had often expressed the determination to execute a new will in favor of her niece, and prior to her death had her attorney draft a new will to such effect.   By means of false representations, undue influence and physical force the beneficiaries under the first will prevented testatrix from executing the second will.   Can the niece obtain any relief against the beneficiaries under the will?

    Answer.   *Yes.   The beneficiaries under the will hold what they receive as constructive trustees for the niece.   By force and fraud the beneficiaries under the first will prevented the testatrix from making a will in favor of her niece.   Where a devisee or legatee under a will already executed prevents the testator by fraud, duress or undue influence from revoking the will and executing a new will in favor of another so that the testatrix dies leaving the original will in force, the devisee holds the property upon a constructive trust for the intended devisee or legatee.   To do so does not annul the provisions of the statute of wills requiring due execution of the will.   The will is given full effect by passing the property to the beneficiary under the will.   Then equity acts upon the gift itself as it reaches the possession of the wrongdoer and imposes a trust on it as soon as it reaches his possession, compelling him to turn over the gift to the intended beneficiary.*

    See Latham v. Father Divine, 229 N.Y. 22, 85 N.E.2d 168 (1949). See also Pope v. Garrett, 147 Tex. 18, 211 S.W.2d 559 (1948); Constructive Trusts in General, Chapter XI, below.

1. There are three kinds of wills:

    (a) written and witnessed;

    (b) holographic (olographic); and

    (c) nuncupative (oral).

2. The authenticity of a written and witnessed will is vouched for by the witnesses.

3. The authenticity of a holographic will is vouched for by the genuineness of the testator's handwriting.

4. The authenticity of a nuncupative will is vouched for by the circumstances in which it is made. See *Wills Not Meeting Ordinary Execution Requirements*, below.

5. The formalities required for each type of will are regulated by state statute, and vary from state to state.

6. Written and witnessed wills are permissible in every jurisdiction.

7. Holographic and nuncupative wills are valid in only some states.

CLASSIFICATION OF WILLS

1. Every state has a statute prescribing the formalities requisite to testamentary disposition. These requirements relate to:

    (a) writing,

    (b) signing,

    (c) publication,

    (d) witnessing or attestation, and

    (e) presence.

2. State statutes are usually based on a provision in the English Statute of Frauds which provided: All devises and bequests of any land or tenement shall be in *writing signed* by the party so devising the same or by some other person in his presence and by his express directions and shall be *attested and subscribed* in the presence of the said deviser by three or four *credible witnesses* or else they shall be utterly void and of no effect. 29 Car. 2, c. 3, § 3 (1676).

3. An attempt to make a will coupled with an intent to do so will not make a valid will unless the terms of the statute are fulfilled.

4. To constitute a writing there must be a readable inscription in any language on a substance which makes the recording thereof relatively permanent.

    (a) A writing on the sand of the seashore would not suffice.

WRITTEN AND WITNESSED WILLS

(b) Inscribing legible material on a slate would be sufficient.

(c) Writing on paper with lead pencil is sufficient.

(d) Pen and ink or typewriter on paper is sufficient.

5. Any mark such as an x, a zero, or check mark or name intended by a competent testator to constitute his signature as authenticating his will is a valid signing. This is likewise true of the signature of a witness.

6. A few jurisdictions require the testator to publish his will. This means that he must declare to the witnesses that the instrument is his will. No jurisdiction requires the witnesses to know the contents of the will.

7. Some states require the signing by the testator in presence of witnesses. The majority, however, require only an acknowledgment of the signature to the witnesses. In some states this must be to all witnesses at the same time; in others acknowledgment to each witness, separately is sufficient.

e. g. If testator takes his will which he has already signed to a witness and shows him the signature acknowledging that it is his signature, it is thus acknowledged. An acknowledgment "this is my will" is usually sufficient as an acknowledgment of signature. See UPC 2–502.

8. The words "in the presence of the testator" or "in the presence of the witnesses" usually mean in the line of vision of the testator or witnesses, not that one must actually see the signing just that he could have seen.

9. Some more liberal cases have held that it is only necessary that the event be close at hand and within general cognizance.

e. g. A blind person may make a will with witnesses subscribing in a place where if the testator did have vision he could see them. See Atkinson, p. 344.

10. The signature of the testator may be affixed:

(a) by himself personally, or

(b) by some other person in the presence of the testator and at his direction.

By the better view the same rule applies in case of a witness.

11. The signature of the testator may appear any place on the will, but if the statute requires it to be "subscribed" or "at the end thereof" then it must be preceded by the contents of the will. This principle also applies to witnesses.

12. A minority of states requires the testator to request the witnesses to attest and subscribe. This may be implied by the testator's permitting them to sign.

13. As between testator and witnesses the order of signing is unimportant if all sign as part of a single transaction. Some cases hold that it is sufficient if the testator signs after the witnesses in their absence, but later acknowledges his signature to them. See Bloechle v. Davis, 132 Ohio St. 434, 8 N.E.2d 247 (1937).

See generally Atkinson, pp. 321–344; Clark, pp. 279–281; Palmer, pp. 19–24; Ritchie, pp. 152–170; and Scoles, pp. 100–110.

Animus testandi must be present in order for an instrument to   Case 25
constitute a will

Prior to his death T executed an instrument in the form of a statutory warranty deed whereby he purported to convey certain lands to S. The instrument was attested by two credible witnesses. He placed the deed in an envelope and delivered it to a friend having written on the envelope that the deed was to be delivered to S after the death of T. The friend delivered the deed after T's death, but subsequently the heirs of T contested the validity of the deed on the basis of want of delivery. Their contention was sustained in a court action. S then offered the instrument for probate as a will. Should probate be granted?

Answer. *No. The rule is that any writing however informal made with the express intent of disposing of one's property after death and if executed in accordance with the statutory requirements will be a valid will. The deed in this case was executed in conformity to the Statute of Wills in that it was signed by T and by two credible witnesses. In addition, however, it must appear on the face of the instrument that it is not intended to take effect until the death of the maker. Where the instrument contains nothing in the writing itself which imparts to it a testamentary character for all evidence is inadmissible to show the intention of the testator. "If an unambiguous deed, which on its face purports to convey a present interest, can be converted into a will by proving animus testandi in the maker by parol evidence, the effect is not only to change the legal character of the instrument, but to engraft upon it one of the essentials of a will."*

See Noble v. Fickes, 230 Ill. 594, 82 N.E. 950 (1907).

NOTE—In Butler v. Sherwood, 196 App.Div. 603, 188 N.Y.S. 242 (1921) the decedent prior to her death executed and delivered a quitclaim deed of all of her real estate and personal property to her husband. In addition to the words of conveyance, however, the deed contained a provision stating "this conveyance and transfer are made upon the condition that the Party of the Second Part survive me, and the same is intended to vest and take effect upon my decease and until said time the same shall be subject to revocation upon the part of the Party of the First Part." The court held that the transfer could not be sustained as an executed gift in that it was not to take effect until the decease of the transferor, when the law prevents a transfer otherwise by a Last Will and Testament. Since the deed did not conform to the requirement for a will the husband did not take the property. See Gulliver and Tilson, "Classification of Gratuitous Transfers," 51 Yale L.J. 1 (1941).

Case 26   *Partnership agreement not subject to the requirements of the statute of wills*

Prior to D's death, D had been a partner in an investment club. The partnership agreement of the investment club provided, "in the event of the death of any partner his share will be transferred to his wife with no termination of the partnership." The executors of D's estate have brought a proceeding claiming that the provision in the partnership agreement is an invalid attempt to make a testamentary disposition of property and that the proceeds should pass under the decedent's will as an asset of his estate rather than to his widow under the terms of the partnership agreement. Who is correct?

Answer. The widow. The partnership provision in effect is a third party beneficiary contract performable at death. It is contractual in nature and need not conform to the provisions of the Statute of Wills. Other transactions are similar in nature such as an inter-vivos trust in which the settlor reserves a life estate, an insurance policy, or a contract to make a will. None of these transactions is invalid as attempted testamentary dispositions.

See In re Estate of Hillowitz, 22 N.Y.2d 107, 291 N.Y.S.2d 325, 238 N.E.2d 723 (1968).

CREDIBILITY OF WITNESSES

1. All state statutes require two or three witnesses to the will. These witnesses are usually required both to sign *and* to attest which are separate functions:

   (a) Attestation connotes the state of mind by which the witness intends to bear witness to the performance of the acts required by the statute to validate the will.

   (b) Signing or subscribing refers to the physical act of the witness and putting his hand to paper.

2. Witnesses are required to be *credible* which means competent to testify. The better view is that competency is determined at the time of the execution of the will. The Uniform Probate Code eliminates the requirement that the witnesses be credible. See UPC 2–502, 2–505.

3. At common law any witnesses having a pecuniary interest in a matter was incompetent to testify, and therefore a beneficiary under a will could not be an attesting witness.

   (a) By the more modern view the words *credible* or *competent* mean competent under the rules of evidence at the time the will is executed.

   (b) Modern rules of evidence usually do not disqualify a witness for interest, but such interest goes only to the witnesses' credibility.

   See Clark, pp. 295–298, 301–304.

4. In order to uphold wills many jurisdictions passed "purging" statutes eliminating the interest of witness-beneficiaries in order that they might testify.

   e. g. T leaves $1000 to W in her will. W serves as a witness to the will. Under a purging statute W's gift would be struck from the will. Then W has no interest under the will. Having no interest, it would not be to her benefit to testify falsely to make sure the will is admitted to probate. It is then assumed that she will testify objectively.

   CAVEAT—Even though modern rules of evidence do not in general disqualify a witness for interest, purging statutes may nevertheless eliminate the interest of a witness beneficiary. See UPC 3–406.

5. If a purging statute is to prevent a witness from taking under a will, the benefit must be direct and financial. If the witness is also an intestate successor under the will, only the interest in excess of the amount he would receive if the will is not valid is usually purged.

6. A purging statute does not affect indirect interests.

   e. g. If the testator leaves $100,000 to St. Paul's church and the witness to the will is a member of the church, the gift to the church will not be invalidated.

7. Interests of creditors, attorneys and executors are usually not sufficient to disqualify.

8. Where the spouse of a witness is a beneficiary, some states allow the witness to testify and the spouse to take the interest; others purge the spouse's interest.

9. A witness must sign with intent to validate the testator's act.

10. An attestation clause is a certificate signed by witnesses to a will reciting performance of formalities of execution which the witnesses observed.

11. An attestation clause is not required for validity of the will but in some states is prima facie evidence that the statements made therein are true.

NOTE—The Uniform Probate Code provides for a will to be "self-proved" by the affidavit of the testator and witnesses reciting the facts of executor before an officer authorized to administer oaths at the time of execution or subsequently. On testator's death the will may be admitted to probate without the testimony of any subscribing witnesses. UPC 2–504.

See generally Atkinson, pp. 346–348; Clark, pp. 295–298, 301–304; Palmer, pp. 37–39; Ritchie, pp. 186–191; and Scoles, pp. 110–11.

Case 27 *Gift to wife of witness does not invalidate will*

A statute provided that a will should be witnessed by two credible witnesses and that if any witness is named in the will as devisee or legatee and is also an heir of the testator, then said witness shall take no more than he would have taken had the testator died intestate. T executed his will before two subscribing witnesses, H and X. T died leaving as his sole statutory heirs, his three sisters, W, A and B, each of whom would have taken by intestacy one third of T's estate. H and W were husband and wife. By the terms of the will T gave half of his property to W and half to X. Should the will be admitted to probate under the above statute?

Answer. Yes. Under the English Statute of Frauds (1677) the word credible meant competent and one who was directly financially interested in the cause was not a competent witness. Under such view neither H, spouse of beneficiary W, nor X would be "credible" witnesses. It is obvious, however, that the above statute is intended not to disqualify the witnesses, but merely to eliminate their financial interests in having the will established. X, therefore, would be a good witness, but his devise or legacy would be void. W, being the spouse of witness H, could take only one third of T's estate and not one half because she is financially interested in having the will established to the extent of the difference between one-third which she would take by intestacy and the one half she would take under the will. In a jurisdiction where the common law disabilities of married women have been removed completely and a married woman may hold her property as if unmarried, W should be permitted to take the entire half given her in T's will because witness, H, her husband would have no interest in her gift under the will. The balance of the estate should pass in equal shares to W, A and B, if the will contains no residuary clause.

See In re Ehrlich's Estate, 158, Misc. 540, 287 N.Y.S. 313 (1936).

1. Many jurisdictions have statutes which recognize certain types of wills which do not meet the usual requirements of either a writing or witnesses. The policy behind such recognition is that such wills are made under circumstances which militate against fraud, such as in the case of a holographic will where peculiarities of handwriting of testator can authenticate the will. These statutes are strictly construed. See *Classification of Wills*, above.

2. Holographic wills are wills, usually unwitnessed, completely written and signed in the handwriting of the testator. Some jurisdictions also require that such wills be dated by the testator's hand. See, *e.g.*, Cal.Probate Code § 53.

3. If a holographic will contains material not in the testator's hand:

   (a) Some jurisdictions hold that the validity depends on whether the testator intended it to be part of the will.

   e.g. An instrument offered for probate having a typewritten introductory clause with the balance entirely in decedent's hand was refused probate when the court found the typewritten portions were intended by testatrix to be part of her will even though such portions contained no dispositive provisions.

   (b) Some jurisdictions hold that the portion not in the testator's handwriting is disregarded if it can be severed without violating the testator's intent.

   See Annotation 89 A.L.R.2d 1198–1209.

4. More modern statutes on holographic wills require only that the signature and material provisions be in the handwriting of the testator. See UPC 2–503.

   See generally Atkinson, pp. 355–362; Clark, pp. 304–305; Palmer, p. 27; Ritchie, pp. 210–211 and Scoles, pp. 117–118.

SPECIAL FORMS OF EXECUTION— HOLOGRAPHIC WILLS

Printed matter does not invalidate holographic will

Case 28

D died domiciled in State Y leaving an unwitnessed will written on both sides of a piece of stationery. The will left D's property to M and N. On the front side toward the top the paper had printed D's name and address. Above the printed letterhead D had written the word "Will" and below the letterhead, written entirely in D's handwriting, were: the date, the body of the will and the signature of D. A statute of State X provided "A holographic will is one that is entirely written, dated and signed by the hand of the testator himself. It is subject to no other form . . . and need not be witnessed." J, D's heir at law claims that the will is invalid as a holographic will and claims D's property by intestate succession. Is J correct in his claim?

Answer. No. *The printed letterhead was not referred to either directly or indirectly in the body of D's will. It formed no part of the will. Extraneous material outside of and not a part of the body, date or signature of the will which does not appear to be intended by testator to be a part of the will will not invalidate a holographic will. It will be ignored by the court as mere surplusage. J, therefore, cannot sustain his claim that the holographic will is invalid.*

See In re Bennett's Estate, 324 P.2d 862 (Okl.1958).

NUNCUPATIVE WILLS—SOLDIERS' AND SAILORS' WILLS

1. A nuncupative will is an oral will.

2. A typical statute on nuncupative wills requires:

   (a) that such will be made during the testator's last sickness,

   (b) that it can dispose of personalty only, not realty,

   (c) that testator must indicate to the witnesses that he wishes them to witness his oral will,

   (d) that there be three (or other number) witnesses over the age of 14 years (or other age), and

   (e) that probate of such will cannot be made after six months from the time the words are spoken unless they are reduced to writing within six (or other number) days after spoken.

3. No special form of words is required either to make the will or to call the witnesses to attest.

4. Several states have statutes relaxing statutory requirements for wills of soldiers and sailors. They usually require that the will be made by soldiers in actual military service or sailors while at sea. These wills are usually limited to disposing of personalty.

5. Where an oral will attempts to dispose of both realty and personalty the personalty will go according to the will and the realty according to the statutes of descent and distribution as if the testator had died intestate. See e.g. Ohio Revised Code § 2107.60.

   See generally Atkinson, pp. 363–374; Clark, p. 314; Rheinstein, pp. 199–201; Ritchie, pp. 166–167; and Scoles, p. 118.

Case 29 *Failure to comply with specific statutory requirement for oral will—not valid*

T on his deathbed instructed his lawyer to draw for him a written will which was done and the instrument sent to T. T was too sick to sign the paper so he told the three persons present after the will was read to him and he understood it, "I want that to be my will.

See that my property goes that way."   *The statute on nuncupative wills was typical of those in number 2, above, and the statute for written wills provided that a will be "signed by the testator, or by some other person by his direction and in his presence."*   *Upon T's death a day later, his property was claimed by both his statutory heirs and the beneficiaries named in the paper drawn by T's lawyer. Who should prevail?*

*   **Answer.**   *The statutory heirs.   T died intestate.   T did not execute a written will because he did not sign personally or by a third person in his presence and by his direction.   Did he execute a nuncupative will?   There was no intent by T that the words spoken should be a will.   He intended to adopt by oral words a writing as his will.   This he cannot do under the statutes mentioned.   Therefore, T died intestate.*

*   See In re Taylor's Estate, 55 Ariz. 211, 106 P.2d 492 (1940).*

1. A will written on a single <del>piece of paper</del> *instrument* and executed by two testators as the wills of both is a *joint will*.   When one dies it is probated as his will and when the other dies it is likewise probated as his will.

JOINT AND MUTUAL WILLS

2. If A executes his will on one piece of paper and B executes his will on another piece of paper and each therein gives all of his property to the other, there are *mutual wills*.   If A dies first his will is probated and his property is distributed to B.   Thereafter B's mutual will has no practical value for the beneficiary thereunder has predeceased the testator, B.

3. Wills may be both joint and mutual with reciprocal provisions.

4. Mutual wills standing alone without more do not constitute a contract between the testators not to revoke;   either may revoke his will at any time.   See *Revocation of Wills,* below.

5. If A and B draw mutual wills in favor of each other and contract not to revoke them, the parties have in effect made both a will and a contract.   If one will is thereafter revoked, in a majority of jurisdictions the remedy is with respect to the contract and not the will.   See *Contracts to Devise or Bequeath Property,* below.

6. In a minority of jurisdictions the courts hold that the contract element is a basis for admitting the joint or mutual will to probate.

7. In the majority of jurisdictions, the contract element will not make the will entitled to probate.

   e.g. A having made a joint and mutual will with B, revokes his will and gives his property to C.   On A's death, B's remedy after

A's later will is probated and the property distributed to C, is either to:

(a) compel C to hold in constructive trust for B according to the terms of the contract, or

(b) to make a claim against A's estate for damages for breach of contract.

8. Reciprocal provisions usually will not be sufficient in themselves without more to show a contract not to revoke. See CASE 30, below; and see UPC 2–701.

See generally Atkinson, pp. 222–227; Clark, p. 355; Palmer, p. 65; and Scoles, p. 168.

CONTRACTS TO DEVISE OR BEQUEATH PROPERTY

1. A contract to make a will is to be interpreted and tested by the law of contracts.

2. Many states have statutes which require an agreement to make a will to be in writing.

3. If the state does not have a statute requiring a writing, an oral agreement to leave personal property by will is valid and enforceable; but an agreement to devise real property is within the Statute of Frauds.

4. The last will of a testator must be probated whether or not it conforms to a previously made contract or constitutes a breach thereof.

5. The remedy for breach of a contract to devise or bequeath property is through the medium of a trust in the court of equity, and not by attempting to enjoin the probate of the last will which constitutes the breach. See Joint and Mutual Wills, above. See UPC 2–701.

See generally Atkinson, pp. 210–220; Ritchie, p. 746; and Scoles, p. 167.

Case 30 *Mutual will revocable in absence of contract not to revoke*

O had four children, two by his first wife X, and two by his second wife, T. Prior to O's death O and T executed wills at the same time before the same attesting witnesses. Each will provided that the residuary estate would go to the spouse, but if the spouse failed to survive, it would go to the four children of O. O predeceased T and T succeeded to his estate. Thereafter T made a new will by which she left everything to her two children and nothing to the two children of X. On T's death her new will was admitted to probate. The children of the first marriage have brought an action seeking to im-press a trust on the property received by T under O's will. Will the court impose a constructive trust on T's property?

Answer. No. T's moral obligation to give the property which she inherited from O to all four children alone is not enough to impress a trust on the property. The only basis on which the court can intervene is to enforce a promise made by T not to alter or revoke the former will and that by reason of that promise her husband gave and bequeathed his property to her. In the absence of proof of an express promise or representation by O that she would not change her testamentary intent as expressed in the prior will, a court will not interfere. The mere fact of a confidential relationship between O and T is not enough to find such a promise. "To attribute to a will the quality of irrevocability demands the most indisputable evi-dence of the agreement which is relied upon to change its ambulatory nature and that presumptions will not, and should not, take the place of proof." Nor will such proof support a constructive trust. More-over, the mere circumstance that T executed the will contempora-neously with the will of O and that both contained similar provisions with respect to the gift.

Oursler v. Armstrong, 10 N.Y.2d 385, 223 N.Y.S.2d 477, 179 N.E.2d 489 (1961).

Trust imposed on property received by beneficiary under will made in breach of contract to make a will

Case 31

T was an elderly man without relatives other than a favorite niece, C. T made an agreement with C that in consideration of C's taking care of him for the rest of his days T would make a will giving all of his property to C. T moved his belonging to C's house and lived with C until his death. C performed her part of the contract fully. T died and it was discovered that he had made a will in C's favor. However, after making such a will, he had made a will in favor of B and had revoked the will in C's favor. May C get the property left by T?

Answer. Yes. The contract which T and C made is valid. So also is the will which T made in favor of B, even though it constituted a breach of his contract with C. So when T died his last will should be probated and his property should be distributed to B. The nicety of probate procedure requires such. B, however, is a mere volunteer and has given nothing for T's property. On the other hand, C has paid in full for such property by caring for T during his lifetime. B then has the legal title to property which equitably and in good conscience belongs to C. By T's will B got what T had which was T's property subject to the terms of his contract with C. To prevent unjust enrichment of B at the expense of C, C can have B declared to be trustee of the property he received from T and can obtain a decree compelling B to convey such property to C.

See Allen v. Bremberg, 147 Ala. 317, 41 So. 771 (1906).

Case 32   *Remedy available for breach of contract created by execution of joint, mutual and reciprocal wills*

H and W executed a joint, mutual and reciprocal will whereby each bequeathed his estate to the survivor and provided that on the death of the survivor the property would go to a certain third person, S. The will contained no language relating to contract nor any express promise that the survivor would carry out the dispositions in the will. After the death of H, W remarried and by inter vivos transfer gave all of her property to her second husband.   On W's death S brings an action against W's second husband for an accounting for the property transferred to him by W.   Can S prevail?

Answer.   Yes.   A contract to make mutual and reciprocal wills may be conclusively presumed from the provisions of the will themselves.   This is especially true in the case of a jointly executed will. Such contract becomes partially executed upon the death of one of the parties to the agreement and the acceptance by the survivor of properties devised or bequeathed under the will and pursuant to the agreement to make such joint will.   At this point the contract becomes irrevocable.   The fact that the testatrix left unrevoked the will she had jointly executed was a compliance in form not in substance with her contract and breached the covenant of good faith accompanying every contract.   In such case equity will give effect to the mutual agreement that the property shall go to the person designated in the joint will by imposing a constructive trust.

See In re Chaika, 47 Wis. 102, 176 N.W.2d 561 (1970).   Contra: Olive v. Biggs, 276 N.C. 445, 173 S.E.2d 301 (1970).

INTEGRATION, INCORPORATION BY REFERENCE, ACTS OF INDEPENDENT SIGNIFICANCE AND TESTAMENTARY ADDITIONS TO TRUST

1. *Integration* means the determination of what papers constitute the testator's will.

   e.g.   T makes a first will giving Blackacre to A, second will giving Whiteacre to B, a third will giving Brownacre to C and a fourth will giving Greenacre and all of the residue of his property to D. T dies.   All four of the above wills together constitute the last will and testament of T since they are wholly consistent one with the other and none containing a revocatory clause.   See Atkinson, p. 380.

2. *Incorporation by reference* means that the testator by provision in his will has legally reached out and caused extraneous material, such as a book, record or memorandum, to become part of the will.

3. For the doctrine of incorporation by reference to apply three propositions must be established:

   (a) that the extraneous material was in existence at the time of making the will;

   (b) that the will on its face refers to such material as being in existence at the time of the making of the will and shows intention to incorporate it, and

   (c) that the extraneous material offered as part of the will is the identical material referred to or described in the will.

   CAVEAT—The general rule is that documents not in existence at the time a will is executed cannot be incorporated by reference. This would be changed by adoption of the Uniform Probate Code provision that a will may refer to a written statement or list to dispose of items of tangible personal property (e.g., jewelry and household goods) if the list is in the testator's handwriting or signed by him and is in existence at the time of the testator's death. See UPC 2–510, 2–513.

4. Although an informal document is not in existence when the will referring to it is executed, a later republication of the will by a codicil will satisfy the existing document rule and will incorporate it by reference if properly identified in the will. See, Simon v. Grayson, 15 Cal.2d 531, 102 P.2d 1081 (1940).

5. A will may dispose of property by reference to certain acts and events which have significance apart from their effect upon the dispositions made by will whether they occur before or after either the execution of the will or the testator's death.

   e.g. The execution or revocation of the will of another person is an act of independent significance. See Case 35, below. See also UPC 2–512.

6. Several approaches are taken to testamentary gifts to a trust in existence at the time of the testator's death.

   (a) If the trust instrument is in existence at the time of the execution of the will and is referred to therein, it will be incorporated by reference and a testamentary trust will be created on the same terms and conditions contained in the trust document.

   (b) If the trust is not in existence or if it is amendable or revocable it cannot be incorporated by reference, either:

(i)   the testamentary gift fails, or

(ii) a trust is created on the terms contained in the trust document referred to at the time of execution

(c) The creation of the trust is an act of independent significance and the gift is valid.

7. Many jurisdictions now have statutes validating gifts to trusts executed before or concurrently with the execution of the testator's will, and which provide that the gift will not be invalid because the trust is amendable or revocable or is in fact amended after the execution of the will.   See Uniform Testamentary Additions to Trusts Act which is identical to UPC 2–511.

8. Under the Uniform Testamentary Additions to Trusts Act, a gift to a trust which qualifies is deemed and administered as a part of the trust to which it is given.   The revocation of the trust prior to the death of the testator causes the devise to lapse.

See generally Atkinson, pp. 380–400; Clark, pp. 334–335; Palmer, pp. 503–506, 515–517; Ritchie, pp. 724–728, 738–741; and Scoles, pp. 124–125, 128–129.

Case 33   *A document not adequately referred to in a will will not be incorporated by reference*

T died leaving a will which contained the following clause: "I give and bequeath unto my wife the sum of $50,000 in trust, however, for the purposes set forth in a sealed letter which will be found with this will."   At the time the will was offered for probate a letter from T to his wife dated the same date of the will was also offered as part of the will.   It provided "it is my desire that the $50,000 conveyed to you in trust by my will be paid to William Jennings Bryan of Lincoln, Nebraska.   I am earnestly devoted to the political principles which Mr. Bryan advocates and believe the welfare of the nation depends upon the triumph of those principles.   .   .   ."   At the probate proceeding evidence was offered tending to prove that the letter in question was in the handwriting of T and was by him placed in a sealed envelope bearing an endorsement to his wife "to be read only by her alone after my death."   Other evidence indicated that T placed the will and the envelope containing the letter in his box in a vault in his New York office building on the day after the date of the will.   The court excluded this evidence.   Subsequently a jury rendered a verdict to the effect that the letter was not a part of the will of T.   Mr. Bryan has appealed the decision.   Should the letter have been admitted as part of the will?

Answer.   *No.   In order for a document to be probated as part of a will under the Doctrine of Incorporation by reference the document* *must be in existence at the time of the execution of the will and the description must not be so vague as to be incapable of being applied to any instrument in particular but must describe the instrument intended in clear and definite terms. The will itself must refer to the informal document sought to be incorporated as a writing existing at the time of the execution of the will. In the will in question there was not any clear explicit and unambiguous reference to a specific document as one existing and known to the testator at the time his will was executed. Any sealed letter setting forth for purposes of the trust and found with the will would have fully and accurately answered the reference. As a result the reference is so vague as to be incapable of being apprised to any instrument in particular as a document existing at the time of the will and therefore may not be admitted to probate as part of T's will.*

See Bryan's Appeal, 77 Conn. 240, 58 A. 748 (1904).

Doctrine of integration will not validate holographic will lacking requirements as such   Case 34

M.T. died leaving an unsealed envelope on the outside of which she had written, "This is my last and only Will (signed) M.T." Inside the envelope was a paper on which she had written in her own handwriting what purported to be her will. But there was no signature on the paper. The envelope and enclosed paper were offered together for probate as her last will and testament. Should they be admitted?

Answer. No. The issue in this case is one of integration. Every holographic will must be signed by the testator and the signature must be on the paper which is the will. Here the only signature is on the exterior of the evenlope which is unsealed and which contains a paper which was without doubt intended to be M.T.'s will because she called it such on its face. The signature may be any place on the instrument unless the statute provides that it must be at "the end" or "foot" thereof. But in this case it is not on the instrument at all. It is on an extraneous piece of paper and there is no connection in the writings on the two which would link one to the other. The signature is an essential part of the authentication of the will and without it there is no will. Further, to admit these two pieces of disconnected papers as the will of M.T. would open the door too far for fraud and imposition. Thus, doctrine of integration will not apply.

See In re Tyrrell's Estate, 17 Ariz. 418, 153 P. 767 (1915).

NOTE 1—Suppose T dies and in a sealed envelope there are found four pieces of paper which appear to have been cut from the provisions of a completed will. On one piece is a paragraph stating an intention to make a will, on another designated "First" debts are directed to be paid, on another "Eighth" is a residuary clause and on another are T's signature, an attestation clause and signatures of witnesses. With no relationship between these pieces of paper and no internal coherence in sense they should not be integrated as T's will. It would open the door wide to fraud. "Any evil-minded person might, with comparative ease, take a will, and, by cutting from it sections or paragraphs, entirely defeat the object of the testator." See In re Seiter's Estate, 265 Pa. 202, 108 A. 614 (1919).

NOTE 2—Suppose T dies leaving four sheets of paper on which he has written what is offered as his will for probate. The top page is signed and if it is placed under the other three there is continuous literary sense from beginning to end and at the end of each of the first three pages there is no period or end of sentence but the sentence continues on in sense from the bottom of the preceding page. These four sheets being obviously connected as a single instrument should be admitted to probate as an integrated whole as T's will. See In re Maginn's Estate, 278 Pa. 89, 122 A. 264 (1923).

Case 35   *Acts of independent significance also dispositions in wills*

T died testate providing in his will, "I give the rest, residue and remainder of my property to the persons who have been in my employ not less than ten years at the date of my death." This will was made in the year 1915. T died in 1945. There were five employees who answered the description in the will and all of them had been employed by T since the making of his will. May the five employees take the residue?

Answer. Yes. Here is a non-testamentary act of T, the testator, such act being the employing of these five employees. The act is not executed by signing or witnessing as required by the wills statute and is therefore non-testamentary. But the five beneficiaries are designated by an act which has significance ordinarily apart from designating them as persons to take under the will. Ordinarily an employer employs persons to get a job done or to accomplish a task, not for the purpose of designating them as beneficiaries under his will. Hence, when T hired these five employees by a non-testamentary act having such independent significance, they are properly residuary beneficiaries under T's will.

See White v. Massachusetts Inst. of Technology, 171 Mass. 84, 50 N.E. 512 (1898). See also Atkinson, p. 394.

NOTE 1—The doctrine in the Case above is broad enough to include an act of a third person. Suppose T in the Case above had given property "to the persons who had been in the employ of X

Company for five years at the time of T's death." This would have been an effective designation of beneficiaries.

NOTE 2—The doctrine also may include an act of a beneficiary. Thus, T leaves property to the girl whom T's son John marries. The girl's non-testamentary act of marrying John, which act has independent significance, makes her a beneficiary under T's will.

Gift to a trust which is amended subsequently is valid as an act of independent significance   Case 36

T's will gave the residue of her estate to a revocable and amendable inter vivos trust established ten years prior to the date of execution of the will. Six months after the execution of the will, T and the trustee of the inter vivos trust signed and acknowledged an instrument amending the trust in accordance with the provisions for amendment in the trust agreement. Following the death of T the executor of her estate asked for instructions under the will as to whether or not the residue passed to the trustees under the trust as amended, or subject to the terms of the original unamended trust. How should the property be distributed?

Answer. *The property should be distributed according to the terms of the amended trust. In a majority of jurisdictions it has been held that a gift from a will to a trust is sustainable in that the inter vivos trust is a fact having significance apart from the disposition of the property bequeathed. The trust is valid even though not executed with the formalities required by the Statute of Wills. The rule changed because the trust in question was amendable and revocable and was in fact amended subsequent to the execution of T's will. "The test is not whether the facts are subject to the control of the testator but whether they are facts which have significance apart from the disposition of the property bequeathed." The Doctrine of Independent Significance does not controvert the underlying policy of the Statute of Wills in that frauds are equally avoided by the formalities attended upon the execution of trust and the solemnity of the transfer of property to trustees.*

See *Second Bank—State St. Trust Co. v. Pinion*, 341 Mass. 366, 170 N.E.2d 350 (1960).

IV REVOCATION, REVIVAL AND CONSTRUCTION OF WILLS

Summary Outline

REVOCATION OF WILLS—IN GENERAL

1. A will is ambulatory, which means that it is always subject to alteration or revocation by a competent testator, until the time of his death.

2. Revocation may be effected in three ways:

   (a) by subsequent instrument;

   (b) by physical acts of burning, tearing, canceiling, obliterating or destroying;

   (c) by operation of law, i.e. by certain changes in the testator's circumstances, such as marriage, divorce or the birth of a child.

3. A revocation is not effective unless there is:

   (a) the intent to revoke, which may be express or implied; and

   (b) an act of revocation, concurrent with the intent to revoke.

4. Declarations made by the testator at or near the time of a physical act of revocation on the will are admissible to reflect on his intent. See generally Atkinson, pp. 419–422; Ritchie, pp. 214–218; and Scoles, p. 148.

SPECIFICS OF REVOCATION OF WILLS

1. Revocation by subsequent instrument may be by:

   (a) a later will

   (i) which expressly revokes the earlier will, or

   (ii) which is inconsistent with the earlier will,

   (b) codicil, or

   (c) revocatory instrument executed with like formalities as a will, but which disposes of no property.

2. Statutes usually designate certain physical acts which are acts of revocation. These frequently include: burning, tearing, cutting, destroying, mutilating, cancelling and obliterating.

3. Most statutes permit the act of revocation to be done:

   (a) by the testator, or

   (b) by someone else:

   (i) at the testator's direction, and

   (ii) in his presence.

4. Many statutes have been construed to permit the revocation of a part of a will by physical act or by the use of language such as: "nor any clause thereof" or "or any part thereof".

5. Jurisdictions vary as to whether or not partial revocation by physical act is effective in the absence of such statutory language.   See UPC 2–507.   See also Ritchie, pp. 251–252; Rheinstein, pp. 243–246.

6. Revocation by operation of law occurs where there is a change in either the family situation or the property holdings of the testator, such as the birth of a child or the sale of property devised in the will.   See Ritchie, pp. 244–248; Rhienstein, pp. 267–272.

   NOTE—At common law marriage always revoked the will of the wife, and a married woman was unable to make a will.   As a result, if she died during coverture she died intestate.   This has been changed by statute in most jurisdictions.

7. Statutes in a number of jurisdictions provide that a will is revoked in its entirety when the make-up of testator's family changes such as marriage, divorce, or the birth of a child.

   CAVEAT—The trend is to limit such statutes to the case of divorce which revokes any disposition to the former spouse when accompanied by a property settlement.   Omission of children or a spouse from a will is usually now treated by provisions giving them their intestate shares unless intentionally omitted.

   See UPC 2–508; 2–301; 2–302.   See also *Protection of Children*, Chapter II, above.

8. After the execution of his will if a testator disposes of property which is the subject of a devise or bequest, at common law, the disposition of the property was said to revoke such devise or bequest.   This is more appropriately considered from the standpoint of ademption by extinction.   See *Ademption*, below.

   See generally Atkinson, pp. 422–452; Clark, pp. 355, 361, 366–368; Palmer, pp. 67, 72–75, Ritchie, pp. 220–222, 224–226, 236–239; and Scoles, pp 155–159.

Acts revoking a will must strictly comply with statutory requirements   Case 37

On September 1, T signed a will typewritten on five sheets of paper the signature appearing on the last page and duly attested by three subscribing witnesses, all in conformance with the State Statute of Wills.   On September 15, at the request of T her attorney took the will to her home where she asked her attorney in the presence of two persons who were also present to destroy the will.   Instead of destroying the papers, however, at the suggestion of her attorney she decided to retain them as a memorandum to be used in the event she decided to execute a new will.   On the back of the manuscript cover which was fastened to the five pages of the will in the handwriting *of T's attorney signed by T the notation was made as follows: "This will null and void and to be only held by my attorney instead of being destroyed as a memorandum for another will if I decide to make the same." T died October 1. The will was offered for probate. Should the will have been probated?*

Answer. Yes. The requirements for revoking a duly executed will are statutory. The statute in question provided: "No will, or any part thereof, shall be revoked, unless . . . by a subsequent will or codicil, or by some writing declared an intention to revoke the same, and executed in the manner in which a will is required to be executed, or by the testator, or some person in his presence and by his direction, cutting, tearing, burning, obliterating, cancelling, or destroying the same, or the signature thereto with the intent to revoke." In this case the notation by T's attorney is ineffectual as a "writing declaring an intention to revoke," because they do not comply with the statutory requirements as to execution. Moreover, the faces of the two instruments bear no physical evidence of any "cutting, tearing, burning, obliterating, cancelling, or destroying." In order to effect a revocation of a duly executed will the statute provides the method for so doing. Two things are necessary: (1) the doing of a specified act, which is (2) accompanied by the intent to revoke, the *animus revocandi.* Proof of one element without proof of the other element is insufficient. In the present case the intention to revoke is clearly shown; however, cancellation within the meaning of the statute contemplates marks or lines across the written parts of the instrument, a physical defacement, or some mutilation of the writing itself with the intent to revoke. If written words are used they must be placed so as to physically affect the written portion of the will not merely on blank parts of the paper on which the will is written. A writing on the back is equivalent to a writing separate from the will. Such an attempted revocation is ineffectual unless executed in the manner in which a will must be executed.

See *Thompson v. Royall,* 163 Va. 492, 175 S.E. 748 (1934).

Case 38   *Specific intention to revoke must accompany mere act of cancellation for revocation to result*

After T's death a will which contained the signature of T was found at her residence in a locked safe. It was apparent, however, from an examination of the document that the signature had been erased first by drawing diagonal lines over the name and then erasing the lines and the name itself. The signature on the will, as it was taken from the safe and was offered for probate appeared to be carefully rewritten over the original signature using ink of a different color from that used in the body of the will. When the will was offered for probate there was no evidence as to when the erasure was made or why it was done. Contestants filed objections to the admission *of the will to probate on the ground that it was duly revoked by T and not legally re-executed and published as T's will. Is the will entitled to probate?*

Answer. *Yes. The applicable state statute provides in part, "no will in writing . . . shall be revoked or altered otherwise than by some other will in writing . . . or unless such will be burned, torn, cancelled, obliterated or destroyed with the intent and for the purpose of revoking the same by the testator himself." It cannot be presumed, as a matter of law that the erasure was made after the execution of the instruments nor that the erasure was made with intent to revoke and destroy the will. The mere act of cancelling is a nullity unless it be done with an intention to revoke which accompanies the act. Had the will been found with the signature of T erased and not rewritten the presumption would have been that it was cancelled and revoked with the requisite animus revocandi, but when found with the signature carefully restored no such presumption arises. The cancellation of a will in and of itself does not necessarily effect its revocation.*

See In re Woods Will, 2 Con.Sur. 144, 11 N.Y.S. 157 (Chenango 1889).

What constitutes an act of obliteration

Case 39

T made a witnessed will and subsequently with intent to revoke he threw it onto the fire in the fireplace. His son, John, jumped and grabbed the instrument off the fire, after there had been a singeing of one corner of the paper, but no part of the writing had been burned. T died and the will was admitted to probate. Was there error?

Answer. *Yes. The will was revoked. A testator may revoke a will by a present intention to revoke accompanied by an act or symbol appearing in the document. When T threw the will on the fire with intent to revoke both the intent and the symbolic act required to effect revocation were accomplished. To constitute a burning the paper and the writing need not be completely consumed. Any burning of the writing or of the paper on which the will is written when done with animo revocandi is sufficient burning. The burning constituted the act showing the intention of the testator and when that appears on the paper whether or not the words are destroyed the evidence is complete. Therefore, the will should not have been admitted to probate.*

See White v. Casten, 46 N.C. 197, 59 Am.Dec. 585 (1853).

Partial revocation effected by cancellation of clauses in will

Case 40

D died in State X leaving a will which had been duly executed under the applicable state law. When D's will was offered for probate it was proved that after execution D drew ink lines across all the words in the sixth and thirteenth clauses with the intension of revoking those clauses and no more. A State X statute provides: "No will shall be revoked, unless by burning, tearing, cancelling or obliterating the same, with the intention of revoking it, by the testator or by his directions, or by some other will, codicil or writing, signed, attested and subscribed in the manner provided for making a will." The will contained a general residuary clause which provided "I give bequeath and devise all the rest, residue and remainder of my estate of every description of which I die seized and possessed to B." B offers the will for probate. He claims that clauses six and thirteen are revoked and that he as residuary legatee is entitled to the property which was included in such clauses rather than D's heirs at law. Is B's contention correct?

__Answer.__ Yes. The power to revoke a will includes the power to revoke any part of it. It is established that a subsequent codicil can effect a partial revocation. There is no distinction between the power to revoke a will in part by a subsequent codicil and the power to revoke in part by cancellation or obliteration. If an act of cancellation and an intent to revoke co-exist the portion cancelled is effectively revoked. D's cancellation of the sixth and thirteenth clauses of the will by drawing lines through them with the intention of revoking the dispositions found in these clauses was a legal revocation of the cancelled material but not of the remainder of the will. The will contained a valid residuary clause, and it is clear from its wording that the intention of D was to give all of the property not otherwise disposed of by the will to the residuary beneficiary. The rule is that a general residuary clause passes all property of the testator not otherwise disposed of unless it is manifestly contradictory to the declared intention of the testator found in other parts of the will.

See Bigelow v. Gillot, 123 Mass. 102, 25 Am.Rep. 32 (1877).

CONDITIONAL REVOCATION AND DEPENDENT RELATIVE REVOCATION

1. Revocation of a will may be expressly conditional, in which case the will is not revoked until the condition has been satisfied.

2. Dependent relative revocation takes place when a testator revokes his will either by physical act or by subsequent instrument and the revocation is induced by a mistake of law or fact. In such cases the revocation is said to be conditional and the will is held not to be revoked.

   e.g. If a testator cancels or destroys a will with a present intention of making a new one immediately and dies before a new will can be executed, it will be presumed that the testator preferred the old will to intestacy.   See LaCroix v. Senecal, 140 Conn. 311, 99 A.2d 115 (1953).

3. The doctrine of dependent relative revocation is held by some courts to be applicable only in cases where revocation is by physical act, but the majority hold it applicable in cases where revocation is by subsequent written instrument as well.   See generally Atkinson, pp. 452–463; Clark, p. 366; Palmer, p. 124; Ritchie, pp. 278–281; and Scoles, pp. 159–161.

Revocation of will which itself revoked a prior will; validity of   Case 41
prior will

T executed a will giving all of his property to A.   Later he executed a second will in which he gave all of his property to B and revoked all former wills.   Still later he destroyed the second will with animus revocandi.   T died and his property is claimed both by A and by T's heirs.   Which should prevail?

Answer.   A.   By the common law, when a second will which revokes a former will is itself revoked or destroyed with animus revocandi, then the first will becomes the last will of the testator.   It is reviewed by the revocation of the second will.   The theory is: no will becomes effective until death and the second will never having become effective by T's death, never did effectively revoke the first will.   Under such theory the first will is effective at T's death and A being the beneficiary takes T's property.

See Atkinson, p. 474.

NOTE—The cases are not at all in accord on this subject.   At common law the revocation of a subsequent will revived the first will but the ecclesiastical courts required proof of testator's intention to revive the former will.   American jurisdictions have a conflict of authority on this matter.   Many states now have statutes which require re-execution of the prior will in order to revive it.   The Uniform Probate Code adopts the view that the first will remains revoked unless it is evident from the circumstances of the revocation or from testator's contemporary or subsequent declarations that he intended the first will to take effect by reversal.   See UPC 2–509.

Doctrine of dependent relative revocation prevents revocation of   Case 42
earlier bequest

T executed a will in New York.   He subsequently moved to California where he executed a new will containing the clause: "I, T, do hereby make and declare this to be my Last Will and Testament, revoking all former wills.".   Both wills named identical persons for identical cash bequests and the Second Church of Christ as residuary legatee. The only change in the later will was the naming of a California executor. T died shortly after executing the second will which was admitted to probate. The charitable bequest violated the California Mortmain provision because of the time period prior to death, and was therefore invalid. Thereafter, a petition was filed to have the earlier will admitted to probate. At the hearing evidence showed that the testator had wanted no change in his will except for the naming of a California executor. Moreover, T had not been advised that he might provide in his later will that the revocation of the charitable bequest by the revocation clause was dependent upon the legal effectiveness of the later will to carry out his bequest. Is the earlier will entitled to probate?

Answer. Yes. "Under the doctrine of dependent relative revocation, an earlier will, revoked only to give effect to a later one on the supposition that the later one will become effective, remains in effect to the extent that the latter proved ineffective. The doctrine is designed to carry out the probable intention of the testator when there is no reason to suppose that he intended to revoke his earlier will if the later will became inoperative. . . ." It is clearly applicable to the present case since the second will was identical with the first in that the only change was to name the new executor. It is therefore clear that the first will was revoked only because the second duplicated its purpose and the testator would have preferred the first will to intestacy as to a substantial part of his estate. "A testator who repeats his purpose and intends to confirm and not revoke it and does not intend to have a new will operate as a revocation independently of its operation as a will."

See In re Kaufman's Estate, 25 Cal.2d 854, 155 P.2d 831 (1945). Contra, Newman v. Newman, 199 N.E.2d 904 (Ohio Probate Court 1964).

Case 43 *Effect of revocation of will revoking a prior will on validity of prior will*

T executed his will giving all of his property to A. Later he executed a second will giving all of his property to B and revoking all former wills. This second instrument was then destroyed by T with animus revocandi, but with the expressed intention on T's part that the first will in A's favor once again be effective. T died and A offered said first will for probate which was contested by T's heirs and by B. Who should prevail?

Answer. A should prevail. This is purely an arbitrary answer for the reason that one can also justify a decision either for B or for T's heirs by both reason and authority. For A it may be said that the very nature of a will is that it is never effective until death. Then

T's revoking will did not completely destroy his first will because the second will itself had not been made effective by the death of T. Such subsequent revoking will then merely made the first will dormant while both wills were extant and T lived. But when T destroyed the second will with intent to revoke it, the second will, including the revocation clause, was rendered totally ineffective as though it has never been made. As a result the first will then became effective as the last will of T when T died. Some cases reach a contrary result in the absence of an expressed intent on the part of the testator that the first will shall again be effective, but in this instance such expressed intent is given as a fact and parol evidence is admissible to establish such. B's case would rest upon the doctrine of dependent relative revocation—sometimes called conditional revocation. He would argue that the second will with its revocatory clause completely and effectively destroyed will number one; that T revoked will number two only on condition that will number one was thereby made effective; that the condition having failed, will number two is still T's will and hence, B, the beneficiary thereunder should take. The heirs of T would argue that will number one had been effectively revoked beyond recall by the revocatory clause of will number two; that will number two was effectively revoked by destruction with animus revocandi and that will number one could not be brought back into existence as a will by a mere expression of intention that such be the case, but rather that a complete re-execution thereof would be necessary to comply with the statutes. The result would be, in their view, that T died intestate. By the better view the revocation of the second will revalidated the first will and therefore A should prevail.

See Onions v. Tyrer, Ch. 1717, 2 Vern, 742; House of Lords, (1924) A.C. 653. See also Atkinson, pp. 386, 414, and 452; UPC 2–507 Comment; Republication and Revival of Wills and Case 41, below.

1. If a will cannot be found at the testator's death and it was last known to be in his possession it is presumed that he revoked it. If, however, it cannot be found and was last known to be in the possession of a third person then there is no such presumption.   **LOST WILLS**

2. The contents of a lost and unrevoked will may be provided by parol evidence.

See generally Atkinson, pp. 506–511; Palmer, pp. 96–98; and Ritchie, pp. 236–239.

Will lost or destroyed without intent to revoke may be probated   Case 44

T executed his will giving all his property to A. He left the original will with his brother, B, and a copy thereof with his lawyer, L. B's house burned and all its contents including T's will was destroyed. A few days later T died. A went to L's office and requested L to petition the probate court for admission to probate of T's will. L complied with the request alleging that T died testate and offered the copy in L's possession to prove the contents of T's will. B was the only heir of T and objected to the probate of the will and claimed T died intestate. Should the will be admitted?

*   **Answer.** *Yes. This case involves the probate of a lost will. When a person dies and it is shown that he made a will and that such will was last in his possession and it cannot be found upon his death, there is a presumption that he destroyed it with intent to revoke it, animus revocandi. But when such will was last known to be in the hands of a third person, then such presumption cannot obtain. In this case it being shown that the will of T was last in the hands of B, of course the presumption of destruction cannot obtain. At common law a lost will, one which existed and has not been revoked but cannot be found, could be admitted to probate like any other will, but its contents in substance had to be proved clearly and convincingly. In such case the burden is on the proponent. In this case the copy can be shown in proof of the contents of the original will. There are statutes which require that the lost will must have been in existence at the death of the testator or that it was fraudulently destroyed.*

*   See Johnson v. Kroc, 156 Minn. 253, 194 N.W. 633 (1923). See also Atkinson, p. 506.*

CODICILS   1. The word codicil means "little will".

2. A codicil is usually executed to bring about a change in the will without the necessity of re-executing the will in its entirety.

3. Codicils usually undertake to revoke, modify, alter or republish a will.

4. A codicil must be executed with the same formalities as any other will.

5. A codicil makes specific reference to the will, identifies it by its date of execution and then states the changes to be effected thereby. Except as to modifications made by the codicil the will is affirmed in all other particulars.

See generally Atkinson, pp. 451–452; Clark, p. 343; Palmer, p. 87; and Scoles, pp. 123–124.

REPUBLICATION   1. Republication is used to describe:
AND REVIVAL
OF WILLS   (a) the validating of a former invalid will; and

(b) the reaffirming of an earlier will by the later will or codicil and making the earlier will speak as of the date of the reaffirming instrument.

2. At common law if a first will was revoked by a second will which second will was in turn later revoked the first will was automatically revived by the revocation of the second will.

3. In most states today once a will has been revoked it cannot be revived except by its re-execution, re-acknowledgment or by executing a codicil republishing it. See e.g., Ohio Revised Code § 2107.38.

   NOTE—When a will is republished by the execution of a codicil it is said to speak as of the effective date of the codicil not of the original will. More modern cases do not apply this doctrine strictly where an unreasonable result would be effected. See Atkinson, pp. 468–473.

4. Some states follow the doctrine which was current in the ecclesiastical courts that whether the prior will is revived depends upon the testator's intent. Such intent may be shown from the circumstances and testator's declarations that he *intended* the first will once again to take affect by the Uniform Probate Code. See UPC 2–509. See also Rheinstein, pp. 262–263.

   See generally Atkinson, pp. 468–479; Clark, p. 343; Palmer, pp. 122–124; Ritchie, p. 264; and Scoles, pp. 156–159.

Codicil effectively republishes prior void will   Case 45

On March 1, 1947, T executed his will in favor of A as sole beneficiary. The will only had one witness. The statute of wills in the jurisdiction required two witnesses to a written and witnessed will. Later T executed an holographic codicil in which he "affirmed the provisions of my will of March 1, 1947." Thereafter T died leaving B his sole statutory heir. Both A and B claimed T's property. Holographic wills are valid in the jurisdiction if they are completely written, signed and dated in the handwriting of the testator. Who should prevail?

Answer. A. Here T's will of March 1, 1947 is no will at all for lack of one witness. It is void. The statute must be complied with or there is no will. But when T executed a valid holographic codicil which referred to his earlier void will and reaffirmed the provisions of such will the will is considered as having been republished as of the date of the codicil. The last will and testament of T becomes the will plus the codicil. Hence, A takes under such last will of T. Strictly speaking there can be no republication when there had been no publication. The will being void was never published at all. This case should be solved by the doctrine of incorporation by reference and will come out to the same result. Here we have a codicil which: (a) refers to the will as an extraneous document; (b) shows *on its face that the will is in existence; and (c) specifically identifies it as the paper referred to. Hence, T's last will is the codicil which incorporates the will and makes A the beneficiary therein. The courts, however, have generally solved the problem under the doctrine of republication of wills.*

See Rogers v. Agricola, 176 Ark. 287, 3 S.W.2d 26 (1928).

EFFECT OF SUBSEQUENT EVENTS ON LEGACIES AND DEVISES

1. Dispositions under wills are classified as:

    (a) specific,

    (b) demonstrative,

    (c) general, or

    (d) residuary.

2. Devises and bequests are classified for purposes of ademption and abatement.

3. A *specific* devise or bequest is a gift of a particular identifiable item of property.

    e.g.   I hereby give my Wedgewood tea set to my cousin Jean.

4. A *demonstrative* bequest is a gift of a certain amount of property out of a certain fund or identifiable source of property.

    e.g.   I hereby give $1,000 out of my bank account at Second National Bank to my cousin Margaret.

5. A *general* bequest is a gift of property payable from the general assets of testator's estate.

    e.g.   I hereby give $5,000 to my cousin Emma.

6. A *residuary* gift is a gift of the remaining portion of the estate after the satisfaction of other dispositions.

    e.g.   I hereby give the rest, residue and remainder of my estate to my cousin Clara.

    See generally Atkinson, pp. 731–737; Clark, p. 381; Ritchie, pp. 884–885; and Scoles, pp. 692–693.

ADEMPTION

1. Ademption operates to invalidate gifts in a will. Ademption is of two kinds:

    (a) by extinction, and

    (b) by satisfaction.

2. Ademption by *extinction* applies to specific devises and bequests where the subject matter is not in the estate at the time of testator's death because it is either:

(a) no longer in the estate at all, or

(b) has been substantially changed in character.

e.g. A by will makes a gift of "my topaz ring" to B. The topaz ring is later stolen, but proceeds of insurance are available. Under the usual rule the gift is adeemed, and the beneficiary is not entitled to the insurance proceeds. See Atkinson, p. 741.

CAVEAT—Under more modern statutes where the testator makes a gift of certain securities the specific devisee is entitled to as much of such securities as is a part of the estate at the time of death plus: (i) additional securities of the same entity owned by testator by reason of either action initiated by the entity (such as a stock split) or as a result of a plan of reinvestment in a regular investment company, and (ii) of another entity owned by testator as a result of a merger, consolidation, or reorganization of the original securities. See UPC 2–607.

CAVEAT—Under some recent cases and statutes the specific devisee may be allowed to take any part of the specific devise remaining in the estate as well as any amounts owing relative to such property which were not paid to the testator prior to his death, such as the balance of the purchase price paid for the sale of the property, condemnation awards, and proceeds from fire or casualty insurance. See UPC 2–608.

3. Ademption by *satisfaction* takes place when the testator in his lifetime gives to his legatee all or a part of the gift he had intended be given by his will. It depends on the testator's *intention* and applies to general as well as specific legacies.

4. Ademption by satisfaction is applicable *only* in the case of testacy.

CAVEAT—Ademption by satisfaction must be distinguished from the doctrine of advancements. Advancement takes place only where the decedent dies *intestate*. See *Advancement*, Chapter I, above.

5. If the subject matter of an inter vivos gift is the same as the subject matter of a testamentary provision it is presumed that the inter vivos gift is in lieu of the testamentary gift where there is a parent-child or grand parent-grand child relationship. In other instances, the presumption is against ademption by satisfaction.

e.g. T makes a will leaving $25,000 to his son, S. Afterward T gives S $15,000 to complete medical school. When T dies, S gets only $10,000, unless there is proof that T had a contrary intention.

See generally Atkinson, pp. 737–748; Clark, p. 372; Palmer, p. 160; Ritchie, pp. 893–895, 899–901; and Scoles, pp. 695–698.

ABATEMENT

1. Abatement is the process of determining the order in which property in the estate will be applied to the payment of debts, taxes and expenses where there is an insufficient amount to pay all claims and all dispositions.

2. If expressed in the will the intention of the testator governs the order in which property will abate.

3. In the absence of an expression of the testator's intention in the will the following order of abatement will be applied:

   (a) intestate property,

   (b) residuary gifts,

   (c) general bequests,

   (d) demonstrative bequests (if the fund is in existence at the time of death; otherwise they will be treated as general bequests), and

   (e) specific bequests and devises.

4. Within the same class gifts abate pro rata.

   e.g.   D, by will, leaves: $1,000 to each of his nephews A, B and C; His 1939 Ford to H; $1,000 on deposit at First National Bank to E; $1,000 on Deposit at Second National Bank to F; and his residuary estate to G.   His residuary estate is insufficient by $3,500 to pay all debts and expenses of his estate.   A, B, C and G will receive nothing; E and F will each receive $750; and G will receive the 1939 Ford.   By virtue of abatement the residuary is first used to satisfy the creditors, then the general legacies to A, B and C are used and then the demonstrative bequests to E and F are abated pro rata.   H receives his special bequest in full.

   See generally, Atkinson, pp. 754–763; Clark, p. 381; Palmer, pp. 155–156; Ritchie, pp. 919–923; and Scoles, pp. 693–694.

Case 46   *Legacies and bequests abate pro rata to make up the elected share when spouse elects to take statutory share*

Prior to her death T executed a will by which she left her husband, H a life interest in the entire estate.   Upon his death ten named legatees were to receive personal effects and cash legacies totaling $53,000, the balance of the estate "to be divided among the children of T's deceased brother."   After T's death H renounced the provision of the will and elected to take under the statute which granted him *one-half of the net estate outright. The executor then petitioned the Probate Court for instructions as to the effect of the election upon the bequest contained in the will. How should the estate be distributed?*

Answer. *The elective share should be charged pro rata against all beneficiaries and the vested remainders should be accelerated as if the life tenant had died as of the date of the testatrix's death. The general rules of abatement are that residuary legacies abate first, followed by general legacies and then specific and demonstrative legacies. This rule is based on an arbitrary presumption as to the probable intent of the testator where the will does not anticipate the necessity for abatement. It may be judicially noticed, however, that modern wills often use the residuary clause to carry out the most significant dispositions intended by the decedent such as provision for close family members or the objects of the decedent's greatest bounty. Where an election hostile to the interest of the named beneficiary creates a substantial distortion of the testamentary scheme a more flexible and equitable standard should be applied. It is clear from the circumstances surrounding the execution of the will that T at all times intended that the residuary legatees, who were her next of kin, be the recipients of a substantial portion of her estate. If H's elective share were to be taken entirely from the residuary, T's desire that her next of kin be her primary beneficiaries would be thwarted. A pro rata abatement is the sound and equitable approach and the one which conforms to the presumed intention of the testator where the diminution in the estate: (1) results from an election by a surviving spouse, (2) in circumstances where it produces a substantial distortion of the testamentary scheme, (3) as it applies to persons who have a natural claim on the bounty of the testator, (4) where there is no evidence that the election was foreseeable, and (5) where there is no contrary intent manifested in the will as to the order of abatement.*

See Kilcoyne v. Reilly, 101 U.S.App.D.C. 380, 249 F.2d 472 (1957).

NOTE—Section 2–207 of the Uniform Probate Code provides for an equitable apportionment among the recipients of the property remaining after satisfaction of the spouse's elective share in proportion to the value of their respective interests.

1. A gift in a will is said to lapse if the beneficiary is living when the will is executed, but the beneficiary subsequently predeceases the testator.

    LAPSE AND ANTI-LAPSE STATUTES

2. A gift by will to a person already deceased at the time the will is made is void.

    CAVEAT—Under UPC 2–605 such a gift is treated no differently from that to a beneficiary living at the time the will was executed who died subsequently.

3. Both void and lapsed gifts pass under a general residuary clause. See UPC 2–606.

4. At common law, a lapsed devise of land passed as intestate property while a lapsed legacy passed through the residuary clause. Under the modern law there is no distinction between lapsed devises and lapsed legacies.

5. When a residuary legacy or devise lapses it passes as intestate property.

e.g.   T died testate leaving a will giving Blackacre to A, $1000 to B and the residuary to C.   Both A and B predecease T leaving no lineal descendents.   As between C and T's heirs at law C takes all of the property.

6. Many jurisdictions have enacted "anti-lapse" statutes.   These generally prevent lapse by the death of a devisee or legatee before the testator if the devisee or legatee is a *relative* and leaves *issue* who survive the testator.   In such cases the statutes usually provide that the surviving issue of the deceased beneficiary take the gift in place of the deceased beneficiary.   See UPC 2–605.

7. Jurisdictions vary as to whether or not anti-lapse statutes apply to the following situations:

(a)   gifts where the devisee is dead at the time of execution of the will, or

(b)   gifts to a class where the devisee would have been a member of the class if he had survived the testator, whether his death occurred before or after the execution of the will.

The better view is that the anti-lapse statute will include the predeceased class member in the class as if the gift were to an individual.   It seems likely that this is the result that a testator would prefer.   See UPC 2–605, *Comment.*

See generally Atkinson, pp. 777–786; Clark, pp. 982–983; Palmer, pp. 182–184; Ritchie, pp. 931–935; and Scoles, pp. 709–710.

Case 47   *Application of the anti-lapse statutes to class gifts*

T died leaving a will containing the following clause: "I will, devise and bequeath all the residue of my property, both real and personal, to my brothers and sisters share and share alike."   T had seven brothers and sisters, three of whom died prior to the execution of the will leaving lineal descendants and two of whom died leaving lineal descendants, after the will was executed but prior to T's death.   The state having jurisdiction over the will had the following statute: "If

*a devisee or legatee dies during the lifetime of the testator, the tes-
tamentary disposition to such devisee or legatee lapses, unless an
intention appears from the will to substitute another in his place;
but, when any property is devised or bequeathed to an adopted child
or blood kindred to the testator, and when such devisee or legatee
dies before the testator, leaving lineal descendants, or is dead at the
time the will is executed, leaving lineal descendants who survive the
testator such legacy or devise does not lapse, but such descendants
take the property so given by the will in the same manner as the
devisee or legatee would have done had he survived the testator."*
How should T's residuary estate be divided?

Answer. The estate should be distributed to the brothers and
sisters who survive T and to the lineal descendants of the brothers
and sisters who were living at the time of the execution of the will.
At common law where there was a testementary gift to a class and
a member of the class died before the death of the testatrix, the gift
went to the surviving members of the class unless the testatrix had
expressed a contrary intention in her will.   In the present case T's
gift of the residuary was a gift to a class and the question involved
is whether or not the anti-lapse statute in effect applies to testamentary gifts made to a class, as well as to gifts made to named beneficiaries.   A majority of the states have held that nonlapse statutes
apply to members of a class who die after the execution of the will,
but prior to the death of the testator.   The basis for such holding is
that a lapse of the testamentary gift is thereby prevented and the gift
will pass to those whom the testator would most likely have wished
to substitute for the deceased member of a class.   This result is
further supported by the language of the statute which by the use of
the term "blood kindred" indicates that the legislature intended that
the statute be applied to class gifts where the class consists of blood
relatives.   On the other hand the majority of the jurisdictions have
held that a nonlapse statute does not apply to a member of the class
who was dead at the time of the execution of the will.   The rule at
common law was that a gift to one already deceased was void rather
than lapsed; therefore, no question of lapse was presented.   The anti-
lapse statute being in derogation of the common law must be strictly
construed and thus does not apply to a void gift.   Where as in this
case there is nothing in the will to indicate that T wanted to provide
for her then deceased brothers and sisters or their lineal descendants,
it is more logical to assume that T intended to include only her living
brothers and sisters.   Therefore, it must be concluded that the lineal
descendants of the brothers and sisters who were deceased at the
time of the execution of the will were not members of the class and
not entitled to share in the estate, but that the lineal descendants of
the brothers and sisters who predeceased after the execution of the
will were members of the class and entitled to share in the estate.

See *Drafts v. Drafts*, 114 So.2d 473 (Fla.Dist.Ct.App.1959).

**WILLS—
MISCELLANEOUS
RULE OF
CONSTRUCTION**

1. Rules of construction in statutes apply only when it is not made clear in the will that a contrary result was intended. In the absence of a clear intent expressed in the document courts have developed a series of rules to supply presumed intent.

2. The general rule is that a will should be interpreted by the language of the instrument in the light of the general circumstances surrounding the testator at the time of its execution.

3. It is only when the testator's intention cannot be ascertained from the language of the will and surrounding circumstances that statutory and court-made rules of construction apply.

4. A will is construed to pass all property which the testator owns at his death, including property acquired after the execution of the will.

   e.g. Testator's only property at the time he executes his will is Blackacre. He provides in his will "I give and devise all of my property to Lucy." Thereafter he acquires Whiteacre. On his death he owns both Blackacre and Whiteacre. Lucy takes both properties.

5. If a devise or bequest fails for any reason it becomes part of the residue.

6. If the residuary is devised to two or more persons and the residuary gift to one of them fails for any reason his share passes to the other residuary devisees in proportion to their interests in the residue.

7. If a gift of the residuary fails in its entirety, the residuary passes by intestacy.

8. Many states have statutes which provide that a devisee who does not survive the testator for a stated period of time (e.g. 120 hours) is treated as if he had predeceased the testator.

PART TWO

TRUSTS

V

TRUSTS— INTRODUCTION AND ANALYSIS

Summary Outline

A. Analysis of Trust Problems

B. Definition and Development of Trusts

    1. fiduciary nature of relationship

    2. split title

    3. trust as property concept

    4. trust as remedy concept

C. Definition of Trust Elements

    1. settlor

    2. trustee

    3. beneficiary (*cestui que trust*)

    4. terms of trust

D. Distinctions Between Trusts and Other Relationships

1. The essential determinations to be made in any trust law fact situation are:

    (a) the existence of a valid trust,

    (b) the terms of the trust with respect to the intent of the settlor, and

    (c) the enforcement thereof.

2. The first step in analyzing whether or not a trust exists is to determine if all elements of a trust are present. See Chapter VI. Basics of Trusts.

3. In order to ascertain the presence of necessary trust elements, the trust should first be classified as to _trust intent_, express or implied.

    (a) If express, whether:

        (i)   private, or

        (ii) charitable.

    (b) If implied, whether:

        (i)   presumed intent (resulting), or

        (ii) imposed intent (constructive).

See *Introduction to Trust Classification*, Chapter VI, below.

4. Once it is determined that all trust elements are present it is then necessary to determine if any rule of law will operate to make the trust (or any trust interest) invalid or unenforceable. See Chapter IX, Limitations on the Creation and Duration of Trusts; *The Requirement of a Writing—The Statute of Frauds; Trusts and the Statute of Wills*, and *Prohibited Trust Purposes*, Chapter VII, below.

5. If a valid trust is established, it is then important to examine the relationships of the various parties:

    (a) to each other, and

    (b) to the trust property.

6. In analyzing relationships in the trust careful distinctions must be made between and among:

    (a) settlors,

    (b) trustees,

    (c) beneficiaries,

    (d) creditors, and

    (e) other third parties.

See Chapter VI.   Basics of Trusts.

CAVEAT—The same person may relate to the trust in more than one capacity.   In answering a question in the area of trusts, reference to an individual must include specific reference to the particular capacity and the rights and liabilities related to each.

7. In every instance the intent of the creator of the trust as to the rights and duties of each party should be identified.

8. The powers, duties, and liabilities of the trustee vis-a-vis the trust property and the various parties related to the trust must be determined with reference to the intent of the creator and applicable provisions of law.

   See Chapter XIV.   The Fiduciary, below.

9. In the event that a trust or any interest in a trust is invalid, it is then important to determine the effect of such invalidity on the trust property.

   See Chapters X, Resulting Trusts and XI.   Constructive Trusts, below.

10. Whenever a breach of trust occurs or an interest in a trust is rendered invalid it is important to consider:

    (a) who has standing to raise the issue; and

    (b) the ability of the court or the parties to change or modify the intent of the creator.

    See Chapter VIII, Charitable Trusts and Chapter XIV, The Fiduciary, below.

11. It is important to keep in mind that the constructive trust is not intent enforcing.   It is a remedial device, because as such it will often be subject to special rules which have little application in the general law of trusts.   See Chapter XI, Constructive Trusts, below.

DEFINITION AND DEVELOPMENT OF TRUSTS

1. A trust is:

   (a) a fiduciary relationship wherein,

   (b) one or more persons,

   (c) hold property,

   (d) subject to equitable duties to hold and deal with the property,

   (e) for the benefit of other persons.   See Bogert, pp. 1–5; Rest. § 2.

2. The concept of a trust is that of split title:

    (a) one person, the trustee, holds *legal title* to particular property for the benefit of another, and

    (b) another person, the beneficiary, is said to hold *equitable* title.

3. The interest of the trustee, or title-holder, is said to be *legal*, while that of the beneficiary is *equitable*.

4. The trust form is adaptable to numerous situations:

    (a) It is a means of holding and disposing of property.

        e.g. S desires to transfer Blackacre to her children who are minors, but does not want them to control legal title until they are sui juris. She therefore transfers title to a trustee to hold and manage the property until her youngest child reaches age 21 and then to convey to her children.

    (b) It is also a mode of reasoning on which to fashion a remedy against persons who are holding title to property in circumstances where it is unjust for them to keep it.

        e.g. A fraudulently induces B to convey Blackacre to him. Although A then holds legal title the property justly belongs to B. A court will declare A a constructive trustee for B.

5. The trust developed out of the common law system of uses, i.e., where one person held land "for the use of another." The system of uses originally involved a transfer from A to B for certain purposes, B agreeing to carry out such purposes, by a gentlemen's agreement.

6. Uses were usually created to achieve the effect of a will for real property (wills not then being allowed) to escape taxes on death and to give the benefit of the land to persons who could not hold title.

7. The common law courts would not enforce agreements with respect to uses, but the courts of equity became increasingly liberal toward affording remedies.

8. The Statute of Uses passed by the English Parliament in 1535 attempted to eliminate uses by "executing" uses, i.e. turning equitable estates into legal estates.

    e.g. If A transferred land to B to the use of C, the use would be executed and thereby B's legal estate would be vested in C who thus became the fee simple owner.

9. The Statute of Uses did not apply to certain transactions involving uses. Exemptions were:

    (a) a use of personal property,

(b) an active use, i.e., one in which the trustee had active duties to perform other than holding and conveying legal title,

(c) a use on a use, i.e., A to B to the use of C to the use of D.

These exemptions allowed the development of the modern law of trusts.

10. Some states have adopted the Statute of Uses either by legislative enactment or consider it adopted as part of the common law.

11. In other states the statute of uses is not in force. Much the same result, however, is achieved by legislation and court rulings providing that when the purpose for which an express trust is created ceases, the estate of the trustee also ceases. See *Active and Passive Trusts*, Chapter VI, below.

See generally Bogert, pp. 5–17; Clark, pp. 433–450; Palmer, pp. 252–253; Scoles, pp. 398–399; and Scott, §§ 1–1.11

DEFINITION OF TRUST ELEMENTS

1. The *settlor* (or *trustor*) is the person who creates a trust.

2. The property interest held by the trustee is the *trust property*. It may also be called the *corpus, res* or *subject matter of the trust*.

3. The *trustee* is the person who holds the trust property.

4. The *beneficiary* (or *cestui que trust*) is the person for whose benefit the trustee holds the trust property.

5. *Terms of the trust* are those duties and powers of the trustee and rights of the beneficiary intended by the settlor at the time of creating the trust.

e.g.   A transfers property to B with the instruction that B is to pay the income to C during C's life.   B has the duty to pay the income to C and C has an enforceable right to such income.   See Rest. § 4.

See generally Bogert, pp. 1–5; Clark, p. 433; Ritchie, pp. 374–375; Scoles, p. 214; and Scott, §§ 3–3.2.

DISTINCTIONS BETWEEN TRUSTS AND OTHER RELATIONSHIPS

1. Trusts must be distinguished from other relationships which resemble trusts in that one person may be acting with respect to or holding property for another, but which are not true trusts. Among such relationships are bailment, guardianship, executorship and administratorship, agency, debt, mortgages, pledges, liens, third party beneficiary contracts, and corporate directorships.

2. It is important to classify such relationships correctly in that frequently the distinctions involved have their origins in the historical difference between several kinds of courts (common law, canon law and equity) and as such remedies will vary depending upon classification.

3. A bailment exists when one person, the bailee, has rightful possession of personal property title to which is in another, the bailor.

  (a) It is *like* a trust in that:

    (i)   The bailee has possession of the subject property.

    (ii) It may be created for the benefit of a third party.

  (b) It is *unlike* a trust in that:

    (i)   The bailee has no title to the subject of the bailment and cannot transfer title to a bona fide purchaser, except in estoppel situations and under certain provisions of the Uniform Commercial Code.　See UCC 2–403.

    (ii) Real property or intangible property not embodied in a document cannot be the subject matter of a bailment.

    (iii) There is no fiduciary duty between the bailee and the bailor or a third party for whose benefit it was created.

    (iv) It is enforced by legal, rather than equitable remedies.

  e.g.　A delivers furniture to B to be stored in B's warehouse for six months while A is in Europe and to be returned to A upon demand.　A bailment is created.　Only possession has passed to B, and not title.　See Rest. § 5.　See also Bogert, pp. 26–28.

4. Executorships and administratorships are limited in purpose to the winding up of the estate of a decedent.　They derive their authority by court appointment.

  (a) Executorships are *like* trusts in that:

    (i)   The executor has a fiduciary duty to the beneficiaries of the estate.

    (ii) The executor holds title to the personal property in the estate.

  (b) Executorships are *unlike* trusts in that:

    (i)   The executor does not hold title to real property in the estate.

    (ii) The duties of the executor are limited in scope to those necessary to collect the property of the decedent, pay decedent's debts and expenses and distribution of the remaining property.

(iii) Executors do not ordinarily have a duty to make investments.

(iv) Executors are always subject to court supervision of their administration while certain trustees are not. See Rest. § 6. See also Bogert, pp. 31–33.

5. Guardianship involves a court appointed official, the guardian or conservator, to deal with the property of a third person, the ward, who lacks legal capacity.

(a) It is *like* a trust in that:

   (i) The guardian has a fiduciary relationship to the ward.

   (ii) The guardian must take possession of and manage the ward's property.

(b) It is *unlike* a trust in that:

   (i) The guardian does not have title to the ward's property; only certain powers to deal with it.

   (ii) The guardians powers and duties are fixed by statute and he is subject to court supervision of his guardianship.

   (iii) The guardianship exists only as long as the ward lacks capacity.

See Rest. § 7. See also Bogert, pp. 37–38.

6. An agency is a relationship wherein one person, the agent, acts for another, the principal, and is in his control.

(a) It is *like* a trust in that the agent has a fiduciary duty to the principal.

(b) It is *unlike* a trust in that:

   (i) The agent is subject to the control of the principal whereas a trustee is under a duty to act for the benefit of the beneficiary but subject to the terms of the trust rather than the control of the beneficiary.

   (ii) An agent does not have title to the property of the principal, except in certain circumstances where it is necessary to have title to carry out the agency.

   (iii) An agent may subject his principal to personal liability whereas a trustee cannot so subject the beneficiary or the trust.

   (iv) An agency is terminated by revocation, death or incapacity of the principal.
     (1) A authorizes B to find a buyer for his house. A

dies prior to B's finding such a buyer. B's agency terminates on the death of A and he is no longer authorized to find a buyer.

(2) A deeds his house to B with directions to sell it and pay the proceeds to C. A dies. B is a trustee and may proceed to sell the house and carry out the terms of the trust.

See Rest. § 8. See also Bogert, pp. 34–36.

7. A debt is a contractual relationship involving a personal obligation on the part of one person, the debtor, to pay money to another, the creditor. It is *unlike* a trust in that:

(a) The debtor has no fiduciary duty to the creditor.

(b) A creditor has only a personal claim against the debtor; he has no interest in the debtor's property.

(c) The creditor's remedies against the debtor are at law in the first instance.

(d) The creation of a debt requires consideration.

See Rest. § 12.

8. Liens and pledges are security interests which are contractual in nature.

(a) They are *like* trusts in that:

    (i) the lienholder or pledgee must have possession of the subject property, and

    (ii) The lienholder or pledgee has certain rights with respect to the subject property.

(b) They are *unlike* trusts in that:

    (i) There is no fiduciary duty between the parties.

    (ii) The lienholder or pledgee acquires no property right in the subject of the lien or pledge.

    (iii) They are dependent upon the existence of a debt and terminate when it has been paid.

9. Mortgages are security interests wherein one person, the mortgagor, grants an interest in property to another, the mortgagee, who holds it for his own benefit as security for the repayment of a debt.

(a) A mortgage is *like* a trust in that:

    (i) The mortgagee, in some jurisdictions, may have legal title to the property.

      (ii) Both legal and equitable duties and remedies are involved in the relationship.

  (b) A mortgage is *unlike* a trust in that:

      (i) There is no fiduciary relationship between the mortgagee and mortgagor.

      (ii) In most jurisdictions legal title remains in the mortgagor with the mortgagee having only a security interest.

See Rest. § 7.

10. A third party beneficiary contract is a mere personal undertaking to make payment to a third party.

  (a) It is *like* a trust in that the beneficiary has the right to enforce the contract.

  (b) It is *unlike* a trust in that:

      (i) The obligor has no fiduciary duty to the beneficiary.

      (ii) The obligee as well as the beneficiary may enforce the contract.

      (iii) The beneficiary has no equitable interest in the property.

      (iv) The remedies of the beneficiary are at law in the first instance.

See Rest. § 14.

11. An equitable charge is created when a person gives, by will or inter vivos transfer, property to another person for his own benefit but subject to a payment to a third party.

  (a) It is *like* a trust in that:

      (i) The transferee of the property holds it subject to an equitable interest in a third party.

      (ii) The transferee of the property can transfer it to a bona fide purchaser free of the equitable interest.

  (b) It is *unlike* a trust in that:

      (i) No fiduciary relationship is created.

      (ii) The transferee has both the legal title and beneficial interest in the property.

      (iii) Once the equitable charge is paid the transferee holds it clear of any interest in others.

         (1) A devises Blackacre to B "subject to the payment of" $100 per month to Mary during her life. B holds Blackacre on an equitable charge in the ab-

        sence of evidence of a different intention.   B holds
        Blackacre beneficially having both legal and equi-
        table title.

  (2) A devises Blackacre to B "in trust" to pay Mary
        during her life $100 a month from the income, and
        to B on Mary's death.   A trust is created.   B only
        holds legal title to Blackacre during Mary's life.

See Rest. § 10.   See also Bogert, pp. 28–30.

12. Directors of corporations are in a special relationship to the corporation.

  (a) The relationship of directors to a corporation is *like* that of
      trustees in that they owe fiduciary duties to the corporation.

  (b) It is *unlike* that of a trustee in that they do not hold title to
      the property of the corporation.

See Rest. § 16A.

13. A *fiduciary relationship* is the relation wherein one person is
under a duty to act solely for the benefit of another within the
scope of the relationship.   See Chapter XIV, The Fiduciary.

See generally Bogert, pp. 26–39; Palmer, p. 341; Scoles, pp.
222–223; and Scott, §§ 4A–8.

Insurance benefits option arrangement does not create a trust   **Case 48**

*Prior to his death D purchased a life insurance policy with NLI In-
surance Company on his life and named his son S as the beneficiary.
Concurrently D executed and delivered to NLI the following document: "To NLI Insurance Company, I hereby direct that in the event
my son S, the beneficiary of record, shall survive me but shall not
have attained the age of 21 years at the time of my death, the amount
payable under said policy upon my death to such son, shall be retained by the company and interest thereon at the rate which the
company may each year declare on such fund shall be compounded
annually at the end of each year until such son shall have attained
the age of 21 years when his share together with the interest then
accumulated thereon shall be paid at once in one sum to him.   I
hereby further direct that my son shall not have the right to withdraw
any amount retained by the company except as hereinbefore provided
nor the right to assign or encumber any payment hereunder."   After
D's death, NLI, upon surrender of the policy, delivered to S a sup-
plemental contract providing for payment of the proceeds of the policy in exact accordance with the directions given by D in the above
statement.   Thereafter S's mother and guardian filed an action in
equity alleging that she was without sufficient funds with which to
properly maintain and educate S and asked that the court order NLI*

to pay her for this purpose such sums from the proceeds of the policy as the court found necessary.   May the court grant the relief requested?

Answer.   No.   In order for a court of equity to grant the desired relief it would have to find that a trust relationship existed between the insurance company and the beneficiary.   A trust relationship only exists when there is an assignment of property to a trustee with the intention of passing title to hold for the benefit of another.   There must be a separation of the legal estate from the beneficial enjoyment. In the present fact situation the provision for the payment of interest on the fund held by the insurance company together with the fact that there was no segregation of any fund from which payment was to be made are not indicative of a trust relationship.   The agreement executed by D concurrently with the issuance of the policy specifically incorporates D's directions and is no more than a contract containing a promise to pay proceeds of the policy in such a manner as the insured has designated.   The relationship existing was that of debtor and creditor rather than that of trustee and cestui que trust. In circumstances such as those pleaded by S's mother an advancement may be allowed from a trust fund for the purposes of maintenance and education of the beneficiary.   The same is not true for a disposition of property fixed by contract.

See Pierowich v. Metropolitan Life Ins. Co., 282 Mich. 118, 275 N.W. 789 (1937).

VI

BASICS OF TRUSTS

INTRODUCTION TO TRUST CLASSIFICATION

1. A trust is classified on the basis of:

    (a) the intent manifested by its creator;

    (b) the duties imposed upon the trustee; i.e. whether it is active or passive, see *Active and Passive Trusts* below; and

    (c) the method by which it is created. See Chapter VII. The Creation, Modification and Revocation of Trusts, below.

2. Trusts are classified as to intent as follows:

    (a) express trusts:

        (i) private trusts,

        (ii) charitable trusts,

    (b) resulting trusts, and

    (c) constructive trusts.

3. The term "express trust" is used when it is necessary to contrast a formal trust with a resulting trust or a constructive trust.

4. The term "private trust" is used when it is necessary to contrast a trust for private purposes with a charitable trust.

5. Every private express trust consists of four distinct elements:

    (a) an intention of the settler to create a trust,

    (b) a trustee,

    (c) a res or subject matter, and

    (d) a beneficiary or cestui que trust.

    See *Definition of Trust Elements*, Chapter V, above.

    See generally, Bogert, pp. 18–26; Clark, pp. 450–451; Ritchie, pp. 374–378; Scoles, p. 261; Scott, § 2–2.2.

ACTIVE AND PASSIVE TRUSTS

1. An "active" trust is one in which the trustee has some affirmative duty to perform, *e.g.* to collect rents and distribute the income to the beneficiaries.

2. A "passive" trust is one in which the trustee is the mere title-holder and has no duties with respect to the trust res.

3. In many jurisdictions either the Statute of Uses (see *Definition and Development of Trusts*, Chapter V, above) or similar legislation is in force which abolishes passive trusts. As a result of such legislation the trustee of a passive trust takes nothing and the beneficiary takes legal title automatically. Most states apply this rule to trusts of personality as well as realty.

4. There is a split of authority among jurisdictions as to whether or not a trust in which the only duty of the trustee is to execute and deliver a deed to the beneficiaries is passive.

5. Some states have statutes which provide that when the purposes for which an express trust is created cease, and the trust becomes passive, the trust automatically ceases.

6. Courts will terminate trusts when the trust purposes are fulfilled. See *The Power to Terminate Trusts*, Chapter VII, below.

   See generally Bogert, pp. 165–170; Ritchie, p. 454; Scoles, p. 22; and Scott, §§ 69–70.

Beneficiary may terminate passive trust after active trust term ends **Case 49**

D died and in his will he left property to T in trust to receive and pay the net income to W and upon W's death in trust for W's children and the issue of such children living at the death of W. No duties were given to the trustee after W's death except to hold the property for the benefit of W's children and issue. W died leaving two adult children and one minor grandchild. The trust property consisted of both real and personal property. W's children and the guardian of the grandchild bring an action asking the court to decree that the trust is terminated. Are they entitled to such a decree?

Answer. *Yes. During W's life the trustee had active duties in that he was to collect the income from the property and pay it to W, while preserving the remaining interest for the persons who were to have the property in W's death. On W's death there is no longer any duty for the trustee to perform other than the passive duty of holding title to the property. The trust is no longer an active trust; therefore, the Statute of Uses "executes the use." The effect of the statute is to transfer the legal title on to the beneficiaries thereby terminating the estate of the trustee. The principle applies equally to both real and personal property. Although the language of the English Statute of Uses was "whenever any person is seised" and the English courts, by a strict construction, held that it did not apply to personal property for the reason that one could not be "seised" of an interest in personalty, it has been long settled that a trust in regard to personal property will only continue so long as the purpose of the trust requires. When all the objects of the trust have been accomplished, the person entitled to the beneficial use is regarded as both the legal and equitable owner and entitled to the possession of the property. Under the will in question, the purpose of the trust was that the trustee should pay the net income to W during her life. This purpose was fully accomplished and upon her death the trustees had no longer any active duty to perform. The beneficiaries entitled to the ultimate* *use, therefore, became absolute owners of the property.   Moreover, the fact that one of the beneficiaries is a minor is no reason to continue the trust in that the minor's guardian is entitled to receive her share of the personal estate.   Minority in itself does not constitute a reason to continue the trust.*

See Hooper v. Felgner, 80 Md. 262, 30 A. 911 (1894).

INTENTION TO CREATE A TRUST— HOW MANIFESTED

1. It is essential to the creation of an express trust that the settlor overtly manifest an intention to create a trust.

2. The settlor must intend to impose enforceable duties on a trustee to deal with the property for the benefit of another.

3. The manifestation of intent necessary to the creation of a trust must be overt, but no particular words or form of conduct are necessary.

4. Intent may be made manifest by words, conduct or both.

   CAVEAT—It is important to remember that although the settlor's intention may be made manifest by words and conduct of the settlor such evidence may, in appropriate cases, be excluded by the parol evidence rule, the statute of frauds, the statute of wills or other rules of law.   Also, statutes in some instances require the intention be shown in a particular form such as the requirement of a writing in the case of trusts of interests in land or testamentary trusts.

5. The use of the words "in trust" or "trustee" are not necessary and conversely the presence of such words does not make it certain that a court will find a trust intent.

   See generally Bogert, pp. 23–25; Rest. §§ 23–24; Ritchie, p. 406; Scoles, p. 232; and Scott, §§ 23–24.

Case 50   *Intention to create a trust where words "trust" not used*

T died testate leaving Blackacre to be divided equally among five of his children.   He instructed his executor to sell the real estate but until it could be sold to rent it and divide the rents among the children.   One child brings an action for partition of the property.   Is he entitled to a decree of partition?

   Answer.   No.   By the language of the will, there was a trust created for the benefit of the children.   It is clear that an outright gift was not intended to the children and it is immaterial that the word trust was not used or that the property was not devised to the executor.

   See Morse v. Morse, 85 N.Y. 53 (1881).   See also Scott § 24.

Power of attorney may be sufficient to indicate intent to declare   Case 51
a trust

Prior to his death D, in a letter, authorized A to purchase an annuity in France for the benefit of D's mistress, M.   A purchased the annuity, but because M was married purchased it in D's name.   Thereafter D sent A a power of attorney to transfer the annuity to M.   D died prior to the transfer of the annuity.   M brings an action claiming that she is entitled to the annuity.   Was a trust created by these transactions in favor of M?

Answer.   Yes.   The issue involved in this case is: does the power of attorney amount to a declaration of trust?   If a party declares himself to be the trustee of property, it becomes the property of the trust beneficiary without any further action.   On the facts presented the power of attorney in the present case constitutes a sufficient declaration that D held the annuity in trust for M, and therefore, the property should be delivered to M.

See *Ex parte Pye*, 18 Ves. Jr. 139 34 Eng.Rep. 271 (Ch.1811).   See also NOTE following CASE 74, below.

TRUSTS CREATED BY PRECATORY WORDS

1. Precatory words are words of *hope, wish,* desire or recommendation.

2. If a transferor of property expresses the wish or desire that the property be used in a particular manner or for the benefit of particular persons whether or not a trust is created depends upon the intent of the transferor to impose enforceable obligations.

   (a) The earlier view was that if the transferor expressed a desire that a certain use be made of the property the expression of desire in itself was sufficient to form a trust.

   (b) Under the more modern view precatory words alone do not create a trust.   See Rest. § 25.

3. Under the modern view, precatory words may create a trust only if it is found that the transferor intended to create enforceable obligations, when the entire language of the instrument is considered in the light of the situation of the transferor, his family and the alleged beneficiaries at the effective date of the document.

   e.g.   "I give $100,000.00 to my wife commending to her the support of my mother."   Was the testator creating a trust for the benefit of his mother using polite language or did he intend a moral obligation at most?   The court could find from all the circumstances (including the facts that testator had supported his mother for many years, that the mother was otherwise destitute and that the amount of support given the mother was a definite amount) that the testator intended to impose enforceable duties on his wife with respect to the support of his mother. In such circumstances, a trust is created.

4. The failure of the transferor to describe clearly any element required for a trust is evidence that he did not intend a trust.

5. Courts tend to find a trust created by precatory words where the beneficiary has a moral claim on the transferor.

e.g. If a testator, having for many years supported his retarded child, Mary, in an institution leaves his entire estate to his other child, "with the hope that he will provide for the comfort and maintenance of Mary," the court, recognizing testator's obligation to his helpless child will hold a trust to have been created.

6. If the transferor makes an absolute gift of property in one sentence and inserts precatory language in a separate sentence or article courts usually find no trust intent.

e.g. "I give, devise and bequeath all the rest, residue and remainder of my property to my wife to be her absolute estate forever. It is my request that upon her death my wife shall devise Blackacre to my brother, John." No trust in favor of John is created. To do so would cut down the prior gift of the fee. See Comford v. Cantrell, 177 Tenn. 553, 151 S.W.2d 1076 (1941).

See generally Bogert, pp. 40–43; Clark, pp. 466–474; Palmer, pp. 314–316; Rest. § 25; Ritchie, pp. 409–411; and Scott, §§ 25–25.2.

Case 52 *Words of recommendation following gift of absolute interest do not create a trust*

T died leaving a will which provided as follows: "I direct that my just debts and funeral expenses be paid by my executrix. My house and home in the town of Williamsburg I give to my beloved wife W. To my daughter D, I give and bequeath the sum of $5,000. All the rest, residue and remainder of my property of every kind and character, including real estate, personal property and mixed, I give to my beloved wife, W. And should my wife have anything left at her death, I recommend to her that the balance if there be any be given to my daughter, D." W subsequently died leaving only her diamond ring to D and leaving the rest of her estate to her own relatives. D brings an action contesting W's will contending that she should receive the residuary of W's estate by virtue of the last item of her father's will. Is D entitled to the proceeds of W's estate?

Answer. No. The solution depends upon the intention of the testator which must be gathered from the language of the will where *it is plain and unambiguous. The general rule is that where an interest is given in absolute terms, precatory words which follow are treated as expressions of wish rather than of will so that no trust is created. Used in their literal sense precatory words can impose no obligation on the first taker. The literal meaning of "recommend" is advisory, not obligatory. Moreover, it is significant that when T desired to make a bequest or mandatory direction he used language clearly expressing such desire as in the other item of the will. Given such facts there is nothing in the contents of the will which would justify a construction that the testator intended a binding obligation on W.*

　　See In re Estate of Hogan, 259 Iowa 887, 146 N.W.2d 257 (1966).

SAVINGS BANK TRUSTS— TENTATIVE OR TOTTEN TRUSTS

1. If a person makes a deposit in a bank in his own name "in trust" for another he may have intended any of the following:

   (a) to create a revocable trust;

   (b) to create an irrevocable trust;

   (c) not to create a trust.

   The Court resolves these questions by examining the situation of the depositor and his relationship to the beneficiary and other facts and circumstances.

2. Where there is no evidence of the testator's intention other than the form of deposit, most states have held that a revocable trust is created. The depositor may withdraw all or any part of the funds during his lifetime and on his death the beneficiary may enforce the trust as to any part remaining on deposit at his death. This is called *a tentative* or *totten* trust. The word "totten" refers to the famous case establishing this principle. Matter of Totten, 179 N.Y. 112, 71 N.E. 748 (1904).

3. In spite of the fact that the depositor has had complete control over the deposits during his life the trust is not held invalid as a testamentary transfer. The trust is considered to arise at the time of the deposit.

4. Many states have enacted statutes validating the Totten Trust. These statutes generally establish a "conclusive presumption" that the depositor intended to create a trust for the beneficiary if the beneficiary survives. See e.g. Conn.Gen.Stat.Ann. § 36–110; Ohio R.C. § 1107.07.

5. A tentative trust may be revoked at any time prior to the depositor's death by:

   (a) withdrawal of any part of the deposit, which operates as a revocation to the extent of the withdrawal;

   (b) the death of the beneficiary prior to the death of the depositor;

   (c) any other manifestation of intention to revoke.

     e.g. The depositor leaves a demonstrative bequest of the funds to another individual.

6. Tentative trusts are subject to the rights of the depositor's creditors.

7. Whether tentative trusts are subject to statutory rights of a surviving spouse in the depositor's estate varies from jurisdiction to jurisdiction. By the better view they are. See Matter of Halpern, 303 N.Y. 33, 100 N.E.2d 120 (1951), Whittington v. Whittington, 205 Md. 1, 106 A.2d 72 (1954).

See generally, Bogert pp. 43–47; Clark, p. 489; Palmer, pp. 346–347; Rest. § 58; Ritchie, pp. 550–554; Scoles, pp. 288–289; and Scott, §§ 58–58.6.

Case 53 *Savings account opened as trustee where no intent to create a trust—no trust created*

Several years prior to his death T deposited $5,000 in a bank account in his name as trustee for his niece Frances. Prior to the execution of his will T informed the executor that the trust account was T's. He stated that he had opened it when a teller at the bank where he had an individual account for the maximum amount allowable advised him that the bank could not accept a new deposit but that a "better way to make the deposit" would be to name himself as trustee. T made deposits and withdrawals from time to time. Frances was never advised of the account. At his death T left Frances a legacy of $5,000. Can the executor of T's estate claim the bank account as part of the estate?

    Answer. *Yes.* It is common for persons to put property in their own names as trustee without any intent to create a genuine trust. Where it is shown by the evidence that the depositor put the account in his name as trustee for another because of the limitation on the size of accounts any presumption that a trust was intended is rebutted.

See Reagan v. Phillips, 345 Mass. 387, 187 N.E.2d 801 (1963).

Case 54 *A tentative trust though valid for some purposes may be ineffective to defeat a surviving spouse's statutory share*

During her lifetime T created a number of savings accounts in which she was named as trustee for the benefit of her two children by a former marriage. The accounts provided for payment to the child *pbbaccounts* or children named therein on her death. She retained control over all of the accounts during her lifetime and made deposits into and withdrawals from them. On her death her husband D filed a petition in the court alleging that the trusts were a fraud on his marital rights and were illusory. He also claimed that the trust, if sustained, would defeat his statutory right to one-third of T's estate and his right to a widower's award under state law. Is D entitled to the proceeds of any of the bank deposits in question?

Answer. Yes. With respect to D's contention that the trusts are invalid in that they are illusory, the general rule is that savings account trusts are valid. They are not substantially different from other revocable inter vivos trusts where the declaration of trust immediately creates an equitable interest in the beneficiaries even though the enjoyment of the interest is postponed until the death of the settlor and may be completely destroyed by withdrawal from the account of all the deposits made by the settlor during his or her lifetime. The later destructibility of the interest does not negate the present existence of a valid trust. A trust may not be valid for every purpose, however. State law provisions protecting a surviving spouse's expectancy from the other's estate are expressions of a public policy to protect the surviving spouse. Such an expressed statutory policy of protecting a surviving spouse's statutory share in an estate should prevail regardless of the intent of the deceased spouse in creating the savings account trust. During her lifetime, T retained the absolute, unqualified control over the bank accounts and possessed and exercised all the incidents of complete ownership. The enjoyment of the proceeds of the accounts by the beneficiaries would arise only upon the death of T with the accounts remaining intact. As such, the control retained over the savings account trust is so complete that even though the trust is generally valid it should not be so against the right of a surviving spouse. The trusts in question were illusory and invalid as to D and did not deprive him of his statutory share in his deceased spouse's estate. In all other respects the trusts are valid and the balance remaining after the satisfaction of D's share should be distributed to the beneficiaries named in the trust accounts.

See *Montgomery v. Michaels*, 54 Ill.2d 532, 301 N.E.2d 465 (1973).

1. A trust requires a present legal transaction not a future one.

2. The manifestation of the settlor's intention to create a trust in the future does not create a trust.

   (a) S the owner of bonds tells T that he intends on the following

LACK OF INTENTION TO CREATE A PRESENT TRUST

day to transfer the bonds to T in trust for B. No trust arises until the transfer is made to T.

(b) S tells B that he intends to purchase 1,000 shares of ABC stock and, when he does, hold them in trust for B. Even if S purchases the shares no trust arises until he declares himself trustee for B. The previous declaration of intent will not suffice.

3. A trust will not arise immediately if the settlor:

(a) manifests an intention it shall not arise immediately;

(b) does not immediately designate the beneficiary, trustee or the trust property.

e.g. A delivers to T bonds to be held in trust for such person as A may designate by letter to T. A dies prior to such designation. No trust has arisen.

4. A promise to create a trust in the future is to be distinguished from:

(a) A present trust of an enforceable promise to be performed in the future.

(b) A present trust where the interest of the beneficiary will not take effect in enjoyment until a future date.

CAVEAT—If there is a manifestation of present intention to create a trust, a trust will arise although by the terms of the trust the interest of the beneficiary is a future interest.

e.g. A declares himself the trustee of 1,000 shares of stock to pay income to A for ten years and then to B for the remainder of B's life. Although B's interest is a future interest a trust is created in presenti. Rest. § 26 Comment g.

5. If one party makes an *enforceable* promise to pay money or transfer property to another person as trustee and if the promisee manifests the intention that his rights under the promise shall be held in trust a present trust is created at the time of the promise. In the absence of evidence of a different intention the inference is that the promisee intended an immediate trust and he becomes trustee of his rights under the promise.

e.g. In consideration of a payment of $100,000 made by S to X, X promises in writing to convey certain property to S in trust for B. There is no other evidence. S holds his rights against A in trust for B. See Rest. § 26, Comment n.

See generally Bogert, pp. 65–68; Palmer, p. 304; Rest. § 26; Ritchie, pp. 400–405; Scoles, pp. 262; and Scott, §§ 26–26.5.

Effect of intent to make property subject to a trust in the future   Case 55

S executed a deed of trust to T as trustee, by which she gave T $5,000 to be held upon the trusts set forth in the trust instrument. S reserved the right to deliver to the trustee additional property during the continuance of the trust. At the time of executing the deed there was pending a proceeding for settlement of an estate of which S was the beneficiary. Simultaneously with the trust deed S executed a power of attorney whereby she authorized T to collect all property to which she might be entitled in the estate proceeding. At the same time S gave T a letter instructing T to receive the property from the estate proceeding and transfer it to T to be added to the trust created under the trust agreement. S died before T had collected the property from the estate. Is T as trustee entitled to the property?

Answer. *No. T had only a power of attorney with respect to the property, which was revoked on S's death. Under the law of agency a power of attorney automatically terminates on the death of the principal. S did not manifest any intention to effectuate a present gift. There was no word of present transfer except as to the $5,000. All that was present was a set of instructions from principal to agent. There was a marked absence of words of present assignment. S had an intention to have the property become subject to the trust in the future but the intention was never carried out.*

See Farmers Loan & Trust Co. v. Winthrop, 238 N.Y. 477, 144 N.E. 686 (1924).

ILLUSORY TRUSTS

1. If a settlor *in form* either declares himself trustee of, or transfers to a third party, property in trust, but by the terms of the trust, or by his dealings with the trust property, *in substance* he exercises so much control over the trust property that it is clear that he did not intend to relinquish any of his rights in the trust property, the trust is invalid as illusory.

   (a) In such cases in a declaration of trust the settlor has not changed his relationship to the trust property.

   (b) In such cases in a transfer in trust he has rendered the trustee his agent in controlling the trust property.

2. The test of whether or not the creation of an inter vivos trust is illusory is whether the beneficiary receives a present interest in the trust property or in fact is to receive only an interest at or by reason of the death of the settlor. In the latter case the trust is testamentary and must comply with the statute of wills. See *Trusts and the Statute of Wills,* Chapter VII, below.

3. The mere reservation by the settlor of income for life will not render a trust illusory.

4. By the more modern view, the settlor's reservation of income for life plus a retained right to revoke will not render a trust illusory.

   e.g.   If S transfers Blackacre to T in trust to pay all rents and income to S for life and on S's death to convey to B and if, in addition, S retains the right to revoke the trust, the trust will be valid.   The rationale is that a present interest passes to B with possession and enjoyment postponed.   The interest may be defeated by a subsequent revocation but until such revocation takes place the beneficiary's interest is a validly existing interest.

5. A reservation of income for life plus both the right to revoke, and additional retained rights of control, such as the right to determine investment, may render the trust illusory.   The results in any given case may depend upon the degree of control actually retained and exercised by the settlor.

6. The actual exercise of retained power used by the settlor will be influential in a court's determination of whether a transfer is real or illusory.

   e.g.   S transferred all of his property in trust including his home and club memberships.   He retained the income for life plus the right to revoke and full power to control investments.   S then used this right to revoke in order to pay bills and in his general business making revocations for as little as $12.00 to pay personal expenses.   The trust is clearly illusory.   The trustee is no more than a depositary and an agent for the settlor.   See Osborn v. Osborn, 10 Ohio Misc. 171, 226 N.E.2d 814 (1966).

7. The central issue in cases involving illusory trusts is the emphasis placed by the court on the degree of control retained by the settlor. This varies from court to court, with the facts of the particular case, and to some extent, on the type of attack made upon the trust.   "The trust may be adequately armored against attack as a testamentary transaction but reserved powers less extensive than those upon which testamentary attacks are usually grounded may provide a foothold for a hostile spouse with whom the court may sympathize."   See also Case 57, below.

   See generally Clark, p. 63; Ritchie, p. 491; and Scott, § 57.1.

Case 56   *Settlor's retained powers do not render trust illusory where present interest passes to beneficiary*

D died intestate.   Prior to his death he had purchased certain securities.   At the time of the purchase he instructed that the stock be registered: "D as trustee for R." At the same time, he signed a document entitled "Declaration of Trust" which recited that he had purchased the stock as trustee for R as beneficiary and that he was holding the stock in trust under conditions whereby he reserved to himself as settlor certain power including: (1) the right to receive during his lifetime all cash dividends; (2) the right at any time to change the beneficiary or revoke the trust, the trust being automatically revoked on R's death; and (3) upon sale or redemption of any portion of the trust property, the right to retain the proceeds therefrom for his own use. He also reserved the right to act as sole trustee and as such had the power to vote, sell, redeem, exchange or otherwise deal in the stock which constituted the res of the trust. D died without having revoked the trust. His heirs at law claim that the declaration of trust is a mere attempt at a testamentary disposition and invalid for failing to comply with the statute of wills, and that the stock passes to them by intestacy. Are the heirs-at-law entitled to the shares?

Answer. No. The issue in this case is whether the trust instrument created a valid inter vivos trust, effective to give R title to the stock on D's death or the trust was an illusory transfer intended to effect a testamentary disposition of D's property without complying with the statute of wills. If D actually intended to part with some incident of ownership in the trust property at the time of the declaration of trust which passed to R as a present beneficial interest the trust even though such interest might be subsequently divested by revocation is valid. It is well settled that the mere retention of a life interest plus the right to revoke a trust will not in itself render the trust illusory. Many other powers may be retained including the right to act as trustee without defeating the trust so long as the retention of such powers is consistent with the beneficiary's having some present beneficial interest in the trust. On the facts of the present case the settlor could only act with respect to the trust property in accordance with the terms of the trust instrument. If he failed to do so he would be liable to the beneficiary for breach of trust. Although D might revoke the trust, as long as the trust existed he must deal with the property as a fiduciary. If for example, not having revoked the trust, D were to pledge it for his personal debt and lose it by foreclosure, the beneficiary would have a claim against his estate for damages for breach of trust. The settlor in this case with due formality declared himself a trustee. By doing so he manifested the intention that an interest should then pass to R and bound himself to act toward the res as a trustee. In such case he has fewer of the bundle of rights which made up his property in the shares prior to his declaration of trust and the transfer is valid.

See *Farkas v. Williams*, 5 Ill.2d 417, 125 N.E.2d 600 (1955).

Case 57 *Trust created to defeat spouse's right in property invalid where transfer illusory*

Three days prior to his death, D executed a trust agreement transferring all of his property to T in trust. By the terms of the trust deed, D retained a life interest in the trust property plus a right to revoke the trust or to change the beneficiary. He also retained the right to direct the trustee in the administration of the trust. At D's death T was to convey the trust property to D's niece N. The trust was created for the purpose of defeating D's wife, W's rights in his property on death. A state statute provided that a surviving spouse would take a one-third share in a decedent's property owned at death. After D's death, W brings an action seeking to obtain the statutory share out of the trust property. Is she entitled to recover?

Answer. Yes. The fact that the trust was created for the purpose of depriving the widow of her rights in D's estate is not controlling. If in fact D has made a valid transfer of his property the trust will stand despite the fact that his acknowledged intention in creating the trust was to defeat his wife's lawful interest in his property. The statute does not prohibit the husband's defeating his wife's expectant interest by inter vivos transfers. It does create a special equity in the wife which allows her to contest the transfer in that D may not defeat her interest by transfers which are not intended to effect a bona fide disposition of property. In this case the husband retained the right to control the actions of the trustee in the administration of the trust. Although the conveyance may not have taken back absolutely everything it gave, it took back so many of the rights over the property that the retention of power is sufficient to render the conveyance unlawful and illusory as to the wife. The key is that the settlor never intended in good faith to part with the ownership of his property until his death. The conveyance to the trustee is an exercise involving only form and not substance.

See Newman v. Dore, 275 N.Y. 371, 9 N.E.2d 966 (1937).

NOTE—In some states the fact that a trust was created with intent to defeat the spouse's share will invalidate the trust. See *Dower, Curtesy and Elective Share,* Chapter II, above.

THE SUBJECT MATTER OF THE TRUST

1. An essential element of every trust is the trust property or res. See *Definition of Trust Elements,* Chapter V, above.

2. The trust property, both at the time of creation and throughout the existence of the trust, must be:

   (a) in existence, and

   (b) definite or definitely ascertainable.

3. At the time of the creation of the trust the trust property must be voluntarily transferable by the owner.

4. An interest in an intangible such as a chose in action, patent, trademark or copyright, if transferable, may be held in trust.

5. Equitable interests, such as a beneficiary's interest in another trust, if transferable, may be held in trust.

6. Contingent interests, such as contingent remainders, if transferable may be held in trust.

CAVEAT—The transferability of contingent remainders depends upon the jurisdiction. See Smith's Review—Property 3d, Chapter XVI, Future Interests.

7. A mere expectancy, such as the interest of a person who expects to receive property as a devisee under a will, cannot be held in trust.

8. A trust ends with the destruction of trust property.

e.g. If the trust property consists solely of lumber which is destroyed by fire and there is no insurance the trust comes to an end although the beneficiary may have a claim against the trustee for breach of trust, if the trustee was negligent in failing to insure.

9. The duration or extent of the trustee's interest in the trust estate in the absence of the manifestation of a different intention by the settlor will be:

(a) in the case of real property, whatever estate in land the trustee must have to accomplish the trust purpose;

(b) in the case of personal property, an interest of unlimited duration.

e.g. A transfers Blackacre and 100 shares of ABC stock to T in trust to pay the income to C for life. T has a life estate for the life of C in Blackacre and a fee simple in the ABC stock.

See generally Bogert, pp. 69–75; Clark, p. 496; Rest. §§ 74–88; Palmer, p. 281; Ritchie, pp. 415–420; Scott §§ 74–88.

A promise to transfer property in trust which is not presently in existence does not create a present trust Case 58

In December of the year prior to the taxable year in question, a taxpayer decided that he would trade in the stock market during the following year. He thereupon stated to his wife and mother that he declared a trust of his stock trading during the following year for the benefit of his family on certain terms and conditions. Taxpayer agreed to assume personally any losses and to distribute the profits in equal shares to his wife, mother and two minor children. During the year in question he did carry on trading operations, deducted compensation for himself which he reported on his income tax return and divided the profits in equal shares as he had stated which amounts were reported in the respective income tax returns of the family members. The Commissioner of Internal Revenue contends that all of the profits are taxable to taxpayer for the year in question. Is this contention correct?

Answer. Yes. The general rule is that an interest which has not come into existence or which has ceased to exist cannot be held in trust. At the time of his declaration the taxpayer had no property interest in the profits in stock trading for the following year because there were none in existence at the time. He therefore had based his declaration of trust upon an interest which at that time had not come into existence and in which no one had a present interest. The trust first attached to the property when the taxpayer credited them to the beneficiaries on his books of account. Since the profits were not impressed with the trust when earned by the taxpayer, they are properly taxable to him in his income for the year in question.

See Brainard v. Commissioner of Internal Revenue, 91 F.2d 880 (7th Cir. 1937). See also Annot. "Creation of express trust of property to be acquired in the future." 3 A.L.R.3d 1416 (1965).

INSURANCE TRUSTS
1. If a person takes out a policy of insurance on his life, he may create a trust of the policy and its proceeds by:

   (a) making the policy payable to a designated person as trustee;

   (b) making the policy payable absolutely to a designated beneficiary who in turn agrees with the insured to hold the proceeds in trust;

   (c) assigning the policy to a third party as trustee; or

   (d) declaring himself trustee of the policy.

2. In each of the cases set forth in number 1, above, a present inter vivos trust is created. The beneficiary of the policy holds his rights as beneficiary in trust for such persons and on such terms as specified by the insured. The one who purchases the policy is the settlor. The beneficiary or assignee is trustee and the rights to the policy are the trust res.

3. An insurance trust is not testamentary and therefore need not comply with the Statute of Wills even though the insured reserves the power to change the beneficiary or to revoke or modify the trust. See *Trusts and the Statute of Wills*, Chapter VII, below.

4. The fact that the beneficiary's rights can be terminated at any time by the insured or may be enjoyed by the *trust beneficiaries* only

after death does not prevent a trust from arising immediately.

5. If an interest in an insurance policy can be transferred only to members of a particular class, a trust of such interest cannot be created for persons outside the class.

   e.g.   The National Service Life Insurance Act of 1940 originally provided that the insurance issued to members of the Armed Forces under the Act should be payable only to certain classes of relatives of the insured.   Soldier A takes out a policy payable to B, a member of the class.   B agrees to hold the proceeds in trust for C, a *non*-member of the class.   The trust for C is invalid.

6. The rights of the beneficiary of an insurance policy may be held in trust even though such beneficiary's rights may be subsequently defeated by the insured's changing the beneficiary of the policy.

   e.g.   H purchases a policy of life insurance on H's life and names W as beneficiary but reserving the power to change the beneficiary.   W declares herself trustee of her interest for her daughter D.   A valid trust is created in which W is trustee for D even though H may later change the beneficiary and defeat W's interest, at which time the trust will terminate.

   See generally Bogert, pp. 74–75; Clark, pp. 507, 511; Palmer, pp. 330–332; Rest. §§ 17(h), 57, 79 84(b); Ritchie, pp. 710–714, 719–721; Scoles, pp. 291–292; and Scott, §§ 57.3, 82.1, 87.1.

Reservation of the right to change the beneficiary of an insurance policy which is the subject matter of an insurance trust will not invalidate the trust

Case 59

Prior to his death, D and Trust Co. entered into a trust agreement under the terms of which D deposited with Trust Co. insurance policies insuring his life and agreed to make Trust Co. the beneficiary of all the policies.   The agreement also provided that D would pay the premiums and that he retained all rights under the policies, including the right to change the beneficiary, to borrow against the policies, and to surrender any policy for its cash value.   He also reserved powers to revoke and amend the trust and twice exercised such power prior to his death.   During D's lifetime the trustee's only duty was to return the policies to D upon his demand.   On D's death the trustee was to collect the policies and administer the proceeds for the benefit of D's beneficiaries under the terms of the trust agreement.   After D's death, C, a creditor of D's estate, brought suit against the insurance companies and Trust Co. seeking to have the trust agreement declared void and to have the trustee ordered to hold the proceeds of the life insurance policies under a resulting trust in favor of D's estate.   C contended that the rest of D's estate was insufficient to pay the claims of creditors and that D had treated the insurance policies as his sole property and that there was no actual corpus of the trust and no transfer of property during D's lifetime. Is C entitled to have the proceeds of the insurance policies declared a resulting trust?

Answer. No. *A life insurance policy is property and may constitute the subject matter of a trust. When the designated beneficiary of a life insurance policy promises the insured to pay either the whole or a portion of the proceeds of the policy to a third person the proceeds will be impressed with the trust to the extent of the promise made. The date of death of the insured merely fixed the time when the obligation of the insurers to pay and the right of the beneficiary to receive the proceeds of the policies became enforceable. The trust agreement and the change of beneficiaries, however, became effective during the lifetime of the settlor. The continuing right to receive the proceeds of an insurance policy is not impaired by the unexercised right of the insured to designate another beneficiary. A policy of life insurance is not an asset of the estate of the insured unless it is made payable to him, his executors or his administrators. The mere fact that the insured may change the beneficiaries does not make the policy or its proceeds a part of the estate. It is settled law that the reservation of a power to revoke an entire trust does not invalidate the agreement presently creating it or render it testamentary. The reservation of a right to name a new beneficiary in a policy of life insurance which is the subject matter of a trust has precisely the same effect as the revocation of the trust with respect to such policies.*

See Gurnett v. Mutual Life Ins. Co., 356 Ill. 612, 191 N.E. 250 (1934).

NOTE—It is possible to view the interests of a beneficiary in a life insurance policy in two ways which may affect the ability to find that the policy constitutes the necessary res for a present trust. One is the view which gives a vested interest to a beneficiary subject to divestment in accordance with the provisions of the policy. Under this view there is no problem concerning the testamentary aspect of the transaction for the beneficiary's vested right is a proper subject for a trust. The other view is that the beneficiary has no more than an expectancy. If considered to be an expectancy, it is more difficult to find the necessary res for the transaction may be construed to be a contract to create a trust at the insured's death. The courts generally, however, have not drawn this conclusion and have generally upheld the usual form of unfunded insurance trust even where the court finds that the beneficiary has no more than a mere expectancy. See Gordon v. Portland Trust Bank, 201 Or. 648, 271 P.2d 653 (1954).

Case 60 *Surviving spouse may not claim statutory dower in proceeds of life insurance policy held in trust*

Prior to his death, D transferred certain policies of insurance on his life to a trustee under a trust agreement providing that the trustee to whom the policies were made payable would hold the policies and on D's death collect the proceeds and hold them in trust for D's wife and children. By the trust agreement, D retained the power to revoke or amend the trust agreement, D retained the power to revoke or amend the trust and retained all privileges under the policies including the right to dividends and to borrow on the policies. The trust agreement provided that the trustee's sole duty during the life of D was to hold the policies in safekeeping. D paid all the premium payments on the policies. After D's death his widow W claims a right to statutory dower in the proceeds of the policies on the ground that the purported trust is illusory and testamentary. Is W entitled to claim dower in the proceeds of the policies?

***Answer.** No. The trust was not illusory. D's intention to create a trust was clearly expressed and he delivered the policies, the trust res, to the trustee who accepted delivery and the duty of safekeeping and collection, and undertook to hold himself in readiness to perform more active duties with respect to the trust on the death of the settlor. Nor was the trust testamentary merely because of the nature of life insurance contracts. The fact that the major benefits to be derived therefrom do not accrue until the death of the insured does not make the interest which passed to the trustee at the time of creation of the trust insubstantial. The trust had a substantial existence during the life of the settlor D and as such defected W's dower claim.*

See In re Estate of Herron, 237 So.2d 563 (Fla.App.1970). See also Ritchie, pp. 720–721.

1. Any person who has the capacity to take, hold and administer property for his own use may take, hold and administer property in trust.

2. Infants and insane persons can take and hold property in trust, but since their contracts are voidable they cannot properly administer a trust and will usually be removed as trustee.

3. Non-residents of the state in which the trust is to be administered may be trustees. In some states, however, by statute courts have discretion to refuse to confirm the appointment of a non-resident as testamentary trustee. See e.g., Ohio Revised Code § 2109.21.

4. Where a non-resident is named as trustee, the court may require the appointment of a resident agent for service of process.

5. At common law the extent to which an alien could take and hold real property was severely restricted and today whether or not aliens may act as trustees is regulated by statute in many states.

6. The extent to which a corporation may act as trustee will depend upon the statutes of the jurisdiction of its incorporation and the purposes for which it is incorporated.

THE TRUSTEE— CAPACITY AND SUCCESSION

7. The United States or a state may take and hold property as trustee but because of the Doctrine of Sovereign Immunity whereby a government cannot be sued without its consent the trust is unenforceable against it in the absence of a statute or special act of the legislature.

8. A partnership may serve as a trustee to the extent it is recognized as an entity by the applicable law of the jurisdiction.   See UPA § 8(3).

9. A trust will not be permitted to fail for want of a trustee.

   e.g.   M by will leaves Blackacre in trust for C.   No trustee is named.   The equity court will approve a trustee to administer the trust and will order the person having the legal title to the property to convey it to the appointed trustee.   In this case, before the court's order, the title would be either in M's heir or residuary devisee.

   See Kale v. Forest, 9 N.C.App. 82, 175 S.E.2d 752 (1970).

10. If a sole trustee dies intestate the title to the trust real property descends to his heir and the title to the trust personal property passes to his personal representative, but such heir or personal representative will not be permitted to administer the trust.   The court will appoint a successor trustee.

    e.g.   T holds Blackacre and bonds in trust for C.   T dies intestate leaving H his sole heir and A is appointed his administrator. The title to Blackacre passes to H and the title to the bonds passes to A.   The equity court will appoint a new trustee and order H and A to transfer Blackacre and the bonds respectively to such newly appointed trustee.   This same principle holds true if T dies testate and devises Blackacre to H and bonds pass to T's executor, A.

11. Two or more trustees always hold the title to the trust property in joint tenancy with the doctrine of survivorship obtaining even in a jurisdiction where tenancy in common is by statute preferred over joint tenancy.

    e.g.   A, B and C hold Blackacre and a herd of sheep in trust for X.   A dies testate or intestate.   B and C by survivorship hold title to Blackacre and the sheep.   B then dies.   C by the doctrine of survivorship holds the title to Blackacre and the sheep.

12. A trustee cannot resign without permission of the equity court unless the trust instrument so provides or all of the beneficiaries being sui juris consent to the resignation.   The court will usually permit the trustee to resign if continuing to serve will be unreasonably burdensome to him and will not cause great detriment to the trust.

13. Whether or not to remove a trustee is within the sound judicial discretion of the equity court. A trustee may be removed for habitual drunkenness, or for dishonesty, or incompetency in handling of trust property, or for dissipation of the trust estate. Mere friction or incompatibility between the trustee and beneficiary is not enough to justify removal unless it endangers the trust property or makes impossible the accomplishment of the purpose of the trust.

14. If the settlor conditions the creation of a trust on the acceptance of a particular person as trustee, upon the failure or refusal of the designated person to act, the trust fails.

See generally Bogert, pp. 101, 103–114; Clark, pp. 710–712; Palmer, p. 368; Rest. §§ 89–111; Ritchie, pp. 424–430; Scoles, pp. 503–506; and Scott, §§ 89–98.

Trust will not fail where trustee is incompetent to take property   Case 61

S executed a deed transferring certain property to St. Clair's Roman Catholic Church, an unincorporated religious society. The deed sought to convey to the church S's farm and lots and contained a provision that the church "shall pay to C the sum of $50 per month beginning one month after my death for and during his life and shall pay the doctors' and hospital's bill if any, and upon his death provide him with a Christian burial . . ." Under state law the deed to the church is void because an unincorporated religious society is incapable of taking by deed. After S's death her heirs seek a declaration that no trust has been created. Are they entitled to such a declaration?

Answer. *No. Even though the deed to the religious society was void for want of a lawful grantee, it can have the effect of impressing a trust upon the property in favor of C. There is no question that had the church been competent to take the property the words used were adequate to establish a trust for C. The incapacity of the church to take the property does not destroy its rights. No particular form of words is necessary to create a trust and any expression which shows unequivocally the intention to create a trust will have that effect. The inability of the trustee to take the property will not invalidate a deed where the settlor and the beneficiary are both competent and the property is of such a nature that it can be legally placed in trust. Although the void deed did not transfer title to the property from S, from the date of its execution a trust was impressed upon the property in S's hands and at her death in the hands of her heirs. Equity will not allow a trust to fail for want of a trustee even though the grantor fails in one purpose, that of devoting the property to religious uses in this instance. In this case the purpose of the* *grantor was clearly manifested and the trust in favor of C clearly created. The trust was declared in the instrument creating it. No further act was necessary to give it effect. Although the deed did not in fact transfer title from the grantor, it was sufficient to impress the trust upon the property.*

See Wittmeier v. Heiligenstein, 308 Ill. 434, 139 N.E. 871 (1923).

BENEFICIARIES AND SETTLORS AS TRUSTEES

1. The extent to which a beneficiary of a trust may also be a trustee of the trust is governed by the following rules:

   (a) The sole beneficiary cannot be the sole trustee. This would vest the same person with identical legal and equitable interests and a merger would take place giving the trustee-beneficiary an absolute interest.

   (b) One of several beneficiaries may be one of several trustees.

   (c) One of two or more beneficiaries can be the sole trustee. The trustee's interest as trustee is different from his intent as beneficiary. No merger results because the same person is not vested with the absolute legal and equitable interests.

   (d) The sole beneficiary can be one of two or more trustees. Absolute title does not vest in the beneficiary upon the death of the other trustees and a new trustee will be appointed based on the implied intent of the settlor.

   (e) If there is more than one beneficiary all the beneficiaries may be all the trustees.

   e.g. A conveyance to B and C in trust for B and C creates a valid trust. As trustees B and C hold as tenants in common so their interests do not merge.

2. The settlor of the trust may be the trustee. This is always the case in a declaration of trust.

   See generally Bogert, p. 95–98; Palmer, pp. 368–371; Rest. §§ 99, 100; Ritchie, pp. 427–428; Scott, §§ 99–100.

Case 62   *A court will appoint a successor co-trustee to prevent merger when a co-trustee dies leaving the sole beneficiary as the sole remaining trustee*

D by will left certain property to B and C in trust to hold for the benefit of C for life and upon her death to W and F for the life of W and upon W's death, C having predeceased, to convey to F in fee simple. B dies and C becomes the sole trustee, W having predeceased D. One of the terms of the trust provided, "the trustees or their successor or successors may sell, mortgage or lease the real property in any manner as he, she or they in their discretion might consider best for the estate." F petitions to have a successor trustee to B appointed. C maintains that on the death of B her legal and equitable life estates merged and there is no trust remaining as to which a successor trustee could be appointed. Should the court appoint a successor trustee?

Answer. Yes. A trust contemplates the holding of property by one person for the benefit of another and the same person may not at the same time be both the sole trustee and the sole beneficiary of the same interest. This does not mean that a merger necessarily occurs if one of two trustees dies leaving the sole beneficiary as the sole trustee. If it is established that the settlor intended the trust to continue for protection of the remaindermen or of the life beneficiary the courts will act to prevent the termination of the trust and appoint a successor co-trustee. In the present case the decedent by the language in his will indicated that he believed a successor would be appointed at any time one of the original trustees died, and the court will appoint such a successor.

See In re Phipps Will, 2 N.Y.2d 105, 157 N.Y.S.2d 14, 138 N.E.2d 341 (1956); In re Hasken's Trust, 59 Misc.2d 797, 300 N.Y.S.2d 711 (Sup.Ct.N.Y.1969).

1. In every private trust there must be

   (a) a specifically named beneficiary, or

   (b) a beneficiary so described that his identity can be ascertained when the trust is created or within the period of the Rule Against Perpetuities.

2. A natural person who has capacity to take and hold legal title to property has capacity to be the beneficiary of a trust. See Scott § 116.

3. Corporations may be beneficiaries of a trust to the extent they are empowered to take and hold legal title to property. A corporation not yet organized may be the beneficiary of a trust to the extent it could be if in existence and if it is certain to come into existence within the period of the Rule Against Perpetuities. See Scott §§ 112.2, 117.1

4. Aliens may be beneficiaries of a trust unless restricted by special rules of the jurisdiction.

   e.g. In some states it is held that although an alien may take title to land the state may bring a proceeding to forfeit the land to the state. In such states the equitable interest of an alien trust ben-

THE BENEFICIARY— CAPACITY

eficiary could also be forfeited.   See Rest. § 117, Comment (n). The question of the constitutionality of state statutes restricting the rights of aliens to inherit has been frequently raised in other contexts.   See Cases 13 and 14, above.

5. The beneficiary may also be a trustee of a trust except that the sole beneficiary may not be the sole trustee.   See *Beneficiaries and Settlors as Trustees*, above.

   See generally Bogert, pp. 120–123; Rest. §§ 116–117; Ritchie, pp. 433–434; Scoles, pp. 238–239; Scott, §§ 112–119.

CLASSES AS BENEFICIARIES

1. The beneficiary may be a class of persons as long as the class is definite or definitely ascertainable.

   (a) If A leaves property in trust for, "my children", the class is definite and the trust would be valid.

   (b) If a trust is designated "for my family" the validity of the trust will depend upon whether the court construes the term to mean immediate family in which case the class is sufficiently definite or all relations in which case the trust would fail since the class is indefinite.

   (c) If a trust is designated "for my relatives" and this is interpreted to mean "next-of-kin", the class is sufficiently definite, and the trust is valid.

2. If the beneficiary is an ascertainable class the fact that the trustee is given power to select from the class does not affect the validity of the trust.

3. If the settlor designates that the trustee may select the members of an indefinite class and the class is such that it is possible to ascertain who falls within it, the trustee may be allowed to carry out the trust.

4. A trust created for the benefit of any person or persons whom the trustee may select is not a trust.   Unless an intent is expressed to the contrary, in such instances the trustee is considered to have an unrestricted power of disposition and takes an absolute gift free of trust.

   CAVEAT—This situation is to be distinguished from that where the settlor manifests an intention that the transferee shall not dispose of property for his own benefit, but fails to name a beneficiary in which case the trust fails and the trustee rather than holding for his own benefit holds on a resulting trust in favor of the settlor's heirs.   See CASE 87, below.   See also Chapter X.   Resulting Trusts.

5. If property is transferred to a person for the benefit of himself and his family, it is a question of interpretation whether the transferor:

(a) intended to create a trust, or

(b) intended to make a beneficial gift to the person named with an expression of the motive for making the gift. See Rest. § 25, comment d.

6. If the settlor's designation of an individual beneficiary or of a class of beneficiaries is so vague or indefinite that the beneficiary or the class of beneficiaries cannot be determined with reasonable certainty, the trust must fail.

7. Even though at common law a partnership as such or an unincorporated association as such cannot hold legal title to real property or be a trustee, either may be a beneficiary of a trust and hold the equitable title to the trust property.

(a) The individual members of any such association at a given instant and who are therefore determinable may be beneficiaries.

(b) The individual members of such an association with indefinite succession may be beneficiaries provided either the trustee or such members or a committee thereof has power to terminate the trust.

e.g. S leaves securities to T in trust "for the members of the Sioux County Bar Association who pay their annual dues but at any time T may, in his discretion terminate the trust and distribute the corpus of the trust property to the members". In this case the trust would be invalid under the Rule Against Perpetuities if T did not have power to terminate it because many members might in the indefinite future pay their annual dues and the equitable title to the trust res would vest in them long after the time allowed by the Rule. The fact that T may at any instant terminate the trust prevents a violation of the policy of the Rule because there is always someone who has power to dispose of the property both legally and equitably.

8. The beneficiaries of a trust hold their equitable interest as tenants in common unless the trust instrument provides that they shall hold as joint tenants.

e.g. S transfers property to T in trust for A, B, and C. These beneficiaries each own an undivided one third of the equitable title in the trust property.

See generally Bogert, pp. 120–123; Palmer, pp. 395–396; Rest. §§ 120–122; Ritchie, pp. 433–436; Scoles, pp. 246–247; and Scott, §§ 119–122.

Case 63   *No trust comes into existence if sole beneficiary is also sole trustee*

On January 1 T, a bachelor, executed a written agreement entitled *"Trust Agreement"*.   By the provisions of the agreement, T declared himself trustee of certain listed securities to accumulate the income thereon for a period of 5 years and add to the principal.   Thereafter the income was to be paid to T during his life and on his death to be distributed among his descendants, if any, and if none to his widow and if none to his heirs at law.   Has a trust been created?

Answer.   No.   A trust may exist where the owner of property declares that he holds it as trustee for designated persons even though he does not part with possession of the property.   In the present case, however, the only beneficiary of the trust who can be ascertained is the trustee himself.   It is the general rule that a trust cannot exist where the same person possesses both the legal and equitable titles to the trust fund at the same time.   Since at the time of the declaration of the trust no person exists who can be identified as a beneficiary in that there are no issue born, no widow that can be ascertained and heirs can only be ascertained on the death of the Settlor, there is no severance of title and the trust does not exist.   To hold that a present trust arises where the owner of property declares that he holds it in trust for himself and other persons who are yet nonexistent or not ascertainable is illogical and incapable of practical application since there is no one other than the trustor to enforce the trust.

See *Morsman v. Commissioner of Internal Revenue, 302 U.S. 701, 58 S.Ct. 20, 82 L.Ed. 542 (1937).*

NOTE—There is a good deal of criticism as to the outcome of the above case on the grounds that it is unnecessary that the beneficiary be known at the time of the creation of the trust as long as such beneficiary is capable of ascertainment from facts which must necessarly be in existence within the period of the Rule against Perpetuities.   The language of the Restatement supports the contrary view. See Restatement § 112.

Case 64   *A bequest to a trustee upon trust not defined in a will but communicated orally to the trustee is invalid.*

D, by a validly executed will, left the residue of her estate to T, "to distribute the same in such manner as in his discretion shall appear best to carry out the wishes which I have expressed to him or may express to him."   D's heirs bring an action asking to have the property held by T in resulting trust for them.   All parties stipulated that D had before and after executing her will expressed her intention and directed that T dispose of the residue for charitable purposes according to his discretion.   Are the heirs entitled to the property?

Answer. *Yes. The residuary bequest to T gave him no beneficial interest. It expressly required him to distribute all of the property bequeathed to him, giving him no discretion upon the question of whether he shall or shall not distribute it, or shall or shall not carry out the intentions of D; but allowing him a discretionary authority as to the manner in which the property is to be distributed. The will declares a trust that is too indefinite to be carried out. Where a trust is shown on the face of the will and it is clear that the devisee takes no beneficial interest, the trust fails if it is not sufficiently defined by the will to take effect. The equitable interest then goes by way of resulting trust to the heirs of D as property of D not disposed of by her will. A trust not sufficiently declared on the face of a will cannot be established by extrinsic evidence. It must be established by those forms of proof which are required as essential to every testamentary disposition.*

See *Olliffe v. Wells,* 130 Mass. 221 (1881).

1. Trusts for unborn children are valid if there is another beneficiary in existence at the time of creating the trust who can enforce the trust from its inception.

TRUSTS FOR UNBORN BENEFICIARIES

e.g. A transfers property to T in trust for A's children then living or born thereafter. A trust is created. The living children can enforce the trust from its inception.

2. If there is no beneficiary in existence at the time of the creation of the trust but a beneficiary may be born thereafter it is important to determine whether or not the trust is created by a transfer in trust or a declaration of trust.

(a) In the case of a *transfer* in trust, the trust is valid. The trustee is considered a resulting trustee for the benefit of the settlor who may enforce the trust until a child is born.

e.g. A transfers property to T in trust for A's children. A has no children at the time of transfer; however, a trust is created.

(b) In the case of a *declaration of trust,* as for example, when A declares himself trustee for his childen, but no children are in existence at the time, there is disagreement as to whether or not a trust is created.

   (i) One view is that since there is no beneficiary in existence who can enforce the trust against A, no trust is created. See Morsman v. Commissioner of Internal Revenue, 90 F.2d 18 (8th Cir. 1937); CASE 63, above.

   (ii) Another view is that as long as the interest must vest in the child within the period of the Rule Against Perpetuities, a valid trust is created.

3. The person who creates an inter vivos trust may be a beneficiary or the sole beneficiary of the trust. The settlor has been held to be the sole beneficiary in the following instances:

   (a) Settlor creates an inter vivos trust to pay income to herself for a period of years and then reconvey the property to her.

   (b) Settlor creates an inter vivos trust to pay income to herself for life and on her death to convey the property to her personal representative or to whomever she shall appoint by deed or will.

   (c) Settlor creates an inter vivos trust to pay the income to herself for life and on her death to pay the principal to her next of kin or heirs.

4. There is a split of authority as to the result where settlor transfers property in trust to hold for the benefit of settlor and "settlor's heirs":

   (a) Some jurisdictions hold that under *the doctrine of worthier title* the disposition in favor of the settlor's heirs creates a reversion in her and no interest in her heirs.

   (b) Other jurisdictions hold that the doctrine of worthier title is not an absolute rule of law and the rule is only a matter of construction. The question here is whether the settlor in the particular case *intended* to create an interest in the heirs.

   (c) Still other jurisdictions hold that the heirs have a remainder. See Smith's Review Real and Personal Property, Chapter XVII. Doctrine of Worthier Title.

5. A third person is the sole beneficiary of a trust in situations where a disposition is made to such third person for life and then to his heirs in the following instances:

   (a) in jurisdictions where the rule in Shelley's case is in force and the trust is realty, and

   (b) where it is found that the settlor intended the entire equitable interest to go to the designated third person.

   See Smith's Review Real and Personal Property, 3d Chapter XVII. Rule in Shelley's case.

   See generally Bogert, pp. 123–125; Rest. § 112; Ritchie, pp. 449–450; Scoles, pp. 238–239; and Scott §§ 112–112.1, 114, 127.

Case 65 *Effect of testamentary trust for unborn children*

S died testate with no residuary clause in his will, devising Blackacre to "T" in trust for the children of my son, X, during the life of X and at his death then the property to be distributed to X's children share and share alike". At the time of S's death his son X was still a bachelor. X is S's sole heir. Does this will, when X has no child or children, create a present existing express private trust?

Answer. Yes. An express private trust can exist without an ascertained beneficiary at the time of the creation of the trust provided such beneficiary must be in being and definitely ascertained, if at all, within the Rule against Perpetuities. With such premise it is clear that X's children can and will qualify as beneficiaries. If X has no child at the time of his death, the trust will fail entirely. But any child which X will have must be born not later than the period of X's life and a period of gestation. Hence, no part of the 21 years allowed by the Rule against Perpetuities is used. The result of such holding in this case is this: The express private trust is valid and existing from the time S's will takes effect at S's death. T is the trustee and Blackacre is the res. T will manage the land and accumulate the net profits therefrom and hold them for the child or children of X if and when they appear. The trust is considered as presently existing even without a living beneficiary. If children are subsequently born to X, they will become beneficiaries as they are born. If no children have been born (or are in gestation) at X's death, the trustee will hold the property as a resulting trustee for S's heirs.

See Folk v. Hughes, 100 S.C. 220, 84 S.E. 713 (1915). See also Ritchie, pp. 411–412; Rest. § 112, Comment (d).

Bequest to trustees for the benefit of "Friends" is too indefinite to sustain a trust **Case 66**

D died leaving a will which provided in part, "I give and bequeath to my trustees all items of personal property such as books, photographic albums, pictures, statuary, bronzes, bric-a-brac, hunting and fishing equipment, antiques, rugs, scrapbooks, canes and Masonic jewels, to distribute such property by way of a memento of myself to such as my friends as my trustee shall select." Is a valid trust established?

Answer. No. In order to constitute a valid trust there must be a beneficiary or a class of beneficiaries indicated in the will capable of coming into court and claiming the bequest. In this case the bequest cannot be sustained as a private trust. Although the beneficiaries under a trust may be designated by class, the class must be capable of delimitation, e.g. "brothers and sisters," "children," "issue," "nephews and nieces." In the present case, however, the beneficiaries are designated as the friends of the testator. The word "friends," unlike "children" has no accepted statutory or other controlling limitation and no precise sense at all. "Friends" is a word *of broad and varied application. The assertion of testator's confidence in the competency of his trustees to wisely distribute the enumerated articles does not furnish a sufficient criterion to constitute a line of demarcation in which to define an ascertainable group. Therefore, the gift fails and the trustees will hold the property in a resulting trust for the next taker under the will.*

See Clark v. Campbell, 82 N.H. 281, 133 A. 166 (1926).

Case 67   *Charitable trustee's discretion to ascertain beneficiaries within a class*

D bequeathed her residuary estate to T, a charitable corporation in trust to, "first use the income for the alleviation of suffering or for the comfortable maintenance and support of any persons who may be living at the time of my decease and who may be connected by blood (but not beyond the tenth degree) with my husband or me." The distribution of the income was to be in the sound discretion of T, both as to the expenditure of the income and in the choice of beneficiary. T was to use the remainder of the income for the charitable purposes of T. D's next of kin claim that the trust is invalid on the ground that the beneficiaries are so numerous that they cannot be ascertained. Are they correct in their contention?

Answer. *No. It is the general rule that, in order to create a valid trust, there must be a designation of beneficiaries or a class of beneficiaries which must be an ascertainable class and the designation must be made with reasonable certainty so as to be capable of identification. Although the class of beneficiaries in this case may be so numerous that it is not an ascertainable group, it is possible to ascertain if a given person is a member of the class. Where the trustee is authorized to select among the class as to who shall take and in what proportions he may select any member of the class in accordance with the terms of the trust, and the trust does not fail for indefiniteness.*

See Ministers and Mission Ben.Bd. of American Baptist Convention v. McKay, 64 Misc.2d 231, 315 N.Y.S.2d 549 (1970). See also Rest. § 121.

THE HONORARY TRUST   **1.** A trust for specific *non-charitable* purposes where there is no definite ascertainable beneficiary is not an enforceable trust. Such distributions are known as honorary trusts. Common examples of such dispositions are trusts for the erection of monuments, the care of graves, the saying of masses, and the care of specific animals.

e.g.   I give $1,000 to T in trust to be used by T during his life for the care of my cat, Fang.

NOTE—In many jurisdictions special legislation exists validating special provisions for the upkeep of graves and monuments.   In many jurisdictions, trusts for saying masses are upheld as charitable trusts.

2. The general rule is that the purported trustee may carry out the intent of the settlor if he chooses to do so.   Since there is no beneficiary who could enforce the trust the carrying out of the trust purposes relies on the *honor* of the trustee.

3. If the trustee does not carry out the trust duties he will be holding the property for the settlor or settlor's heirs on the theory of a resulting trust.

4. Jurisdictions vary as to the extent to which honorary trusts will be recognized, if at all.

5. Honorary trusts are limited by considerations of public policy in that:

   (a) They may not exist beyond the period of the Rule Against Perpetuities.

   (b) The amount must not be unreasonably large for the purposes to be accomplished.

   (c) The purposes must be those of a reasonably normal testator, and purposes may not be capricious.

   e.g.   "I leave $1,000,000 to T in trust to burn $1,000 on each anniversary of my death."   This would be a capricious purpose and the trustee could not be allowed to carry out the trust purposes.

   CAVEAT—Honorary trusts for the benefit of specific animals which are sustained in some jurisdictions are to be distinguished from charitable trusts having as their trust purposes the benefit of animals in general, which are sustained everywhere.   See *Charitable Trusts Distinguished from Honorary Trusts*, Chapter VIII, below.

   See generally Bogert, pp. 125–127; Clark, pp. 648–650; Palmer pp. 404–405; Rest. § 124; Ritchie, pp. 450–452; Scoles; pp. 407–409; and Scott §§ 124–124.7.

Honorary trust for reasonable sum and purpose sustained; for capricious purpose fails   Case 68

S bequeaths to T $1000 with which to care for S's horse, Dobbin, and his dog, Rover, and $1000 for the purpose of maintaining S's dwelling *house in the same condition as of the instant of S's death for 20 years thereafter with all windows and doors blocked shut. L is S's residuary legatee and claims both these sums of money on the ground that S has attempted to create a private trust which is invalid in that there is no beneficiary to enforce it. Does L have the right to either sum?*

Answer. *(a) L has no right to the $1000 left for Dobbin and Rover unless T refuses to carry out the obligations of caring for the dog and horse. (b) L has the right to the other $1000. Neither of these provisions of S's will can be sustained as creating a private trust. The beneficiary of a private trust should be competent to come into court either in person or by guardian and enforce the trust duties against the trustee. Neither the horse, nor the dog can appear in court and neither is a human being. Some cases, however, permit, provision for specific dogs and horses for a reasonable sum to be valid as an honorary trust on the theory that the purpose not being contrary to public policy may be carried out on the honor of the trustee. If the trustee fails to do as the trust provides, then he must hold the property in resulting trust for the heirs or next of kin of the decedent. In this case the sum is reasonable and there is nothing contrary to public policy in permitting T to care for Dobbin and Rover. If he does so and spends the $1000 for such purpose he is not liable, but if he fails he must turn it over to L as the beneficiary of a resulting trust. On the other hand if the purpose of an intended honorary trust is capricious it will fail. In this case there is no legitimate end to be served by keeping S's dwelling house closed up for 20 years. The purpose is capricious and the trust fails. Hence, T holds the $1000 in resulting trust for L and should deliver it to L.*

See *Willett v. Willett*, 197 Ky. 663, 247 S.W. 739 (1923); In re Searight's Estate, 87 Ohio App. 417, 95 N.E.2d 779 (1950).

PROTECTING THE BENEFICIARY'S INTEREST FROM CLAIMS OF CREDITORS AND OTHERS

1. A beneficiary's interest in a trust is freely transferable to the same extent that the same legal interest is transferable unless there are express or implied restraints on transfer. The interest can be reached by creditors of the beneficiary in the absence of such restraint.

2. Neither consideration nor notice to and consent of the trustee is necessary for the transfer of the beneficiary's interest.

3. Various devices have been developed to protect the beneficiary's interest from alienation. The most common are:

    (a) the spendthrift trust,

    (b) a forfeiture provision,

    (c) discretionary trusts, and

    (d) support trusts.

4. Such devices are directed to protecting the trust interest while it is still in the hands of the trustee. Once funds have been paid over to the beneficiary any attempt at imposing a restraint on alienation is invalid.

See generally Bogert, pp. 140–142; Rest. §§ 132–137; Ritchie, pp. 455–457; and Scott, §§ 132–137.

1. A spendthrift clause in a trust is an express provision against alienation, voluntary, involuntary or both, of the beneficiary's right to receive principal, income or both.

> e.g. A typical spendthrift clause would read: Each beneficiary hereunder is hereby restrained from alienating, anticipating, encumbering or in any manner assigning his interest hereunder nor shall such interest be subject to his liabilities or obligations nor to judgment or other legal process, bankruptcy proceedings or claims of creditors or others.

2. In a majority of jurisdictions spendthrift provisions are held valid on the theory that the settlor who had the entire interest in property can give away a qualified interest if he chooses.

3. Some jurisdictions hold spendthrift provisions invalid on the theory that a person should not be able to live according to the standards to which he claims to be accustomed and at the same time repudiate any obligation to pay for anything that he purchases on credit. See Utley v. Grey, 258 F.Supp. 959 (D.D.C.1966).

4. Any form of words which shows the settlor's intention to impose a direct restraint on alienation of the beneficiary's interest may be used to create a spendthrift trust.

5. Courts often will hold that the settlor intended to restrain both involuntary and voluntary alienation although settlor expresses only one or the other. It is thought contrary to public policy to permit a settlor to restrain involuntary alienation without restraining voluntary alienation.

6. A settlor may not create a spendthrift trust for himself. See Ware v. Gulda, 331 Mass. 68, 117 N.E.2d 137 (1954).

7. In jurisdictions where spendthrift trusts are valid exceptions are often made to the rule that creditors and other claimants may not reach the income of the trust.

   (a) Some jurisdictions hold that only restraints on income are valid and invalidate restraints on the corpus.

   (b) Some jurisdictions hold restraints valid only to the amount of income necessary for the support of the beneficiary and hold additional income subject to creditors.

SPENDTHRIFT TRUSTS

8. In a number of states spendthrift provisions are governed by specific statutes. See e.g., Ala.Code Title 58 § 1; 12 Del.C. § 3536; and N.Y. EPTL 7–1.5.

9. The modern trend is to allow certain special classes of claimants to reach the beneficiary's interest in a spendthrift trust on the ground of public policy. These include:

(a) persons the beneficiary is bound to support,

  e.g. Claims for alimony and child support.

(b) persons who render necessary personal services to the beneficiary,

(c) persons whose services preserve the beneficiary's interest in the trust,

  e.g. S leaves property to T to hold the income for C, but C to have no power to assign such income and it not being subject to the claims of C's creditors. C's wife and minor children who are entitled to support from C may reach the income because they are not ordinary creditors but those which C is bound by law to support. C's physician who nurses him back to health and his lawyer who saves the trust income for C in court also may reach the trust income. Permitting these types of creditors to reach the trust income is considered as carrying out the intent of the settlor in establishing the spendthrift trust, and thus all may do so despite the spendthrift provisions.

(d) tort claims, and

(e) claims by the United States or a State.

See generally Bogert, pp. 147–158; Clark, pp. 512–521; Rest. §§ 152–153; 521; Palmer, pp. 414–419, 425–426; Ritchie, pp. 462–464; Scoles, pp. 451–460; and Scott, §§ 151–153.

Case 69 *Public policy does not invalidate spendthrift trust*

D died leaving a will which provided: "I give the sum of $75,000 to T in trust to pay the net income thereof semi-annually to my brother B during his natural life, such payments to be free from the interference or control of B's creditors, my intention being that the use of said income shall not be anticipated by assignment." C, a creditor of B has brought a bill in equity to reach and apply the income from the trust fund to the debts due C from B. Is C entitled to reach the trust fund?

  Answer. No. *At common law it was not possible to attach to a grant or transfer of property a condition that it should not be alien-*

ated. It remained the English rule that when the income of a trust is given to any person for life the equitable estate for life is alienable by and liable in equity to the debts of the beneficiary. The English rule has been adopted in a minority of American jurisdictions. The majority of American jurisdictions on the other hand have held that the grantor of a trust may secure the benefit of it to the object of his bounty by providing that the income shall not be alienable by anticipation nor subject to be taken for his debts. The general view is that it does not violate any principle of sound public policy to permit a testator to give property so as to provide against the improvidence or misfortune of the beneficiary. It is said that such a grant should be against public policy in that it defrauds the creditors of the beneficiaries. The answer is, however, that creditors have no right to rely upon property thus held and to give credit upon the basis of an estate which by the instrument creating it is declared to be inalienable and not liable for debt. In this case, therefore, under the provisions of the will the income of the trust fund created for the benefit of B cannot be reached by B's creditors either at law or in equity before it is paid to him.

See Broadway Bank v. Adams, 133 Mass. 170, 43 Am.Rep. 504 (1882). Contra, Utley v. Graves, 258 F.Supp. 959 (D.C.1966). See also Spendthrift Trusts, above.

CAVEAT—The Case above cites the rule in a majority of jurisdictions. In some jurisdictions spendthrift provisions are held to be against public policy and void. See Sherrow v. Brookover, 174 Ohio St. 310, 189 N.E.2d 90 (1963).

Spouse suing to enforce order for support may reach spendthrift trust   Case 70

D is the beneficiary of a testamentary trust from which he receives annual payments. The terms of the trust contain a spendthrift provision as follows: "The interest of a beneficiary in the trust property or in the income therefrom shall not be subject to the rights of creditors of such beneficiary and shall be exempt from execution, attachment, distress for rent and all other legal or equitable process instituted by or on behalf of such creditors and the interest of such beneficiary in the trust property or in the income therefrom shall be unassignable." P is D's former wife. As a result of a court action between P and D for divorce, a court entered an order requiring D to pay P $400 a month for support and P alleges that D has refused to make such payments. P brings an action to reach the income from the trust. She alleges that she is a dependent of D and seeks a judgment against him and an order to the trustee to pay into the court the amount of the judgment to the extent of payments due her for support. Is P entitled to reach the trust?

Answer. Yes. The state law applicable to the provision of D's trust provides: "The creditors of a beneficiary of a trust shall have only such rights against such beneficiary's interests in the trust property or the income therefrom as shall not be denied to them by the terms of the instrument creating or defining the trust or by the laws of this state. Every interest in trust property or the income therefrom which shall not be subject to the rights of the creditors of the beneficial, as aforesaid, shall be exempt from execution, attachment, distress for rent and all other legal or equitable process instituted by or on behalf of such creditors." A wife, however, suing for support or on a court order directing that her husband pay support to her is not a creditor as that term is commonly defined. She sues rather to compel performance of a duty which the law imposes upon a husband. It is arguable that since the will only insulates the trust property from claims by creditors, claims by dependents for support are not included. Even if the language of the will were considered to bar a claim by the wife, it is against public policy to give full effect to the provision in most American jurisdictions. This policy is based on the theory that a beneficiary should not be permitted to have the enjoyment of his interest under a trust while neglecting to support his dependents. Thus, in this case, P may reach the assets of the trust to the extent necessary for support on grounds both of trust interpretation and public policy.

See *Wife, J.B.G. v. Husband,* 286 A.2d 256 (Del.Ch. 1971). Contra, *Erickson v. Erickson,* 197 Minn. 71, 266 N.W. 161 (1936). See also Rest. § 157.

SUPPORT AND DISCRETIONARY TRUSTS

1. A trust containing a direction that the trustee shall pay or apply only so much of the income and principal as is necessary for the education and support of the beneficiary is a *support trust*. The interest of the beneficiary cannot be transferred because of the nature of the beneficiary's interest.

   e.g. A typical support trust clause would read: I hereby transfer $100,000 to T in trust to pay or apply so much of the income as is necessary for the education and reasonable support of C during C's life.

2. In a trust for support restrictions on alienation are implied only to the extent actually necessary to effect the settlor's purpose of providing support for the beneficiary. If the beneficiary has a right to any additional amount from the trust such additional interest is freely alienable.

3. A support trust must be distinguished from a trust wherein the settlor has expressed support and education as the motive for the trust but which does not limit the beneficiary's interest to an

amount necessary to his support. In such cases the interest of the beneficiary can be transferred and is subject to his creditors.

e.g. A transfers property to T to pay the annual income to B during his life for his comfort and support. B is entitled to the entire income and can assign it and his creditors can reach it. See Rest. § 154.

4. Support trusts are subject to the same exceptions for alimony, child support and necessaries as are spendthrift trusts. See *Spendthrift Trusts*, number 7, above.

5. A trust which provides a direction that the trustee shall pay to or apply for a beneficiary only so much of the income or principal "as the trustee shall determine in her absolute discretion" is a *discretionary trust*.

6. In a discretionary trust the beneficiary has no vested interest in the trust which can be alienated or reached by creditors until the trustee has elected to make a payment to the beneficiary. An assignee of the beneficiary, however, may hold the trustee liable for any future payment to the beneficiary by giving the trustee notice of his assignment, such assignment being considered an assignment of a future payment.

e.g. S delivers $5,000 to T in trust for C, any and every payment or no payment at all to C from corpus or income to be in T's sole discretion. Before T has elected to make any payment to C as beneficiary, C assigns to X a right to $25 of payment T elects to make to C. X notifies T of such assignment and demands that if T elects to pay C any amount up to $25 that T make the payment thereof to X and not to C. T need make no election to pay C and if he does not do so, then X has no right to receive anything from the trust; however, if T thereafter elects to pay C $25, he is liable to X for such amount.

7. If a settlor creates a support or discretionary trust for his own benefit his creditors can reach the maximum amount which the trustee could apply for or pay to him under the trust terms.

8. A forfeiture provision in a trust may provide that the interest of the beneficiary immediately ceases, or that the trust automatically changes to a discretionary trust, if he attempts to assign or his creditors try to reach his interest. A gift to another is provided for in such case.

e.g. P transfers property to T in trust to pay the income to B during B's life and then to pay the principal to C. The trust instrument provides that if at any time B should attempt to assign his interest or be adjudicated a bankrupt or if a creditor should attempt to subject the interest to creditors claims then B's interest under the trust will cease and the property be paid to C. If a creditor brings an action to reach C's interest the interest automatically terminates and is vested in D and C has no further interest in the trust.   See Rest. § 150.

See generally Bogert, pp. 159–164; Clark, p. 544; Palmer, pp. 438–440; Rest. §§ 154–156; Ritchie, p. 478; and Scott, §§ 150, 154–156.3.

Case 71   *A trust interest assignable unless settlor manifests an intent to prohibit alienation by beneficiary*

S transferred property to T in trust to collect the proceeds therefrom and to apply the same in T's full and uncontrolled discretion for the use and benefit of M during her natural life.   The trust agreement further provided "T shall at all times pay over monthly, if convenient, if not all the net income, a sum sufficient for the needs, comfort and maintenance of the beneficiary in the style she has been accustomed, or according to the means at hand."   M subsequently assigned her interest in the income of the trust to W.   Thereafter, she filed an action to set aside the assignment alleging that, under the terms of the trust, she had no right to assign the income of the trust.   Is the assignment to W valid?

Answer.   Yes.   *The classification of a trust as a support or discretionary trust depends on the interest of the settlor determined from the language of the trust instrument.   Here the language used by the settlor does not limit B's interest in the income of the trust to her needs for support.   Where the whole of the income is to be paid to the beneficiary or applied to his use, his interest is alienable even though the settlor provides that the trust is created for the support of the beneficiary.   This is the rule unless the settlor manifests an intention that the interest of the beneficiary should not be alienable.   Here the settlor intended that the entire net income of the trust should be applied for the use or benefit of M during her life.   The trustee is not to apply just so much of the income as is necessary for the support of the beneficiary.   Language in the trust agreement allowing the trustee to provide for the proper maintenance of the property and the corpus of the trust and pay legal and administrative expenses and, if necessary, to set up a reserve fund for M's education and unusual needs that might arise are objectives for which the trustee may limit distributions to the beneficiary but for no other purposes. The provision that the trustee shall pay over such sums as are necessary for the needs, comfort and maintenance of the beneficiary shows an intent not to limit the interest of the beneficiary but to enlarge it by requiring the trustee to pay such amounts monthly if he does not distribute the entire net income.   A trust is not a support trust where the amount to be paid or applied by the trustee is a specified sum or is not limited to what is necessary for the education* and support of the beneficiary, although by the terms of the trust it appears that the settlor's motive in creating the trust is to provide for the education or support of the beneficiary. Nor is a trust a discretionary trust where the trustee has discretion merely as to time of payment and where the beneficiary is ultimately entitled to the whole or to a part of the trust property. The trust in this case is neither a spendthrift trust, a support trust, nor a discretionary trust. Therefore, the interest of the beneficiary is freely alienable.

See Philp v. Trainor, 100 So.2d 181 (Fla.Dist.Ct.App.1958). See also Rest. §§ 154, 155.

NOTE—The authors of one casebook have made the following observation as to discretionary and support trusts:
> "The Trusts Restatement does not adequately distinguish between discretionary and support trusts. Support trusts involve a restriction of the trustee's power, whereas discretionary trusts involve its expansion. Support trusts generally have all the characteristics of spendthrift trusts (but, unlike them, do not require the use of language prohibiting alienation or rendering creditor process ineffective), and are generally enforced as such even in states not otherwise recognizing the effectiveness of spendthrift restrictions." Clark, p. 544.

U.S. government may satisfy lien against beneficiary out of income from support trust Case 72

Testator left property to Trustees to pay or apply for the benefit of his son "so much of the net income as the trustees may from time to time deem necessary or advisable for his proper care, maintenance and support". The will further provided, "if from any cause whatsoever the net income, or any part thereof, shall or but for this proviso, would at any time become payable to or pass to or for the benefit of any person, firm, political subdivision, state or federal government, other than such beneficiary, the beneficiary's rights hereunder shall be forfeited. Notwithstanding any forfeiture by a beneficiary my trustees in their uncontrolled discretion but without any obligation to do so, may from time to time apply or direct the application of so much of the income as seems to them best to the use of the beneficiary." The U.S. Government has an unpaid judgment against the son and a lien upon all his "property and rights to property." Is the Government entitled to satisfaction of its lien out of the trust?

Answer. Yes. The son has a beneficial right to receive payments from income to the extent needed for his support, which the state courts will enforce. Such a property right differs from any other property right in that it has no permanently fixed dollar value. But such a value can be assigned a reasonably accurate dollar value by *assessing the taxpayer's current needs and living demands. It follows that Government liens have attached to and subsist against that right. Nor does the forfeiture clause defeat the tax lien in that the trustees still have discretion to pay income to the beneficiary. The public policy which recognizes a testator's right to dispose of his property as he sees fit does not extend to his giving property in trust for a beneficiary on the condition it not be used to pay the beneficiary's federal tax obligations.*

See *United States v. Taylor*, 254 F.Supp. 752 (N.D.Cal.1966).

Case 73 *Creditors cannot force surviving spouse to elect statutory share instead of spendthrift trust*

H is the beneficiary of a testamentary trust containing spendthrift provisions created under the will of his deceased wife. Spendthrift provisions are valid in the jurisdiction. Under applicable local law H, at the death of his wife, had an election to take either under a statute entitling a surviving spouse to a specified share of decedent's estate outright or under the will creating the trust. He elected to take under the will. C, H's creditor, claims the income of the trust is subject to his claim on the ground that the surviving spouse who surrenders his statutory share is in effect the creator of the trust. Is C's contention correct?

Answer. No. Although the rule is that one may not create a spendthrift trust for himself, and thus put it beyond his creditors, the mere fact that one surrenders a right to a distributive share does not make him the creator of the trust.

See *American Security and Trust Co. v. Utley*, 382 F.2d 451 (D.C.Cir., 1967). See also Rest. § 156, Comment g.

NOTE—There are some older cases which in the case of a surrender of curtesy or dower hold to the contrary. See Scott § 156.3.

VII CREATION, MODIFICATION AND TERMINATION OF TRUSTS

Summary Outline

METHODS OF CREATING A TRUST— INTRODUCTION

1. A trust may be created in any of the following ways:

   (a) declaration of trust,

   (b) transfer in trust, either

       (i) inter vivos, or

       (ii) by will,

   (c) exercise of a power of appointment,

   (d) contractual agreement, or

   (e) statute.

2. The method used for creating the trust will depend upon the relationship of the settlor to the property interest which is to constitute the trust res. The following explain the various relationships and the various ways in which trusts may be created.

   See generally, Bogert, pp. 21–22; Rest. § 17; Ritchie, p. 374; Scoles, p. 261; and Scott, § 17.

DECLARATION OF TRUST

1. A trust is created by a declaration of trust when the owner of property *declares* that he holds it as trustee for the benefit of another.

   e.g. S is the owner of 100 shares of stock. S declares himself trustee of the shares for the benefit of B. S is trustee for B.

   See *Intention to Create a Trust—How Manifested*, Chapter VI, above. See also Case 74, below.

2. In the case of a declaration of trust there is no need for a transfer of title since the trustee already has legal title and an oral declaration is usually sufficient to transfer equitable title. But an oral declaration may be ineffective as to land.

   See *The Requirement of a Writing—The Statute of Frauds*, below.

3. Where the owner of property executes an instrument conveying property to himself as trustee the instrument has the same effect as if he had declared himself trustee.

   e.g. S, the owner of Greenacre executes, acknowledges, and records a deed in statutory form conveying Greenacre to S as trustee for B. S is the trustee of the property for B.

   See generally Bogert, pp. 23–25; Rest. § 17 Comment on Clause (a); and Scott, § 17.1.

OTHER METHODS OF CREATING TRUSTS

1. A trust is created when property is transferred in trust to a trustee for the benefit of a third person or of the settlor.

(a) S is the owner of Greenacre. He conveys it to T in trust for the benefit of B. Legal title is passed to T who is trustee for B to whom equitable title has passed. There is no interest left in the settlor S.

(b) S is the owner of Greenacre. He conveys it to T in trust for S. Legal title is passed to T who is trustee for S who has retained equitable title.

2. A transfer in trust may be either by deed, called an inter vivos or living trust, or by will, called a testamentary trust.

3. A person holding a general power of appointment may appoint to anyone including himself or his estate. He can create a trust by appointing to a person as trustee for himself or for others.

4. A person holding a special power of appointment can only appoint among particular persons or classes or persons. He can create a trust by appointing to a trustee for the benefit of such persons depending upon the intent of the donor of the special power of appointment.

(a) D devises real property to S for life with a testamentary power of appointment in S to appoint the remainder among A, B and C in such shares and interests as S shall determine. S appoints to T in trust for A and B during their joint lives and on the death of the first to die to convey to the survivor. A trust is created. The exercise of the special power of appointment is within S's power because it is to be inferred that S is to have the same power of disposition in making the appointment as he would have in property he owns outright when the donor has not instructed him to the contrary.

(b) D devises real property to S for life with a power to appoint the remainder outright among A, B and C. S may not appoint to T in trust for A, B and C. The testator has manifested the intention that the property pass outright.

See Rest. § 17, comment f.

5. Trusts may be created by various kinds of contractual arrangements such as:

(a) The promise of an enforceable promise to transfer property in trust may hold the promise in trust.

(b) The insured under an insurance policy who has the right to change or designate the beneficiary directs the beneficiary to hold the proceeds in trust for a third person.

6. Statutes may provide for the creation of trusts in various instances. In the case of wrongful death the statute often provides that a right of action exists in the widow or executor of the decedent. Any recovery, however, is to be held in trust for designated beneficiaries.

See generally Bogert, pp. 21–22; Rest. § 17; and Scott, §§ 17–17.5.

Case 74   *Inter vivos trust created by oral declaration*

For a number of years prior to his death D made statements to a number of members of his family that he was setting up trusts taking advantage of the gift exclusion under the tax law. He kept an account book listing names of various persons with amounts credited to them from time to time. In his will he indicated he was holding certain funds belonging to others. After D's death the persons listed in the accounts claim them as beneficiaries of a trust. Are they entitled to such funds.

Answer. Yes. *D has established a series of inter vivos trusts by oral declarations to do so. The settlor need only manifest his intention to hold property in trust. An oral trust is rarely, if ever, declared in words of technical and definitive meaning. It is not necessary that any particular form be followed or that the words "trust" or "trustee" be used if the court after considering all the evidence determines that there is clear and convincing evidence that a trust was intended.*

See Gardner v. Bernard, 401 S.W.2d 415 (Mo.1966). See also Scott §§ 17 and 24.2.

NOTE—In Ex parte Pye, 18 Ves.Jr. 139, 34 Eng.Rep. 271 (Ch., 1811), Lord Eldon declared that what had been characterized as an imperfect transfer to be a declaration of trust in the following situation. Prior to T's death, T instructed B's son-in-law to purchase an annuity for B's benefit and to draw on T's account for the purchase. S followed T's instructions but at the time he purchased the annuity in T's name in order to protect B's interest since she was under an incapacity to hold property at that time. T in turn gave S a power of attorney authorizing him to transfer the annuity to B. After T's death but before S had learned of T's death, S exercised the power and delivered a deed of the annuity to B who was no longer under a legal incapacity. T's executor attempted to have the annuity made a part of T's personal estate on the ground that the power of attorney was revoked by T's death. The Chancery court, however, found that T had made a sufficient declaration that he held the annuity in trust for B so that the equitable interest had been in B prior to then. See Case 51, above.

1. The capacity required in the settlor to create a trust is that which would be required for the same transfer of property outright.

2. A settlor must have testamentary capacity to create a trust by will.

3. A settlor must have capacity to make an inter vivos transfer of legal title to the trust property if he declares himself the trustee of property for the benefit of another.

4. A settlor must have capacity to make an inter vivos transfer of legal title of the trust property to the trustee in order to make a transfer in trust.

See generally Bogert, p. 19–20; Rest. §§ 18–22; and Scott, §§ 18–22.

CAPACITY TO CREATE A TRUST

1. A present declaration of trust as to chattel property is valid and enforceable without any consideration.

   e.g. T, owner of sheep, a promissory note signed by X, and a year lease on Blackacre, orally declares himself trustee of all of such property here and now for the benefit of C.   C can enforce the trust.

2. A promise to create a trust to take effect in the future is unenforceable unless it is supported by a consideration as required in contracts.

   e.g. T, being the owner of 10 cows, gratuitously promises C that beginning one week from now he, T, will hold such cows in trust for C.   There is no enforceable trust and no enforceable contract for lack of consideration.   For a trust to exist it must be complete and the trustee must have presently enforceable duties to perform.

3. An owner of real property can create a trust of such property by his declaration, or a conveyance, even though it is unsupported by either good (relationship by blood or marriage) or valuable consideration.   However, the declaration or conveyance must comply with the Statute of Frauds.

   (a) By a writing signed by T, owner of Blackacre, T declares, "I hereby make myself trustee of Blackacre for the benefit of C and his heirs".   This is a presently created trust enforceable by C.

   (b) S, owner of Blackacre, executes a deed and delivers it "to T and his heirs in trust for C".   The trust is valid and enforceable by C even though S receives no consideration.

   See generally Bogert, pp. 65–68; Clark, p. 485; Rest, §§ 28–30; Ritchie, pp. 404–405; and Scott, §§ 28–30.1.

NECESSITY FOR CONSIDERATION IN TRUST CREATION

NECESSITY FOR NOTICE TO AND ACCEPTANCE BY TRUSTEE AND BENEFICIARY

1. It is not necessary that the beneficiary have notice of the creation of a trust or that he accept it.

2. It is not necessary that the trustee have notice of the creation of a trust or that he accept the trust.

3. Either the trustee or the beneficiary may disclaim if he has not by words or conduct manifested acceptance of the trust. Disclaimers are retroactive to the date of creation of the trust.

See generally Bogert pp. 99–105, 128–131; Palmer, p. 361; Rest. §§ 35–36; Ritchie, p. 429; Scoles, pp. 341–342; and Scott, §§ 35–36.1.

THE PAROL EVIDENCE RULE

1. If a written document evidences the transfer of legal title to property a question may arise as to the admissibility of extrinsic evidence to show that the transferor intended (or did not intend) to create a trust. Under the parol evidence rule where the writing is adopted by the settlor as a complete expression of his intention, extrinsic evidence (absent fraud, duress or mistake) is not admissible to contradict or vary the writing. If the meaning of the writing is unclear or ambiguous, extrinsic evidence may be admitted to determine its interpretation.

2. As applied to trusts the parol evidence rule operates as follows:

   (a) If the writing provides that the transferee is to take the property for his own benefit, parol evidence is not admissible to show that the transferee was intended to hold the property in trust. See Case 75, below.

   (b) If the writing provides that the transferee is to hold the property in trust for a particular purpose parol evidence is not admissible to show that the transferee was intended not to hold the property in trust or to hold the property on some different trust.

   (c) If the writing does not provide either that the transferee is to take the property for his own benefit or that he is to hold it in trust parol evidence is admissible to show that the transferee was intended to hold the property in trust either for the transferor or for a third party.

   (d) Where the owner of property by a writing has stated that he holds property upon a trust parol evidence may not be admitted to show that he intended to hold free of trust or for a different trust.

   See Smith's Review, Contracts, 3d, Chapter XVII, The Parol Evidence Rule.

   See generally Bogert, pp. 53–54; Rest. § 38; Ritchie, p. 511; Scoles, p. 270; and Scott, § 38.

Extrinsic evidence to prove existence of express trust excluded   Case 75
by parol evidence rule

B and E were tenants in common of an undivided interest in land, which was about to be sold for non-payment of taxes. B quitclaimed her interest to E who borrowed money to pay the taxes and sold the property. B's deed to E recited "B releases and quitclaims to E her heirs and assigns," and that, "E is to take the property for her own benefit." B seeks to prove that E had expressly held the land and certain proceeds of the parcels which were sold in trust for her benefit to the extent of B's proportionate interest. Is B entitled to the property?

Answer. No. The deed to E was absolute on its face. It contains no ambiguity and in the absence of any fraud, duress, mistake or other ground for rescission the parol evidence rule excludes introduction of any extrinsic evidence to prove an express trust in such case.

See *Trover v. Kennedy*, 425 Pa. 294, 229 A.2d 468 (1967).

THE REQUIREMENT OF A WRITING—THE STATUTE OF FRAUDS

1. An enforceable trust can be created without a writing *unless* otherwise provided by statute.

2. An oral trust of personal property is valid and enforceable in all common law jurisdictions.

3. Almost all jurisdictions have statutory provisions requiring that express trusts of real property be evidenced by a writing.

   NOTE—A few jurisdictions do hold oral trusts in land enforceable.

4. Statutes requiring a writing for the enforcement of a trust in land are usually based on the English Statute of Frauds of 1677 which required that an express trust of real property be "manifested and proved" by a writing signed by the party enabled to declare such a trust or it shall be, "utterly void and of none effect".

   NOTE—In states which have not adopted the Statute of Frauds provision with respect to trusts, statutes requiring a writing either in the case of a contract as to land or a conveyance of land have been held applicable to the creation of a trust in land.

5. The Statute of Frauds applies to both:

   (a) declarations of trusts, and

   (b) transfers in trust.

6. The Statute of Frauds has been construed to make oral trusts only voidable not void.   Only the trustee has standing to set up the

Statute of Frauds. No other person may do so. Therefore, the trustee may perform the oral trust, but he may not be forced to do so.

7. In order to satisfy the Statute of Frauds the memorandum does not need to be in any special form. It need only contain the essential terms of the trust (the description of the trust property, the beneficiaries and the purpose) and be signed:

   (a) in the case of a *declaration* of trust—by the owner of the property prior to, at the time of, or subsequent to the declaration of trust (but prior to any transfer of the interest to a third party),

   (b) in the case of a *transfer* in trust—

       (i) by the transferor prior to or at the time of the transfer;

       (ii) by the transferee prior to, at the time of or subsequent to the transfer but prior to any transfer to a third party.

   NOTE—A minority of states has held that the Statute of Frauds does require that the trust be created by a writing not merely proved by it. In these jurisdictions a memorandum prepared after the transfer of the property would be insufficient. See Rest. § 40.

8. Part performance by the trustee of an oral trust concerning real property may take it out of the Statute of Frauds in some jurisdictions. Such part performance may consist of:

   (a) the trustee's delivering possession of the land to the beneficiary,

   (b) the trustee's permitting the beneficiary to make valuable improvements on the land, or

   (c) any act of the beneficiary in reliance on the trust with the trustee's consent which irrevocably changes the beneficiary's position.

   See generally Bogert, pp. 48–55; Clark, pp. 593–595; Palmer, pp. 465–466; Rest. §§ 39–52; Ritchie, pp. 507–508, 511–516; Scoles, pp. 271–272; and Scott, §§ 39–52.1.

Case 76 *Part performance takes oral trust out of the State of Frauds*

D died having title to certain land which he and his brother had purchased as a gift for their mother P. D had also furnished money to P to make improvements on the property. At the time of purchase, P's husband and she were having marital problems; therefore, D took legal title in his name. During D's life, P had possession of the property and received all the income. She expended her own money in addition to monies received from D on improvements. She paid all accounts. On numerous occasions, D spoke of the houses as P's and after P's divorce from her husband, D stated that he would deed the property to her when he visited her in two months. He died before the visit took place. After D's death, P brought an action to establish her title to the property on the ground that D held the property pursuant to an oral trust. The property is in State A which has held that an oral trust of land is within the Statute of Frauds. Is P entitled to the property?

Answer. Yes. Even though an express parol trust of land is within the Statute of Frauds, it may be taken out of the Statute by part performance. The parol agreement is not void; it is merely voidable, and where there is part performance, evidence of the parol trust is admissible to prove the trust. Here the performance was sufficient to satisfy the part performance exception. P took possession of the property and made valuable improvements thereon. These improvements were made with her money and money recovered as a gift from D which gift was completed before being applied to the improvements. Thus, all of the requisites are present to take the case out of the Statute of Frauds and to enforce the trust, i.e., an agreement to convey, a present gift, possession thereunder and the making of valuable and lasting improvements at the expense of the donee.

See Stewart v. Damron, 63 Ariz. 158, 160 P.2d 321 (1945).

Letter acknowledging beneficiary's interest in property is   Case 77
sufficient memorandum for statute of frauds

B and S were brother and sister. They inherited an undivided interest in certain real estate. B had a position which subjected him to requests to provide bail for persons in trouble. In order to escape the importunities he executed a deed conveying his undivided interest to his sister S. The property was later sold and S received the proceeds. She used the proceeds and invested in two parcels of real estate. The jurisdiction has a statute requiring a trust of real property to be evidenced by a writing. There were repeated declarations by S that, although the title was in her name, a half interest was B's. Subsequent to the purchase of the two parcels of real estate, S wrote a letter to B as follows: "Now I want you to fully understand that I would not sign a lease or give a two years privilege to anyone without seeing and talking to you first—not much—no siree—why should I? Are you not as much interested in the houses as myself—surely yes— so 'put that in your pipe and smoke it,' old chap." After the death of both B and S, B's heirs bring an action to establish a trust in favor of B to the extent of an undivided half interest in the real property. Are B's heirs entitled to the property?

Answer. Yes. S's statement that her brother had as much interest in the houses as herself can be fairly interpreted by the triers of fact as an admission that her title was subject to a trust. A letter may be a sufficient memorandum to evidence a trust. The rule is that the recognition of the trust must be found in the writing and not elsewhere; however, the general rules of interpretation are to be applied to the writing, and it is to be construed in the light of the facts and circumstances. S had received a deed of B's interest in land for which she paid nothing. She had received it because he wished to put title in a form where his ownership would be secret. If from such a conveyance a trust did not arise, at least the situation was one in which the recognition of a trust became natural and probable. B trusted to S's sense of honor. The letter must be read in this setting. Thus viewed, its assertion of equality between brother and sister is something more than a tribute to brotherly affection. It is the recognition of a right and the declaration of a duty. Nor is the memorandum inadequate because, while referring to the houses, it does not otherwise describe them. The parcels in controversy were the only ones she owned and were bought at a time when she had no other resources. She left no other real estate at her death. In such a case, the description that might otherwise be indefinite becomes definite when applied to the only subject matter that can reasonably fit it. "A description will be rejected as inadequate if the signer is the owner of two or more parcels, to any one of which it may be applied with equal fitness. It will be accepted as sufficient if he is the owner of only one."

See *Sinclair v. Purdy,* 235 N.Y. 245, 139 N.E. 255 (1923).

TRUSTS AND THE STATUTE OF WILLS

1. Only a valid will can create a testamentary trust of either real or personal property.

2. To comply with the Statute of Wills all of the elements of the testamentary trust must be ascertainable either

   (a) from the face of the will; or

   (b) from the face of the will and from an existing document properly incorporated by reference; and/or

   (c) from facts which have independent significance apart from the intended testamentary disposition.

   See *Integration, Incorporation by Reference, Acts of Independent Significance* and *Testamentary Additions to Trust,* Chapter III above. See also Case 79, below.

3. A trust is testamentary when the transfer in trust becomes effective only upon and by reason of the death of the settlor.

4. If an heir agrees with his ancestor to hold inherited property in trust for a third person and the ancestor refrains from making a will in reliance on the heir's promise, the express trust is unenforceable. Relief may be given the intended beneficiary by a constructive trust on the theory of unjust enrichment.

5. If a legatee or devisee orally agrees with the testator to hold property given him by will in trust for a third person and the testator leaves the property to such promisor in reliance on such promise, the express trust is unenforceable because it does not comply with the Statute of Wills. Nevertheless, relief may be given the intended beneficiary by imposing a constructive trust on the theory of unjust enrichment.

6. If no one has an interest in trust property other than the settlor prior to the settlor's death, the disposition is testamentary and must comply with the statute of wills.

   e.g. S executes and delivers to T a deed transferring to T in trust for B such shares of stock as S shall own at his death. No trust is created either at the time of the deed or at S's death.

7. The fact that the settlor of an inter vivos trust reserves a life interest, the power to revoke, alter, modify or control the administration of the trust during his life does not make a trust testamentary if an interest is created in a beneficiary during the settlor's lifetime. The mere fact that the beneficiary's enjoyment is postponed does not make the trust testamentary. See Case 56, above.

   See generally Bogert, pp. 55–61; Rest. §§ 53–57; Ritchie, pp. 538–540; Scoles, pp. 308–311; and Scott, §§ 53–57.6.

Oral evidence to identify beneficiaries of testamentary trust   **Case 78**
inadmissible

T died testate providing in his will as follows: "I give all the rest, residue and remainder of my property to A to be held by him in trust for equal distribution among the persons whose names I have given him orally in a private conversation with him". A offers to testify that T had requested him to accept the residue of his estate and to distribute it equally among three of T's favorite nieces, X, Y and Z. H is T's heir to whom the residue will pass by intestate succession if the trust is invalid. Is the offered oral testimony of A admissible in a suit by X, Y and Z to enforce the trust?

     Answer. No. *The Statute of Wills requires that a will be in writing. Oral evidence is admissible for the purpose of explaining but not for the purpose of altering or enlarging the provisions of a will. To admit oral evidence for such purpose would be to violate the Statute of Wills. For any person to take under a will he must* *be described therein in such a way that he can be identified. And for a person to be a beneficiary of a trust created by will he must be described in the will so that he can be identified from the face of the will. To permit X, Y and Z to be identified not from the language on the face of the will but by oral evidence would be a clear violation of the Statute of Wills. It would permit X, Y and Z to take through oral testimony and not through the writing on the will. An incomplete testamentary trust cannot be made complete by oral testimony. On the other hand, A cannot keep the property which is given him by T's will because the face of the will discloses that he is to take such property "in trust" and is not intended by T to take beneficially. Hence, the express trust fails and T must hold the residue of T's estate in resulting trust for T's sole statutory heir, H. He does so under the principle that when an express trust fails the trustee holds in resulting trust for the settlor or his successor.*

See Moore v. Garvey's Adm'r, 290 Ky. 61, 160 S.W.2d 363 (1942); In re Brown's Estate, 122 N.Y.S.2d 640 (1953).

Case 79 *Extrinsic evidence admissible to identify beneficiaries of testamentary trust*

M was a very wealthy man who operated a large factory for many years and had many faithful employees who had worked for him over a long period of time. M died testate and his will provided, "I give all the rest, residue and remainder of my property to T in trust for such of my employees who at the time of my death have worked for me for not less than five years". The residue of M's estate amounted to $500,000. There were 20 employees working for M at the time of his death who had worked for him faithfully for five or more years, 15 of whom had been employed by M after the making of his will. M's estate is probated and the residue is delivered to T. The 5 older employees insist that all those who were employed by M after the making of his will cannot take. They claimed they are identified not by the terms of the will when it was drawn but by the hiring process after the making of the will. This is a non-testamentary act not complying with the Statute of Wills. Are the 15 employees hired after M's will was executed entitled to share as beneficiaries in the trust?

Answer. *Yes. Of course every will is ambulatory and takes effect not when executed but at the death of the testator. When M died 20 of his employees were reasonably identified by the description of them in M's will. Those 20 had been working for M for more than 5 years at the time of M's death. No will is wholly self-sufficient in its description of either property to pass or persons to take. Even in the most obvious cases some extrinsic evidence is necessary to identify the property and the beneficiaries. It is true that 15 of the*

20 employees who qualify under the trust were hired after the execution of M's will. It is true that such act of hiring those 15 employees was a non-testamentary act which does not comply with the Statute of Wills. However, if such non-testamentary act performed subsequent to the making of the will has significance apart from identifying the persons as those who are to take under the will, then such beneficiaries may take. In this case M surely did not hire those 15 employees merely and solely to make them beneficiaries under his will and the testamentary trust therein and particularly 5 years before his death. He hired them because he had work to do and thought they could do it. Such hiring therefore had significance apart from making those employees take under M's will. Therefore, all 20 employees, including those hired after the making of M's will may participate as beneficiaries under the testamentary trust. It may be observed that in this case the non-testamentary act was performed by the testator himself. Such non-testamentary acts also may be the acts of a beneficiary under a will by the testator himself.

See Rest. § 54. See also Integration, Incorporation by Reference, Acts of Independent Significance and Testamentary Additions to Trust, Chapter III, above.

Illusory inter vivos trust not a substitute for a will   Case 80

S, during his life, transferred all of his property to T in trust for S, the trust agreement providing: "the settlor and beneficiary, S, to have power to revoke the trust at any time while he lives, shall have control over all investments and reinvestments and in all respects T shall do with the trust property as S shall direct so that S shall during his lifetime have as much control over such trust property as though no trust were established and upon S's death T shall hold such property for C". S signed and acknowledged the trust instrument, but there were not two witnesses thereto as required by the Statute of Wills. During S's life, he exercised complete control over the trust. It, in fact, served as a combination bank account and safety deposit box. He used trust assets as collateral for personal loans and listed trust income as personal income on his income tax returns. Upon S's death the property is claimed by S's sole statutory heir, H. Is H's claim well founded?

Answer. Yes. This is a plain case of S attempting to use a living trust as a substitute for a will. The fact that a settlor retains power to revoke a trust does not itself make the trust invalid or make it testamentary. The trust is valid until it is revoked as a condition subsequent. The fact that the settlor retains other powers over the trust property such as the reinvestment thereof also does not prevent the trust from being valid. Moreover the facts in this case go far beyond any of these propositions. Here the settlor, S, retains com-

plete control over both the trust property and over the trustee for all purposes until his death. This prevents there being anything more than a colorable trust and in reality makes T a mere agent of S. In this case S has retained as much power over the property as he had before executing the so-called trust agreement and T has no power other than to do S's bidding. On these facts there is no trust, only an agency. S cannot dispose of hs property in trust and have it too. Looking at the total picture the arrangement was merely a custodial account and in the nature of a testamentary disposition. Neither can the trust agreement be a will for the reason that it does not comply with the Statute of Wills, not having the requisite witnesses. Therefore, the attempt to dispose of the property at death in favor of C must fail and S is held to have died intestate. The property passes to H by intestate succession.

See *Osborn v. Osborn, 10 Ohio Misc. 171, 226 N.E.2d 814 (Cuy.Com.Pl.1966).* See also Illusory Trusts, Chapter VI, above; Rest. § 57.

PROHIBITED TRUST PURPOSES

1. A trust may not be created for an illegal purpose.

2. Trusts for illegal purposes include:

   (a) trusts which involve the commission of a crime or tort by the trustee,

   (b) trusts the enforcement of which would be against public policy:

   (i) provisions which encourage conduct against public policy, such as encouraging divorce, preventing marriage, restraining religious freedom, or discouraging performance of public duties,

   (ii) provisions which direct that property be used in a manner prohibited by public policy, such as holding property in trust for a period longer than the Rule Against Perpetuities, providing for unreasonable periods of accumulation of income, unreasonable restraints on alienation or for capricious purposes.

   (c) trusts created for the purpose of defrauding creditors or other third parties, or

   (d) trusts for which the consideration is illegal.

3. If the illegal provision goes to the whole trust, the trust fails in its entirety.

4. If the illegal provision does not affect the whole trust, only the illegal provision is stricken and the balance of the trust is given effect without it.

See generally Bogert, pp. 175–180; Rest. §§ 60–65; Ritchie, pp. 390–391, 396–397, 399; Scoles, pp. 251–252; and Scott, §§ 60–65.3.

Marriage conditions in trust valid unless general restraint against marriage or encouraging divorce   Case 81

Testator by will left (a) his business to his three eldest sons on condition that each such child marry one of "true Greek blood and descent and of orthodox religion;" (b) $2,000 to D (who had married one not of the Greek Orthodox religion) conditioned upon her remarrying a man of their Greek blood and descent and of Orthodox religion after her first marriage was terminated by death or divorce. Are the conditions valid?

Answer. As to (a) Yes. As to (b) No. Marriage conditions are valid unless the scope of legatee's choice is so limited that the restriction becomes one against marriage in general. On the other hand, the condition in (b) is one which tends to encourage divorce in that it is not logically related to the changed circumstances of the beneficiary. In fact the condition in (b) is conducive to the disruption of the family and thus invalid.

See In re Estate of Kzffalas, 426 Pa. 432, 233 A.2d 248 (1967).

1. In general if the settlor has not expressly reserved the power to revoke or modify a trust, the power to do so does not exist.

   POWER OF SETTLOR TO REVOKE OR MODIFY

2. If the trust is written and unambiguous the parol evidence rule will apply to exclude evidence that the settlor intended a power to revoke. See *The Parol Evidence Rule*, above.

3. If the terms of the trust instrument are ambiguous or the trust is oral, factors which may show that the settlor reserved power of revocation include:

   (a) improvidence of setting up the trust without such a power,

   (b) relationship between the settlor and beneficiary,

   (c) purposes for creating trust,

   (d) nature of the trust property, and

   (e) impact of federal taxes on provision as drafted.

4. General rules with respect to rescission and reformation will be applied if it is claimed that the provision for revocation was omitted through fraud or mistake.

5. The power to revoke usually also includes the power to revoke in part and to modify.

6. Whether the power to modify includes the power to revoke depends on all the circumstances.

7. If the settlor reserves the power to revoke or modify only in a particular manner he may only revoke or modify in such manner.

   e.g.   The power to revoke with the consent of a third party.

8. If no method is specified the power may be exercised in any way sufficient to manifest the intention to revoke or modify.   See Case 82, below.

9. In many states statutes have been enacted which provide that in the absence of an express provision to the contrary the trust is presumed to be irrevocable.   Others presume it to be revocable in such circumstances.

   See generally Bogert, pp. 531–536; Clark, pp. 553–554; Palmer, p. 329; Rest. §§ 330–333; Scoles, pp. 364–366; and Scott, §§ 330–333.

Case 82   *Revocable trust is revoked by conduct which sufficiently manifests settlor's intention to revoke*

Prior to his death S executed a form contained in a book entitled "How to Avoid Probate," headed "Declaration of Trust."   In this form S declared himself to be the trustee of his shares of capital stock in ABC, Inc., for the use and benefit of B.   It further provided that upon S's death, B was to be appointed as successor trustee and was to transfer all of the trust assets to B.   Another provision stated: "I hereby reserve to myself the power and right at any time during my lifetime, before actual distribution to the beneficiary hereunder, to revoke in whole or in part, or to amend the trust hereby created without the necessity of obtaining the consent of the beneficiary and without giving notice to the beneficiary.   Any of the following acts shall be conclusive evidence of such revocation of this trust: (a) the delivery to the issuer or transfer agent of the shares by me with written notice that this trust is revoked in whole or in part; (b) the transfer by me of my right, title and interest in and to said shares; (c) the delivery by me to the issuer or transfer agent of the shares of written notice of the death of the beneficiary hereunder."   Subsequently difficulties arose between S and B who was his wife.   S consulted with his attorney and discussed both his will and his marital problems.   S told his attorney that ABC, Inc. was his corporation, that his efforts had created it, that it was separate property and that his wife owned no interest and that he wanted his son to succeed to his interest.   S executed a will in which he specifically referred to ABC, Inc. as being solely owned by himself.   S subsequently made various declarations that ABC, Inc. belonged wholly to him and that his wife

B had no interest in it whatsoever.   S subsequently died.   B claims the property by virtue of the inter vivos trust.   Is B entitled to the property?

Answer.   No.   By the terms of the trust instrument, it gave the settlor the power to revoke without the necessity of obtaining the consent of and/or giving notice to the beneficiary.   Although the trust provisions set forth certain acts which would be deemed conclusive evidence of revocation, they are by no means the exclusive ways in which the trust could be revoked.   The rule is that if a settlor reserves the power to revoke the trust but does not specify any exclusive mode of revocation, the power can be exercised in any manner which sufficiently manifests the intention of the settlor to revoke the trust. It may be sufficient that he manifest his decision to revoke by communicating it to beneficiaries or to third parties.   In the present case, since the settlor is also the trustee, he merely had to manifest his intention to revoke the trust either by some communication to the beneficiary or to a third party to that effect.   Since the trust instrument stated revocation could occur only during the lifetime of the settlor, the will he executed did not take effect during his lifetime and cannot be considered as a revocation of the trust.   The statements made to his attorney, however, prior to the time of the will, manifested his decision to revoke the trust.   Nor is it necessary that the intention to revoke be evidenced by a writing.   Where no method of revoking a revocable trust is set forth in the instrument, the trust may be revoked informally and orally.   Thus S had effectively revoked the trust by his statements evidencing his intent to do so and B is not entitled to the property.   See *Barnette v. McNulty, 21 Ariz.App. 127, 516 P.2d 583 (1973).*

THE POWER TO TERMINATE TRUSTS

1. Whether or not the terms of the trust include a power to revoke, the trust will be terminated in the following instances whether or not the settlor, trustee or beneficiaries consent:

   (a) upon the expiration of the period for which the trust was created,

   (b) upon the fulfillment of the condition upon which the trust is to terminate,

   (c) where the purposes for which the trust was created become impossible or illegal, and

   (d) if the continuance of the trust would defeat the purposes for which the trust was created.

2. If the settlor is the sole beneficiary of the trust, he can compel termination of the trust although there has been no reservation of

a power to revoke and the trust purposes have not been accomplished.

3. If the trustee conveys the legal title to the trust property to the beneficiaries, the trust will terminate even though the trust purposes may not have been accomplished and there may be a claim against the trustee for breach of trust.

4. If *all* of the beneficiaries and the settlor consent to termination, even though the trust purposes have not been accomplished, the trust will be terminated.

5. If all of the beneficiaries of a trust consent to its termination:

   (a) The trust will be terminated *unless* the trust is an active trust and its material purposes have not been accomplished.

   (b) The trust will *not* be terminated if it is an active trust and its material purposes have not been accomplished.

   e.g. A spendthrift trust will not be terminated while the inalienable interest still exists.

   NOTE—In England and a minority of U.S. jurisdictions the rule is that in such circumstances the trust will be terminated whether or not its purposes have been accomplished.

6. If all of the beneficiaries do not or *cannot* consent to its termination, the trust will not be terminated.

   NOTE—In such case a court may decree a partial termination if the interests of the non-consenting beneficiaries or the fulfillment of a material purpose will not be affected.   Some states now have statutes making it possible to terminate a trust with the consent of the settlor and all living beneficiaries.

   See generally Bogert, pp. 539–552; Clark, pp. 565–566; Palmer, pp. 451–452, 456–459; Rest. §§ 334–340; Ritchie, pp. 565–566, 569, 577, 581–584, 587–589; and Scott, §§ 334–340.2.

Case 83 *Effect of possible unborn beneficiaries on right to terminate trust*

Settlor established an inter vivos trust in which she retained the income for life and reserved a general testamentary power of appointment over the remainder.   In default of appointment the remainder was to go to her "next of kin" under the state law of intestate succession.   The settlor did not retain a power to revoke.   Settlor is seeking to terminate the trust, her economic circumstances having changed, on the ground that she is the sole beneficiary in that the limitation of the remainder to her heirs is presumed to be a reversion in her.   Is she entitled to terminate the trust?

Answer. *Yes or No, depending upon the jurisdiction. The general rule is that an inter vivos trust can be terminated even though its purpose as stated in the trust instrument has not been accomplished if the settlor and all the beneficiaries join in seeking a termination of the trust. The problem in this case is in determining who the beneficiaries are under the trust instrument. This will in turn depend upon whether settlor's next of kin have a remainder interest. If they do not, the settlor will be the sole beneficiary and can compel a termination. This in turn depends on the rule of the jurisdiction. Some jurisdictions hold as a rule of law that a disposition in favor of settlor's heirs creates a reversion in the settlor and no interest in the heirs. Others hold that the interest created is presumed to be a reversion but it may be rebutted and shown it is a remainder depending upon the intent of the settlor in creating the interest. Elements to be considered in determining intent are: whether settlor has made a full and formal disposition of the corpus of the estate, whether settlor has made no reservation to grant or assign during his lifetime and whether he has reserved only a testamentary power of appointment. Still other jurisdictions hold that as a rule of law the heirs or next of kin have a remainder. If the next of kin are held to have a remainder, settlor cannot obtain a termination without their consent. If there is a possibility that some of the heirs are unborn their consent cannot be obtained unless the court is willing to appoint a guardian ad litem to represent unborn heirs.*

See Hatch v. Riggs National Bank, 361 F.2d 559 (D.C.Cir.1966). See also Doctor v. Hughes, 225 N.Y. 305, 122 N.E. 221 (1919) and Richardson v. Richardson, 298 N.Y. 135, 81 N.E.2d 54 (1948).

NOTE—Many states now have statutes which attempt to resolve this issue, e.g. New York makes it possible to terminate a trust with the consent of the settlor and all living beneficiaries. See N.Y.EPTL 7–1.9 (McKinney's 1967, 1970 Supp.).

Court will not terminate trust where material purpose of settlor   Case 84
will be thwarted

By the terms of his will, D left all of his personal property to T in trust "to sell and dispose of the same and to pay the proceeds to my son Albert in the following manner: $10,000 when he is of the age of twenty-one years, $10,000 when he is of the age of twenty-four years and the balance when he is of the age of thirty years". Albert was not quite 21 at the death of his father. When he reached 21 he received $10,000. Prior to reaching 25 Albert brings an action against the trustee to compel the payment of the remainder of the trust fund. He contends that the provisions of the will postponing the payment of money beyond his twenty-first birthday are void because the trustee has no duties other than to hold the property. Is Albert entitled to the entire res of the trust?

Answer. No. There is no doubt that Albert's interest in the trust is vested and absolute and that no other person has any interest in it. A court will order trust property to be conveyed by the trustee to the beneficiary where there is a passive trust or when the purposes of the trust have been accomplished or when there is no reason why the trust should continue and all the persons interested in it are sui juris and desire that it be terminated. When, however, the continuation of the trust is necessary to carry out a material purpose of the settlor, a court will not decree termination even though the sole beneficiary or all the beneficiaries desire termination. In Albert's case it is clear from the testator's will that he did not want Albert to have the corpus or income except as therein specified. Even though the interest of Albert in the trust is alienable by him and can be reached by his creditors, the restrictions imposed by testator are not altogether useless, "For there is not the same danger that he will spend the property while it is in the hands of the trustees as there would be if it were in his own." The restrictions postponing the beneficiary's right to possession and control are within the testator's right to provide and there is no reason why his intent should not be carried out.

See *Claflin v. Claflin*, 149 Mass. 19, 20 N.E. 454 (1889).

Case 85 *Beneficiary estopped from holding trustee liable for wrongful termination of trust*

D by her will created a trust for her grandson S and provided that income should be paid to him in monthly installments until he reached age 31 at which time the principal was to be conveyed to him. After S reached age 21, he induced the trustee to transfer the principal to him. S then lost and wasted the principal and brings an action against the trustee for restitution of the trust principal. Will S prevail?

Answer. No. The general rule is that a trustee and beneficiary acting together have no power to terminate the trust unless a power to terminate is given them by the terms of the trust. If, however, the trustee transfers legal title to the beneficiary, a merger of legal and equitable title occurs in the beneficiary and the trust is terminated despite the fact that a judicial termination could not be had. The termination in such case is clearly a breach of trust and the trustee is liable therefor. If the beneficiary is sui juris and demands that the trust terminate, however, he is estopped from later holding the trustee liable for a breach of trust to which he consented.

See *Hagerty v. Clement*, 15 La. 230, 196 So. 330 (1940).   See also Rest. § 342.

NOTE—In the case above had S not attained the age of majority at the time of the transfer to him, the court would have reached the opposite result and S would have prevailed since S was under an incapacity at the time of his consent to the transfer.   See Rest. § 216.

Trust cannot be terminated if a material purpose of the settlor will be defeated   Case 86

D died leaving his entire residuary estate to T in trust to pay the income to A and B during their lives.   At the death of the survivor of A and B, the trust was to terminate and the corpus was to be distributed to charity C.   D's heirs at law commenced an action to set aside the will.   Subsequently, A, B, C and the heirs entered into a compromise agreement providing for 20% of the estate to A, 20% to B, 30% to C and 30% among D's heirs.   All of their heirs as well as A, B and C, were sui juris and agreed to the compromise but the executor and trustee opposed it.   The trustee argued that the court should refuse to approve the settlement on the ground that the trust cannot be terminated upon the consent of A, B and C, because a material purpose of the settlor would therefore be defeated.   Is the trustee correct?

Answer. Yes.   The effect of the compromise agreement, if approved by the court, would be to abolish the trust.   The rule with respect to the right of beneficiaries of a testamentary trust to have it terminated is that a testamentary trust can only be terminated by judicial decree if: (1) all the parties in interest unite in seeking the termination, (2) every reasonable ultimate purpose of the trust has been accomplished, and (3) if no fair and lawful restriction imposed by the testator will be nullified or disturbed by the result.   A court's function is not to remake a trust instrument or to modify the size of gifts made or accord the beneficiaries more advantage than the donor directed;   it is to ascertain what the donor intended that the donee should receive and to secure to the donee the enjoyment of that interest only.   The reason for this rule is the protection of the reasonable desire of testators.   In this case the first condition, that all the interested beneficiaries have joined in the agreement, is satisfied;   however, the second and third conditions are not.   The obvious objective of the decedent was to provide an assured life income for A and B and, after their deaths, an intact corpus for charity C.   In order to achieve these objectives, D placed the management of the trust in a trustee selected by her and in whose financial judgment she is presumed to have had confidence.   Any expenditure of principal by the life beneficiaries was precluded.   These steps taken by D in all *reasonable probability would have achieved her objectives. To abolish the trust and turn over a part of the corpus outright to the life beneficiaries would enable them in a moment to lose the protection of the assured life income provided by D. These objectives cannot be fully accomplished prior to the death of the life beneficiaries. Had D intended to entrust beneficiaries with the handling of any part of the corpus she would have provided so by a simple and outright gift. Nor does the fact that the circumstances in this case involved the settlement of a will contest change the result. The power to set aside or terminate a testamentary trust is not such that its applicability would be affected by the mere fact that the motivation of a trust termination is the compromise of a will contest. Although will contests are frequently compromised by agreements involving the transfer of legacies or devises by beneficiaries under the will, in such case the gifts are alienable and no violence is done to the provisions of the will. That is not the case here where the provisions of the will itself would be drastically changed so as to abolish a trust. It therefore follows that the court should deny the approval of the agreement.*

See *Adams v. Link*, 145 Conn. 634, 145 A.2d 753 (1958).

NOTE—Generally, when a trust is created under which the income is payable to one beneficiary for life and on his death the principal payable to another and it does not appear that the settlor had any other purpose than to enable the beneficiaries to enjoy the trust property successively, the beneficiaries can compel a termination if both consent and both are sui juris. See Richie, p. 577.

VIII CHARITABLE TRUSTS

HISTORY OF CHARITABLE TRUSTS

1. Charitable trusts developed in England out of the desire of individuals to make gifts for religious purposes. At the time, direct gifts to charity were either:

   (a) forbidden by restrictions on mortmain; or

   (b) unacceptable because of the vows of poverty of the Franciscan friars.

2. Initially the duties of the trustee (feoffee to uses) were merely honorary being unenforceable in the courts.

3. As early as the fifteenth century, charitable trusts were being enforced by the Chancellor.

4. The Statute of Charitable Uses was adopted in 1601 to provide for the enforcement of charitable trusts. It authorized the Chancellor to appoint Commissioners from time to time to inquire into abuses and to make orders for the redress of abuses involving charitable bequests and donations. This remedy was seldom used in England and never in the United States. See 43 Eliz. I, c. 4 (1601).

5. Charitable trusts have been upheld and enforced in the various states of the United States whether or not the statute of Charitable Uses is held to be in effect therein.

ELEMENTS OF A CHARITABLE TRUST

1. A charitable trust is a public trust and must have six distinct elements to be valid:

   (a) an intention of the settlor to create a trust,

   (b) a trustee to administer the trust,

   (c) a res or subject matter,

   (d) a charitable purpose expressly designated,

   (e) a definite class to be benefited, and

   (f) indefinite beneficiaries within the definite class who are the persons who actually receive the benefit.

2. The requirements of:

   (a) the intention,

   (b) the trustee, and

   (c) the res,

   are the same in a charitable trust as in a private trust.

   e.g. S, by will, leaves the residuary of his estate to, "T in trust for the purpose of furnishing food, clothing and shelter for the poor children of City X." A charitable trust is created in that (a)

S is the settlor whose intention to create a charitable trust is expressed in clear language; (b) T is designated as trustee; (c) the property in S's estate constitutes the res or subject matter of the trust; (d) furnishing food, clothing and shelter for the children is an express charitable purpose which has as its object benefitting, uplifting or developing mankind, mentally, morally, physically or spiritually; (e) "poor children of City X" is a specifically designated class of persons to be benefitted; and (f) the specific children who will receive food, clothing and shelter from the trust remain indefinite at the creation of the trust which takes place when S's will becomes effective upon his death. See Rest. §§ 348, 351.

3. A charitable trust is created in the same manner as a private express trust. See Rest. § 349.

4. A private express trust to be valid must have definite beneficiaries who can enforce it. By contrast, a trust having indefinite beneficiaries to be valid must be for a charitable purpose, and as such, enforceable by the attorney general.

See generally Bogert, pp. 199–206, 244–247; Rest. §§ 348–350; and Scott, §§ 348–351.

1. A charitable purpose is one the object of which is to benefit, improve or uplift mankind mentally, morally, physically or spiritually. Charitable purposes include relief of poverty, improvement of government, advancement of religion, education or health, and other purposes which will benefit the community.

CHARITABLE PURPOSES

(a) A trust "for the benefit of the poor" or "for widows" is construed to be "for poor people" and "poor widows" for the relief of poverty and therefore charitable.

(b) A trust "to erect and maintain a bridge, a street and a park" is construed to improve government and therefore charitable. These benefit taxpayers as a class and within the class the particular taxpayers who would be taxed for such improvements.

(c) A trust "to prevent cruelty to animals", "to build a monument to Abraham Lincoln", "to beautify Town X" or "to improve the U.S. Constitution"—these inculcate kindness to animals, patriotism, community happiness and promote better government and are charitable.

(d) A trust "to build a statute of St. Paul", "to distribute Bibles", or "to support foreign missionaries", tends to promote religion and is charitable.

(e) A trust "to provide scholarships", "for educational purposes", "to establish a public golf course", "to promote Boy Scouts and Girl Scouts", "to promote birth control", "to encourage vivesection", "to discourage vivisection", or "to set up a fund for low interest loans to needy students" promotes education and is charitable.

(f) A trust "to study cancer", "to provide a sewage disposal plant for Town Y", "to encourage vegetarianism" or "to prevent cruelty to children"—these promote health and are charitable.

2. The definition of charitable purposes is derived from the preamble to the Statute of Charitable Uses adopted in England in 1601 (43 Eliz. I C. 4) which enumerated charitable purposes. It was early determined that the list contained therein was not a complete list and other purposes of the same general character are also charitable. See Rest. § 368, Comment a.

3. The Statute of Charitable Uses is part of the common law in many states. Other states uphold and enforce charitable trusts under general equitable jurisdiction or specific statutes. Some states have during periods of their history prohibited charitable trusts, but all now generally uphold them.

4. A trust for "benevolent" purposes may or may not be a charitable trust. If the word is construed to be the equivalent of "charitable", the trust is valid. On the other hand if it is found to mean objects of "good will toward man" or mere liberality, the trust fails.

5. The class to be benefitted in a charitable trust must be definite, that is, it must be large enough so that the community in general is affected and interested in the enforcement of the trust, yet it must not include all of mankind. Furthermore, within this class the specific persons to benefit from the trust must be indefinite. Note the application of these two requirements in specific cases:

(a) A trust "for the benefit of orphans of veterans of World War II" is charitable. The class is definite, that is, the orphans of the veterans of World War II. The indefinite persons within the class are the ones who are ultimately selected by the trustee to be paid the provided benefits. The class is large enough so that the community is interested in the enforcement of the trust.

(b) A trust "to establish an athletic field for the X High School" is charitable. If this be considered a trust for governmental purposes because it furnishes a facility which would otherwise have to be paid for at government expense, then the class to be benefited is all taxpayers of the school district and the indefinite persons as beneficiaries within the class are the particular taxpayers who would otherwise be taxed to pay for the field. If this be considered a charitable trust for educational purposes as part of the physical education program of the high school, then the class to be benefited is the entire class of high school students and the indefinite beneficiaries within the class are the students who actually are benefited by using the athletic field.

(c) A trust "to erect and maintain a monument of George Washington in the yard of the County Courthouse of Z County" is charitable as inculcating patriotism. The class to be benefited is the entire immediate community and within that class the actual indefinite beneficiaries are the people who actually view the monument.

(d) A trust "to charity" is valid but leaves to the trustee the selection of the particular charitable purpose to which the trust's res will be applied. If he elects to set up a "hospital for stray dogs and cats", it is charitable because it is for all dogs and cats generally and not for specifically named ones. Such an institution engenders a general feeling of kindliness towards animals. The class of persons which is benefited is the people in the immediate community and the indefinite persons within the class to be benefited are those who come in contact with such institution and are affected thereby.

6. A trust for named persons or a trust for profit cannot be a charitable trust.

See generally, Bogert, pp. 206–240; Palmer, pp. 519–520, 524–525; Rest. §§ 368–375; Ritchie, pp. 590–599, 607–609, 620–621; and Scott §§, 368–377.

Gift in trust with an unlimited power of dispossession in the trust—fails　　　　Case 87

By will D bequeathed all of her estate to the Bishop of her diocese in trust to dispose of it "to such objects of benevolence and liberally as the Bishop in his own discretion shall most approve of." D's heirs filed an action asking that the bequest be held void and that the Bishop is holding the estate as a resulting trustee for them. Are D's next of kin entitled to the property?

Answer. *Yes. The intended trust is not a charitable trust in that the terms "benevolence" and "liberality" are broad enough to include non-charitable purposes. Therefore, the Attorney General cannot enforce the trust and there is no beneficiary who can enforce it. Nor does the bequest show an intention to make an outright gift to the*

Bishop. Since the transfer creates neither a charitable trust nor a gift to the Bishop, he may not be permitted to retain it but holds it for the decedent's next of kin on a resulting trust.

See Morice v. Bishop of Durham, 9 Ves. 399 (1804), 10 Ves. 522 (1805). See also Chapter X. Resulting Trusts.

NOTE 1—In a few cases trusts for general non-charitable purposes are held valid on the theory that if the transferee is authorized or directed to apply the property for such purposes he has a power to so apply it. See Rest. § 123, Comment (a). See also The Honorary Trust, Chapter VI.

NOTE 2—If property is transferred and the transferor manifests an intention that it be disposed of in any manner the trustee may choose the gift is one of a beneficial interest and no trust is created. The key query is: Did the transferor *intend to create a trust?* See Rest. §§ 26, 125. See also Chapter VII. Creation Modification and Termination of Trusts.

Case 88   *Uncertainty of beneficiaries does not invalidate charitable trust*

D died leaving a will giving her residuary estate to T to be used by him at his discretion for religious and educational purposes. The heirs at law of D have brought an action to hold the residuary clause invalid because the beneficiaries of the purported charitable trust are so uncertain that they cannot with certainty be ascertained. Is the trust invalid?

Answer. *No. A gift for religious and educational purposes is a gift for charitable purposes. That the beneficiaries of a charitable trust are indefinite does not invalidate it since a trust is not a charitable trust where all the beneficiaries are definitely ascertained. By the weight of authority a trust provision which gives to the trustee discretion in applying trust property to specified charitable purposes is valid. While a court cannot specify the charities to be selected it can compel the trustee to exercise that discretion and may restrain a diversion or threatened diversion from the religious and educational purposes. In this case the devise to be used in the trustee's discretion for religious and educational purposes created a valid charitable trust. The beneficiaries are sufficiently certain when the trust is for educational purposes and provides that the individuals to benefit therefrom are to be selected in the discretion of a named trustee who is ready, able and willing to act. When so selected such purposes become fixed and definite. Religious and educational purposes are the very essence of a charitable trust. Such a provision is valid even though the instrument creating the trust does not limit in any way the possible charitable appointees.*

See *Yeager v. Johns*, 484 S.W.2d 211 (Mo.1972).   See also Rest.
§ 396.

Trust for the benefit of school children in certain grades is not a   **Case 89**
charitable trust

T died leaving his entire estate to Bank in trust with instructions that
the trustee should invest and reinvest the principal, collect the income and pay the net income on the last school day of each calendar
year before Easter and before Christmas equally to the children in
the first, second and third grades of the city's elementary school, such
gift to be used by each child in the furtherance of his or her obtainment
of an education. Does the will create a charitable trust?

Answer.   No.   The question presented in this case is whether T's
dominant intent was charitable or merely benevolent.   If the disposition is only benevolent, though meritorious and generous the
trust is a private and not a charitable trust and is invalid because it
violates the rule against perpetuities.   In order to create a charitable
trust the settlor must manifest an intention to benefit charity.   Charitable purposes include the relief of poverty, the advancement of
education, the advancement of religion, the promotion of health,
governmental or municipal purposes, and other purposes the accomplishment of which is beneficial to the community.   In the present
case it may be maintained that the trust is either for the advancement
of education or purposes the accomplishment of which is beneficial
to the community; however, in his disposition the testator mandated
that the trustee was to make cash payments to each individual child
just before the Easter and Christmas holidays.   The trustee has no
other duties.   Even though language is added that the payments are
to be used by each child in the furtherance of his or her obtainment
of an education the trustee is given no power, control or discretion
over the funds received by the child.   Nothing toward the advancement of education is attained by the ultimate performance by the
trustee of its full duty.   It therefore appears that testator's dominant
intent is not to create an educational trust but to bestow upon the
children gifts that would bring them happiness on two holidays.   Nor
can it be said that the gifts to the children promote public benefit in
that the income is to be paid without regard to whether the recipients
are poor or in need.   It is, in fact, a mere benevolence and may not
be upheld as charitable.   Payment to the children will bring them
pleasure and happiness and would cause them to think of their ben-
efactor with gratitude and thanksgiving.   "Laudable, generous and
praiseworthy though it may be it is not for the relief of the poor or
needy nor does it otherwise so benefit or advance the social interest
of the community as to justify its continuance in perpetuity as a
charitable trust."

See *Shenandoah Vall. Nat'l Bank of Winchester v. Taylor, 192 Va. 135, 63 S.W.2d 786 (1951).*

TRUSTS FOR BOTH CHARITABLE AND NON-CHARITABLE PURPOSES

1. A trust for both charitable and non-charitable purposes will fail if the two are inseparable.

   e.g. S bequeaths $100,000 to T "to hold in trust for the benefit of all the schools in City X". P is the residuary legatee. Some schools in City X are public and charitable institutions and some are private and operated for profit. S has not indicated how much of the $100,000 may be used for the public schools and how much may be used for the private schools. The valid part being inseparable from the invalid part the whole must fail as a charitable trust and T holds in resulting trust for P.

2. If the primary purpose of the trust is charitable and the whole of the corpus may be applied to such charitable objects unless the trustee chooses to apply it to non-charitable objects, a valid charitable trust is created. Since the power to apply to non-charitable objects is invalid, the trustee must apply the entire property to the intended charitable purpose.

3. If a trust has both charitable and non-charitable purposes and it is possible to determine the maximum amount which could be used for non-charitable purposes, the trust fails only to that amount and the remainder is a valid charitable trust.

4. If a number of purposes are specified for a trust some non-charitable and some charitable, the court may direct a division of the trust into as many equal shares as there are trust objects. The shares for charitable objects then create a valid charitable trust; the shares for non-charitable objects fail.

   e.g. S bequeaths to T $10,000 for the following purposes: (a) to pay the hospital bills of children who become infected with rabies, and (b) to spread rabies among dogs and create a scourge on the people of the Town of X; $5,000 to be used for each purpose. The trust for purpose (a) is charitable and will be enforced. The trust purpose in (b) is vicious and injurious to mankind and that part of the trust will fail and T will hold the $5,000 for that purpose in resulting trust for S's statutory heir or residuary legatee.

   See generally Bogert, pp. 240–243; Rest. § 398; and Scott, § 398.

CHARITABLE TRUSTS DISTINGUISHED FROM HONORARY TRUSTS

1. Trusts for saying masses are generally held valid as charitable but in some jurisdictions, particularly where the trust is for the purpose of having masses said for the soul of the settlor, such trusts are held to be private trusts which fail for want of a beneficiary.

Where this is so they may be upheld as honorary trusts. See *Honorary Trusts*, above.

2. A trust for the erection of monuments to the testator or his family is usually private and may only be upheld as an honorary trust. If, however, the monument is to recognize an individual who has performed great service to the public, it may be charitable.

3. Trusts for the care of cemetery plots are usually not charitable and must be sustained either as honorary trusts or under special statutes. Trusts for the maintenance of a public cemetery, however, may be charitable.

4. Trusts for the benefit of specific animals are private and fail for the lack of a beneficiary. They may be upheld as honorary trusts. See also *The Honorary Trust*, Chapter VI, above.

See generally Bogert, pp. 125, 220–223; Clark, p. 626; Rest. § 371g; and Scott, § 371.5.

1. A charitable trust may last for an indefinite or unlimited period.

2. In a private trust the beneficiary named or designated is the proper person to enforce the trust. By contrast, in a charitable trust the Attorney General of the State, representing the public, is the proper person to enforce such trust.

ENFORCEMENT AND DURATION OF CHARITABLE TRUSTS

3. A suit for the enforcement of a charitable trust cannot be maintained by:

   (a) the settlor,

   (b) the settlor's heirs or personal representatives,

   (c) members of the general public, or

   (d) possible beneficiaries, not identifiable as being entitled to a benefit under the trust.

   e.g. A leaves property in trust for the poor children of Cleveland. No particular poor child may enforce the trust. See number 4, below.

4. In addition to the Attorney General, those who may have a right to enforce the charitable trust are:

   (a) particular persons entitled to receive a benefit under the trust,

   e.g. A leaves his home in trust to be used as a residence for the Dean of the Yale Law School. The Dean of the Law School, for the time being, may enforce the trust.

   (b) members of an unincorporated association or a small class for whose benefit the trust is created, e.g.   A leaves property in trust for the benefit of the Sunlight Chapter of the Daughters of World War II Veterans.   Any member of the chapter may maintain a suit to enforce the trust on behalf of himself and of the other members.

　(c) co-trustees.

NOTE—The modern trend is to enlarge the group who may enforce the trust.   A recent Wisconsin statute gives standing to established charitable entities to which principal or income of the trust is to be paid to the settlor and co-trustees.   In a few cases a member of a class of potential beneficiaries has been allowed to bring an action on behalf of the whole class.   See Wis.Stat.Ann. § 701.10.

5. Under the Doctrine of Deviation (which is also applicable to private trusts) a trustee may deviate from a term of a charitable trust if compliance is impossible; or, due to circumstances not foreseen by the settlor, compliance would impair accomplishment of the purposes of the trust.   See Case 122, below.

6. The doctrine of deviation is to be distinguished from the doctrine of Cy Pres, below, in that it has to do with the methods of accomplishing the trust purposes whereas, the doctrine of Cy Pres involves devoting the trust property to different purposes.

7. Many jurisdictions place limitations on charitable trusts in the form of statutes of Mortmain.   See Chapter II, *Gifts to Charity*, above.

8. A charitable trust will generally not fail for want of a trustee.   If the person named as trustee is unable or unwilling to serve in that capacity, the court will appoint a successor.

9. If the duties of the trustee are personal to a particular trustee, and that trustee dies or refuses to serve the trust will fail.

e.g.   D dies leaving $300,000. to T in trust for the benefit of such charity as T and D shall select.   If T is dead at the time of D's death the trust will fail since only T could make the selection.

See generally Bogert, pp. 557–560; Clark, p. 647; Palmer, pp. 530–531; Rest. §§ 381, 391; and Scott, §§ 381, 391.

THE DOCTRINE OF CY PRES

1. If a settlor establishes a trust for a charitable purpose and evinces both a general intent that the trust fund shall be used for charitable purposes in any event and an intent to apply the fund for particular charities, and it becomes impossible or impracticable to apply the fund to the particular charities named, then the equity court may order it applied to another charity "as near as may be" to the particular ones designated by the settlor. This is the doctrine of judicial cy pres and is applied *only* in charitable trusts.

2. At common law there was "prerogative" cy pres in addition to judicial cy pres. This doctrine allowed the crown to apply the property of a charitable trust which failed to any other charitable purpose it might select regardless of how close it was to the settlor's specific purpose. This doctrine is not accepted in the U.S.

3. In prerogative cy pres it is not necessary that there be a finding of general charitable intent or that the property be applied to a purpose like the particular one designated by the settlor. Both are necessary for judicial cy pres.

4. The modern trend in judicial cy pres is to expand the ability of the court to choose among several schemes and not be limited to the one most like that designated by the settlor.

5. If property is given in trust to be applied to a particular charitable purpose and it is provided in the trust that the trust is to terminate if the purpose fails cy pres will not be applied. The fact that the settlor specifies that the property is to be used for the specific purpose "forever" or "upon condition" it be applied for such purpose will not preclude the use of cy pres although it may be evidence of the settlor's specific intention.

6. Where the specific trust purposes have failed and the court finds a general charitable intent the court usually directs a plan be presented for application of the trust property within the settlor's general charitable intent. In choosing a plan the court will consider the language of the trust as well as other circumstances to attempt to achieve the probable choice of the settlor.

   CAVEAT—If the court does not find a general charitable intent, then a resulting trust in favor of the settlor or settlor's heirs will be raised. See *Resulting Trusts—General Principles*, Chapter X, below.

7. Cy pres may be ordered without the consent of either the settlor, if living, or the trustee.

8. Where the charitable purpose to which trust property is to be applied is accomplished with a surplus remaining the court will usually direct the surplus to be applied to a charitable purpose which fails within the settlor's general intent.

9. Frequent causes for failure of specific charitable purposes are:

   (a) amount of property insufficient for the purpose,

   (b) specific purpose already accomplished,

   (c) third person whose consent is necessary refuses to give it, e.g.   A gift of a historical house in trust to be open to the public if the town consents to maintain it and the town refuses consent, will fail as to the specific charitable purpose.

(d) useless purpose,

(e) illegality,

(f) gift to a corporation which is incapable of taking and holding as a trust beneficiary,

(g) where specific site is impracticable, or

(h) particular purpose impractical due to changed circumstances.

e.g. A gift to establish an orphanage when orphanages are no longer considered a sociologically sound way of caring for parentless children, would be an impractical purpose due to changed circumstances.

See generally Bogert, pp. 523–531; Palmer, pp. 550–552, 555–556; Rest. §§ 395–400; Ritchie, pp. 629–631, 664; and Scott, §§ 395–400.

Case 90 *Gift for research to prove existence of soul is a gift for a charitable purpose*

D at his death left a will providing as follows: "This is my first and only will and is dated the second day in January 1946. I have no heirs have not been married in my life, after all my funeral expenses have been paid and #100. (sic) one hundred dollars to some preacher of the gospial (sic) to say farewell at my grave and sell all my property which is all in cash and stocks with E. F. Hutton Co. Phoenix some in safety box, and have this balance money to go in a research or some scientific proof of a soul of the human body which leaves at death I think in time their (sic) can be a Photograph of soul leaving the human at death."   Was a charitable trust created by the residuary provision of the will?

Answer. Yes.   A charitable trust is a "fiduciary relationship" with respect to property arising as a result of a manifestation of an intention to create it, and subjecting the person by whom the property is held to equitable duties to deal with property for a charitable purpose.   Whereas the settlor must manifest an intention to create a charitable trust, it is not necessary that any particular words or conduct be manifest to create a trust and it is possible to establish a trust as D did here without using the words "trust" or "trustee". Where the testator manifests the intention to create a charitable trust and no trustee is named, the trust will not fail for lack of a trustee; the court will appoint a trustee.   The purposes expressed by the testator are charitable in that they are to encourage scientific research *into new realms, which encourages the advancement of knowledge which is of benefit to the community.*

Answer. In re Estate of Kidd, 12 Ariz.App. 58, 467 P.2d 770 (1970).

Trust to perform public function on a racially segregated basis   Case 91
violative of equal protection clause of U.S. Constitution

In 1911 United States Senator Bacon of Georgia executed a will devising his estate to the mayor and council of the City of Macon. A portion was to be used as a park for White persons only, stating in the will that while he had only the kindest feeling for Negroes he was of the opinion that "in their social relations the two races (White and Negro) should be forever separate." The city kept the park segregated for a number of years but in time let all races use it. Individual members of the Board of Managers then brought a suit asking that the city be removed as trustee. The city resigned as trustee and asked that a new trustee be appointed since it could not legally enforce racial segregation in a public facility. Several Black citizens of Georgia intervened asking that the court refuse to appoint private trustees. Heirs of the Senator also intervened asking for a reversion of the trust property if the park cannot be operated as set out in Senator Bacon's will. (a) Can the court allow the city to resign and appoint private trustees to operate the park on a segregated basis? (b) If the park cannot be operated on a segregated basis so as to carry out the specific intent of the testator, are the testator's heirs entitled to the property?

Answer. (a) No; (b) Yes. The Equal Protection Clause of the Fourteenth Amendment forbids any form of state sponsored racial inequality. The city cannot act as a trustee under a private will which fosters racial segregation. Even if the court were to appoint new trustees, if the operation of the park has become so entwined with the governmental function that the new trustees would be performing governmental activities, the court cannot allow private persons to perform them on a segregated basis without violating the Constitution. In the circumstances after many years of city control the character the park had acquired as a public facility is not dissipated by the appointment of private trustees. Moreover, the service rendered even by a private park is public in nature and is in the public domain and the courts cannot aid private parties to perform segregated acts.

Since the park cannot be operated on a segregated basis the trust will fail and the trustees will be holding as a resulting trust for the owners of the reversion unless by applying the Doctrine of Cy Pres the Court will strike the racial restrictions and open the park to all on a non-segregated basis. The application of the Doctrine of Cy

*Pres is a question of state law and the United States Supreme Court
cannot overturn its application by the State Court to a particular case
unless it finds either that the state law is not racially neutral or that
the state judges are motivated by racial prejudice.   The state law
will only apply the Doctrine of Cy Pres where the testator had a more
general charitable intent than the accomplishment of the particular
purpose.   Where from the language of the will the state court con-
cludes that the testator's charitable intent is not general but extends
only to the establishment of a segregated park for the benefit of White
people only Cy Pres cannot be used.   The trust fails therefore as
being one for an illegal purpose and the reversion goes to the testator's
heirs.*

See Evans v. Newton, 382 U.S. 296, 86 S.Ct. 486, 15 L.Ed.2d 373
(1966) and Evans v. Abney, 396 U.S. 435, 90 S.Ct. 628, 24 L.Ed.2d
634 (1970).

NOTE—The validity of a private charitable trust which discriminates against a group on a basis which is contrary to public policy
still is not clear.   If the trustee chooses not to abide by the discrim-
inatory restrictions the doctrine of Shelley v. Kraemer, 334 U.S. 1, 68
S.Ct. 836, 92 L.Ed. 1161 (1948), which held that courts of equity will
not enforce racially restrictive covenants, may apply to make such
trusts unenforceable.   This appears to be applicable particularly to
the enforcement of charitable trusts where not only must the courts
enforce the trust but also a state official is charged with the duty of
enforcement.   See Commonwealth v. Brown, 392 F.2d 120 (3d Cir.
1968), cert. den. 391 U.S. 921 (1968);   Coffee v. William Marsh Rice
University, 408 S.W.2d 269 (Tex.Civ.App.1966);   Sweet Briar Institute v. Button, 280 F.Supp. 312 (W.D.Va.1967).

Case 92   *Cy pres applicable where specific charitable purpose made
impractical by change of circumstance where general charitable
intent present*

*Testator died in 1861 leaving $10,000 to certain trustees in trust to
use in their discretion for the preparation of books, giving of lectures
and other means to create a sentiment to put an end to Negro slavery
in this country.   By the time the estate was settled the Thirteenth
Amendment to the U.S. Constitution abolishing slavery had been
adopted.   Testator's heirs claim that the bequest cannot be carried
out since slavery has been abolished.   Does the trust fail its purpose
having been accomplished?*

Answer. No.   Under the Doctrine of Cy Pres if property is given
in trust for a specified charitable purpose and afterwards by change
of circumstances the scheme of the testator becomes impracticable,
if the testator's charitable purpose is general, the fund does not go

to testator's heirs as a resulting trust but is to be applied by a court exercising equitable jurisdiction as near the testator's directions as possible to carry out his general charitable intent. "The charitable bequests of . . . [Testator] cannot . . . be regarded as so restricted in their objects or so limited in point of time as to have been terminated and destroyed by the abolition of slavery in the United States. . . . Neither the immediate purpose of the testator—the moral education of the people; nor his ultimate object— to better the condition of the African race in this country; has been fully accomplished by the abolition of slavery. . . ." The court will direct the trustees to submit a scheme which will carry out the general charitable intent and purpose of the testator as nearly as possible.

Jackson v. Phillips, 96 Mass. (14 Allen) 539 (1867).

IX

LIMITATIONS ON CREATION AND DURATION OF INTERESTS IN TRUSTS

Summary Outline

THE RULE AGAINST PERPETUITIES

1. The Rule Against Perpetuities, where in effect, applies to both legal and equitable interests created in trust.

2. The common law rule may be stated: "No interest is good unless it must vest, if at all, not later than twenty-one years after some life in being at the date of the creation of the interest." Gray Rule Against Perpetuities, p. 191 (4th Ed. 1942).

3. The rule is directed entirely against remoteness of *vesting, i.e* definite identification of the person who owns the interest. The sole tests is: Must the interest vest, or fail, within the period of the Rule.

4. Any interest which may remain contingent beyond the period of the rule is invalid.

5. Lives in being are any person(s) identifiable with the disposition. Their lives must span *both* the creation of the interest and the vesting thereof.

   e.g. By will A leaves property in trust to T to hold for the benefit of A's children during their lives and on the death of the last survivor of A's children, to distribute the principal to A's grandchildren then living. At A's death he has three children living, C_1, C_2, and C_3. It is certain that the remainder to the grandchildren will vest at the death of one of the three whose life will span both the time of the creation of the interest (A's death) and the vesting of the interest (his own death). It is unnecessary to determine whether it will be C_1, C_2, or C_3.

6. The Rule Against Perpetuities only applies to *contingent* interests created in *transferees, i.e.* contingent remainders and executory interests.

7. The Rule does not apply to interests created in transferors, *i.e.* a reversion, a possibility of reverter, right of re-entry for condition broken.

8. In a charitable trust, a gift over from a first charity to a second charity on a condition precedent is not void by reason of the fact that the condition may not occur without the period of the Rule. This is an exception to the Rule Against Perpetuities.

   e.g. A leaves property to T in trust to pay the income therefrom to St. Paul's Church so long as it conducts its regular services in accordance with the Book of Common Prayer, 1789 Version; and if at any time it should discontinue to so conduct its services, then to St. James Church. This is valid.

9. All other charitable interests are subject to the Rule.

   (a) Property transferred to a non-charity and then over to a charity on a remote contingency; the remote gift is void.

e.g. A leaves property in trust to hold for Mary's children for life and on the death of Mary's last surviving child to Mary's female grandchildren then living, if no female grandchild is living then to the Cathedral School for Girls. Mary is living at the time of A's death. The gift to the Cathedral School is void.

(b) Property transferred to a charity and then over to a non-charity on a remote contingency.

e.g. A leaves property to T in trust to pay the income to St. Paul's Church so long as it conducts its regular services in accordance with the Book of Common Prayer, 1789 Version; and if at any time it should discontinue to so conduct its services to Robert or Robert's heirs then living. The gift over is void because it may remain contingent for a period longer than the Rule Against Perpetuities. It makes no difference that it is preceded by a gift to charity.

(c) Property transferred to a charity on a remote contingency without a prior gift.

e.g. A leaves property to T in trust to hold for the benefit of St. Paul's Church if it should adopt a new liturgy proposed by the convention of 1970. The gift is void. The contingency may not occur within the period of the Rule. There is no exception for a gift to charity under such circumstances.

10. In recent years many states have adopted legislation designed to eliminate the harsh effect of the common law Rule Against Perpetuities. These are generally of two types:

(a) *Wait and See*—The court decides the validity of future estates only at the time the prior estate terminates and then tests whether the interest violates the rule by the events which have actually happened rather than possibilities existing at the time the interest was created. See e.g. Merchant's Nat'l Bank v. Curtis, 98 N.H. 225, 97 A.2d 207 (1953).

(b) *Cy Pres*—Allows the court to reform the interest within the limits of the Rule to approximate most closely the intention of the creator of the interest.

NOTE—The *Wait and See* and *Cy Pres* approaches have been adopted by the American Law Institute as to the traditional Rule Against Perpetuities. See Restatement, Second, Property §§ 104–105 (Tent.Draft No 2, 1979). See also Leach, Perpetuities: The Nutshell Revisited, 78 Harv.L.Rev. 973 (1965). See generally Smith's Review, Real and Personal Property, Conveyancing and Future Interests Chapter XV. Future Interests; Bogert, pp. 183–186, 252–255; Clark, pp. 828–835, 885–889; Rest. §§ 62(l)(,(m), 401; Ritchie, pp. 1028–1034, 1045–1050, 1099–1101; Simes, pp. 263–282, 296–297; and Scott §§ 62.10, 401.

Case 93 *In determining whether or not a disposition violates the Rule Against Perpetuities all remote possibilities must be taken into consideration.*

D died and provided in his will "I give One Thousand Dollars which shall be placed out at interest during the life of my wife, W, which interest I give her during her life and at her death I give the said $1,000 to my niece, M, and the issue of her body lawfully begotten and to be begotten and in default of such issue I give the said $1,000 to be equally divided between the daughters then living of my relatives J and his wife, E." At the time of the death of the testator J and E were living but of a very advanced age. They had four daughters and no sons. M was unmarried and of the age of 40 and W was dead. Is the gift to the daughters of J and E valid?

> ***Answer.*** *No. The gift of the daughters of J and E is void by reason of the Rule Against Perpetuities as being too remote. The gift is to take effect on the general failure of the issue of M and by its terms the gift to the daughters of J and E is not confined to daughters living at the death of D. Nor can it be assumed that J and E although of an advanced age will have no other children. The determination must be made at the time of the creation of the interest not on events that actually happen. As the limitation stands it may take in afterborn daughters. In that they may be included there is a possibility that it will vest too remotely in that J and E might have children born ten years after D's death and then M might have issue which fails fifty years afterwards, in which case the Rule Against Perpetuities would be violated.*

See Jee v. Audley, 1 Cox 324, 29 Eng.Rep. 1186 (Chancery, 1787).

RULE AGAINST THE SUSPENSION OF THE POWER OF ALIENATION

1. Some states have adopted provisions invalidating any attempt to suspend the power to alienate property for more than a specified period, e.g. two lives in being. The purpose of such provisions is to facilitate the transfer of property.

2. Trusts may offend the rule against suspending alienation if:

   (a) the trustee is prohibited from selling the property, either by reason of the terms of the trust instrument or by reason of having no implied power to sell the property, for a specified period longer than the period of the rule, or

   (b) the beneficiary of a spendthrift trust is restrained from alienating his interest for longer than the period of the rule.

See generally Bogert, pp. 187–190, 255–257; Clark, p. 830; Rest. § 62(p); Ritchie, pp. 1082–1086; Simes, pp. 237–303; and Scott, §§ 62.12.

Where trustee has power to sell trust property, will not violate   Case 94
rule against suspension of the power of alienation

Testatrix' will contained the following provisions: "The remainder of my estate is then to be held in trust until such time as the youngest of my great nephews and nieces is fifty (50) years old. The interest from it is to be divided among them every year. At the time the youngest great nephew or niece is fifty years old the residue of my estate is to be divided among them all share and share alike." At the time of her death Testatrix had two nephews living, one had five children and one had two children. The testatrix left both real and personal property. A state statute provided that any suspension of the absolute power of alienation with respect to property for a longer period than lives in being and thirty years was void. The will contained no express power of sale. Testatrix' nephews (and heirs at law) contend that the trust is invalid since it may last longer than the period of the statute in that children may be born after the death of testatrix, which would be included as beneficiaries of the trust. Are the nephews entitled to the property?

Answer. No. As to the personal property the direction to divide the interest from the trust annually shows that testatrix intended the trust to be productive. This requires investment of the trust res and the power to shift investments by purchase and sale as conditions alter. With respect to realty, the more modern rule is that "the inference is that the trustee has a power to sell land unless it appears from the language of the trust instrument as interpreted in the light of all the circumstances that the settlor intended that the land should be retained in the trust." Since testatrix did not distinguish between realty and personalty and clearly intended the res to be productive, there is no reason to say testatrix wished to withhold power of sale from realty. The trustee therefore has an implied power to sell both the realty and personalty in the estate. Since the trustee may sell the property, there is no suspension of the power of alienation to offend the statute.

See *Estate of Walker*, 258 Wis. 65, 45 N.W.2d 94 (1950).

1. Rules governing the duration of trusts and accumulations are to be distinguished from the Rule Against Perpetuities which governs only the vesting of interests not their duration.   **THE DURATION OF TRUSTS AND ACCUMULATIONS**

   e.g. A leaves property in trust to pay the income to B and his successors for fifty years and then to distribute the remainder to St. Paul's Church. All interests are vested so there is no violation of the Rule Against Perpetuities, but the trust may last longer than allowed by a statute restricting the duration to lives in being plus twenty-one years.

2. Some states have statutes limiting the duration of either:

   (a) all private trusts, or

   (b) certain types of trusts, *e.g.* voting trusts for corporate stock.

3. Where no statute is in effect the general rule is that private trusts are not limited in duration.

   NOTE—Some older cases have held as a matter of common law that the private trust is limited in duration to the Rule Against Perpetuities. This has been rejected in the more recent cases.

4. In the majority of jurisdictions honorary trusts are restricted in duration to the period of the Rule Against Perpetuities.

5. Charitable trusts are not limited to the duration of the rule; they may last forever.

6. An accumulation trust is one in which the trustee is directed to retain all or part of the trust property and add it to trust principal for distribution at some future time.

7. A few states have statutes with special rules limiting the duration of provisions for accumulations in private trusts. Some of these statutes forbid accumulations which exceed the period of the Rule Against Perpetuities; others are more restrictive.

   e.g. Legislation passed by English Parliament in 1800 restricted accumulations to one of four periods:

   (a) the life of the donor,

   (b) twenty-one years after the donor's death,

   (c) the minorities of persons living at the donor's death, or

   (d) minorities of persons entitled to income in the absence of a provision for accumulation.

8. In states where there are no statutes, most courts have held that provisions for accumulation in private trusts which exceed the period of the Rule Against Perpetuities are invalid.

9. Courts often hold the direction to accumulate invalid only to the excess time over the maximum period of allowed accumulation.

   See gnerally Bogert, pp. 190–198; 255–260; Clark, pp. 863–865; Rest. §§ 62(n), (t), 365, 401 (k); Ritchie pp. 1086–1087; Simes, pp. 321–328; and Scott, §§ 62.11, 401.9.

Case 95 *Accumulations valid if limited to the period of the Rule Against Perpetuities*

Testator provided by the terms of his will for a testamentary trust. The trustee was directed to accumulate income for 21 years after the *death of the survivor of his nieces Ruth and Esther at which time the trust was to cease and the principal and accumulations be divided into five parts and be distributed to the issue of each Ruth and Esther and to three others or their issue. The trustee asked the court for instructions on three issues: (1) Does the future interest created violate the Rule Against Perpetuities? (2) Does the will creating future interest violate the statutory provision limiting the period for which the power of alienation may be suspended to lives in being plus twenty-one years because the takers may be infants who would not have capacity to alienate the property? (3) Is the provision that income be accumulated for lives in being plus twenty-one years valid as unreasonable in the light of the size of the estate ($1,600,000) and the length of time involved (estimated at 55 years)? The lower court answered no to each of the questions propounded. Was it correct in so answering?*

Answer. *(1) Yes. (2) Yes. (3) No. (1) As to the question of whether or not the interests violate the Rule Against Perpetuities all interests will clearly vest twenty-one years after the death of either Ruth or Esther and so are clearly within the rule. (2) As to the question of suspension of power of alienation the period used in the disposition is co-extensive with the statutory period allowing suspension. The fact that some of the takers may be minors who could not alienate does not extend the period of suspension. Inability to alienate due to the taker's legal status does not countervene the alienation statute. (3) As to the question of accumulations, it is generally assumed that the common law permitted accumulations for lives in being plus 21 years. Where other periods have been adopted it has been due to legislative action not a court made rule. It is impractical for a court to adopt a new rule for it has no guidelines as to amount to be allowed, property to which the rule should apply, length of period to adopt, whether the whole accumulation should be invalid or only excess, or exceptions to be included. Therefore, the accumulation provision being within the accepted common law period is valid.*

See Gertman v. Burdick, 75 U.S.App.D.C. 48, 123 F.2d 924, cert. den. 315 U.S. 824, 62 S.Ct. 917, 86 L.Ed. 1220 (1942).

NOTE—The modern trend is for states which have adopted special statutes relative to accumulation to abandon them in favor of the period allowed for the vesting of estates. See Ritchie, p. 1098.

Accumulation of income for an unreasonable period of time which is merely incidental to a primary charitable purpose is invalid   **Case 96**

D died leaving the residuary of his estate in trust with instructions to his trustee to invest and reinvest the principal, collect the income and accumulate and pay over the net income for the use of Masonic Homes for the Ages. He further directed that the income be distributed as follows: At the expiration of twenty years from the date of his death and every twenty years thereafter, fifty percent of the net income received to date was to be distributed to the beneficiary and the remainder of the net income was to be added to principal and invested and reinvested therewith; 220 years from the date of his death the percentage of income payable was to be increased to 75% with 25% added to the principal of the trust and invested and reinvested. The manner of distribution was to continue every 20 years until 400 years from the date of his death when the trust was to terminate and the principal be paid over to the beneficiary. The trustee has filed a petition to deviate from the terms of the trust asserting that the provision for accumulation of income is unreasonable and illegal and asked for the Court to allow an annual distribution of income. Can the Court allow the deviation?

Answer. Yes. The trust in question is charitable and the general rule is that statutory provisions under which accumulations of income are declared void does not apply to accumulations of income for charitable purposes. This rule however, does not allow accumulations which are absurd, impossible of execution or unreasonable. The will supplies no indication of a purpose for the 400 year accumulation provision; nor does it reveal any particular plan or need for retaining accumulation over such an extended period of time; nor does the distribution period of accumulation for twenty years have any apparent practical or reasonable purpose. It is clear, however, that the plan was merely incidental to the primary charitable intention of D to create a source in the nature of an endowment fund for the Masonic Homes. The testator's primary charitable intention is therefore best attained by making available to the beneficiary the income of the trust on a current basis.

See Estate of James, 414 Pa. 80, 199 A.2d 275 (1964).

X | RESULTING TRUSTS

Summary Outline

RESULTING TRUSTS—GENERAL PRINCIPLES

1. A resulting trust arises in situations in which: (a) property is disposed of (b) under circumstances which raise an *unrebutted* inference (c) that the transferor does not intend the transferee to have the beneficial interest therein, and (d) such beneficial interest is not disposed of otherwise.   In such cases the person holding the beneficial interest is not entitled to it so the interest not being otherwise disposed of "results" to the transferor.   The person having legal title holds it in a "resulting trust" for such transferor.

2. The resulting trust attempts to do with the property what it is presumed the transferor would have wanted if he had anticipated the situation.   See Rest. Chap. 12, Introductory Note.

3. Every resulting trust is like an express private trust, except that the intention is *inferred* from the circumstances instead of being *expressed*, and has the four elements:

   (a) an inferred intention to create the trust,

   (b) a trustee,

   (c) a trust res, and

   (d) a beneficiary.

4. A resulting trust is distinguished from a constructive trust in that a constructive trust is not based on intent whereas a resulting trust is based on presumed or implied intent.

   See Chapter XI.   Constructive Trusts.

5. A resulting trust arises in three general situations:

   (a) where an express trust fails;

   e.g.   S conveys Blackacre to T to hold in trust for C.   Without S's knowledge C has predeceased the conveyance to T.   The express trust fails for want of a beneficiary because the beneficiary is dead.   T holds Blackacre in resulting trust for the settlor, S.   See Rest. § 411.

   (b) where an express trust does not use all or exhaust the trust property;

   (i)   S transfers $100,000, in trust to pay Bonnie $1000 a month from principal during her life and makes no further disposition.   Bonnie dies after having received $25,000.   The trustee is holding the unexpended funds in a resulting trust for S.

   (ii) S conveys Blackacre to T in trust for the purpose of selling Blackacre and paying S's creditors in full, such creditors consisting of X, Y and Z.   S owes X, Y and Z each $1,000.   T sells Blackacre for $5,000.   After the creditors are paid in full, T still has in his hands $2,000 from the proceeds of the sale of Blackacre. T holds this $2,000 in resulting trust for S. See Rest. § 430.

(c) where property is purchased and paid for by one person and title is taken in the name of another, usually referred to as a purchase money resulting trust.

e.g. A, B and C each pays $1,000 to X for Blackacre and X is instructed to and makes the deed to T as grantee. T holds one third of Blackacre in resulting trust for A, one third for B and one third for C. This is true whether the payment be made in money, goods, credit or anything of value. See Rest. § 440.

6. A resulting trust is always a dry, naked or passive trust. The trustee has no active duty to perform except this: he is duty bound to transfer the legal title to the trust property to the beneficiary and the court should order him so to do.

7. The Statute of Frauds has no application to the creation of a resulting trust. Its existence can be proved by parol evidence showing the failure of an express trust, the performance of an express trust without exhausting the trust property, or that a conveyance has been made to one person and the payment therefor has been paid by another.

8. A transfer by the beneficiary of his equitable interest in land held in resulting trust must comply with the Statue of Frauds.

e.g. T holds Blackacre in resulting trust for S. S makes an oral agreement to sell his equitable interest in the land to P. P seeks specific performance and S sets up as a defense the Statute of Frauds. The defense is good. Such equitable title held by S is an interest in land requiring a writing signed by S to be enforceable. See Rest. § 407, Comment c.

9. A purchase money resulting trust may be extinguished by parol, but resulting trusts of land which arise from failure of an express trust or performance of an express trust without exhausting the trust property require for their extinguishment a compliance with the Statute of Frauds.

10. If a gratuitous transfer of property is made to a trustee and the express trust fails or it does not exhaust the trust property then the resulting trust is based on the theory that the grantor did not intend to give away his property except for the purpose for which the express trust was created.

e.g. S transfers Blackacre to T in trust for C. C disclaims any interest in the property. This causes failure of the express trust because there is no beneficiary. It is inferred that S intended to transfer his property only for C and therefore if C will not or does not take, then T holds in resulting trust for S. This express trust is created by a deed in writing, but the resulting trust is created by the inferred intention without compliance with the Statute of Frauds. See Rest. § 411.

See generally, Bogert, pp. 261–286; Clark, pp. 614–615; Palmer, p. 567; Rest. §§ 407, 411, 430, 440; Ritchie, pp. 516–524; Scott, §§ 404–406, 411, 413, 430, 440.

THE RESULTING TRUST—SPECIAL PROBLEMS

1. When a charitable trust fails, a resulting trust will be raised *only* if the Doctrine of Cy Pres is found not to apply. See *The Doctrine of Cy Pres.* Chapter VIII; Case 68, above.

2. If the settlor creates an express trust for an illegal purpose and it fails for this reason a resulting trust does not arise if the policy against giving relief to a person who has committed an alleged act outweighs the policy against unjust enrichment.

   e.g. if settlor conveys money to a trustee to defraud his creditors or the government.

3. The inference that a resulting trust arises where one person takes title and another pays the purchase price may be rebutted by showing the existence of an intention to the contrary.

   e.g. if A pays the purchase price of Blackacre to V and has title conveyed to B a resulting trust does not arise in A if:

   (a) A pays as a loan to B,

   (b) A pays in discharge of a debt to B,

   (c) A pays as a gift to B,

   (d) A pays in discharge of a debt to a third party, or

   (e) A pays as a loan to a third party.

   See Rest. §§ 444–453.

4. A resulting trust will not be raised in favor of a grantor who has been paid for the trust property.

   e.g. T wishes to establish a trust in Blackacre, which is owned by S, for T's son, C. T pays S $5,000 for Blackacre and has the deed made to "T in trust for C". C rejects the trust entirely which causes the express trust to fail. T holds Blackacre for his own benefit and not in resulting trust for S, because T has paid for the property and S has no right both to the $5,000 and to the equitable interest in the land.

5. A purchase money resulting trust does not arise if the person by whom the purchase price is paid manifests an intention that no resulting trust should arise.

6. If the payor of the consideration is the wife, child, or other natural object of the payor's bounty, the presumption is that a gift was intended. This presumption is rebutted by showing that no gift was intended.

e.g. H purchases Blackacre from V and has title conveyed to W, his wife, who orally agrees with H to hold the property in trust for their son, C. The presumption of gift can be rebutted by evidence of the oral trust and a resulting trust (or in some circumstances a constructive trust) arises. See Rest. § 442.

CAVEAT—Husbands and parents are not considered natural objects of bounty and no presumption of gift arises where property is conveyed to them.

7. If a part of the purchase price is paid by the resulting trust claimant he is presumed to have intended a trust in a proportionate part of the property to the extent of his contribution to the purchase price. See Rest. § 454.

8. If the person paying part of the purchase price of property which is conveyed to another orally agrees with the person taking title that he shall have a greater share than that proportionate to his contribution, a resulting trust only arises to the extent of his contribution.

e.g. A pays one-half the purchase price for a conveyance to B. A and B orally agree that A is to have a three-quarters undivided interest. B holds one-half the property on a resulting trust for A and one-half free of trust. The oral agreement is unenforceable because of the Statute of Frauds. See Rest. § 454, Comment i.

9. If the person paying part of the purchase price of property which is conveyed to another orally agrees with the person taking beneficial title that he shall have a *lesser* share than that proportionate to his contribution a resulting trust arises only to the extent of the intended fraction.

e.g. A pays one-half the purchase price for a conveyance to B. A and B orally agree that A is to have a one-quarter interest. B holds one-quarter on a resulting trust and three-quarters free of trust. The oral agreement may be used to rebut the presumption of resulting trust in part.

See Rest. § 454, Comment b.

10. If the person paying part of the purchase price of property which is conveyed to another agrees orally with the person taking title that he shall have a specified interest in the property, there is a resulting trust to the extent of the specific interest agreed upon.

e.g. Such a specified interest in property could be the northern one-half of the property, a life estate, the southern three-quarters, or the western one-quarter. Since the person making the part payment manifested an intent to acquire a different interest a resulting trust arises only to that extent. See Rest. § 454, Comment j.

11. A few jurisdictions hold that a resulting trust claimant must either pay the entire purchase price or a part that represents an *aliquot* share of the purchase price. "Aliquot share" has been held in different jurisdictions to mean:

   (a) capable of being divided into the total price without leaving a remainder, or

   (b) "a particular fraction of the whole as distinguished from a general contribution to the purchase money." Skehill v. Abbott, 184 Mass. 145, 68 N.E. 37 (1903).

   See Bogert, pp. 275–279.

12. A number of jurisdictions have abolished the purchase money resulting trust by statute, because it has the effect of rendering land titles uncertain.

   See generally, Bogert, pp. 266–286; Palmer, p. 568; Rest. §§ 442, 444–454; Ritchie, pp. 517–524; Scott, §§ 442, 444–460.

Case 97 *Presumption of gift to wife rebuttable by evidence of oral agreement*

H and W are husband and wife. H buys Blackacre from S and pays him $6,000 therefor and has S make the deed in favor of W as grantee. At the time of the conveyance H advised W orally that he was having the title put in her name for his convenience and W orally agreed to convey to H on his request. H held the deed in his possession and paid all taxes on the land and for improvements thereon. H attempts to establish a purchase money resulting trust in his favor. May he succeed?

Answer. Yes. When a husband pays for land and takes title in the name of his wife, there arises a presumption that a gift was intended. However, the presumption may be rebutted by evidence showing that no gift to W was intended. The agreement by W to hold the land for the benefit of H cannot be used to establish an express trust in favor of H because of the rules of the Statute of Frauds. The oral agreement can be shown to rebut the presumption of gift and since H paid the purchase money a purchase money resulting trust arises in H. The fact that the implied resulting trust which arises is the same as the oral express trust which cannot be established does not affect this result.

A resulting trust arises in favor of one furnishing purchase money where title is taken in the name of another

Case 98

H and W, husband and wife, purchase property for the sum of $5,500. H furnished $1,900 and W $1,100. They gave a note secured by a mortgage for an additional $2,500. Because of H's work at the time, he was unable to accompany his wife to the lawyer's office to have the deed made out so the deed was made out in her name alone. W said that the deed could be changed later to both their names. Subsequently, H furnished an additional $2,000 to pay off the mortgage and W furnished $500. H and W often talked about straightening out the deed but this was never done. W died. H claimed that W was a trustee for him to the extent of $3,900. Is H entitled to a part of the property proportionate to his contribution?

Answer. Yes. The rule is that where a person pays a part of the purchase money of property and title is taken in the name of another, the law will presume a trust arises for the benefit of the person who paid the money. Another presumption, however, is that where the parties are husband and wife, the husband furnishes the money with the intention that it should be gift to the wife. But this presumption is a rebuttable presumption and may be overcome by evidence to show that no gift was intended. From the facts given in the present case a jury would have been free to determine that the presumption of gift was overcome and that the husband was entitled to a fractional share of the property.

See Fox v. Shanley, 94 Conn. 350, 109 A. 249 (1920).

XI CONSTRUCTIVE TRUSTS

Summary Outline

A. Constructive Trusts—In General

   1. Nature of constructive trust as remedy

   2. Common applications

      a. title obtained by fraud, duress, mistake or undue influence

      b. murder of another to obtain victim's property

      c. obtaining property with notice of trust

      d. obtaining property by oral promise to hold in trust

CONSTRUCTIVE TRUSTS—IN GENERAL

1. The constructive trust is a remedy created by courts of equity to obtain title from a person who ought not to have it and force him to convey to the one who should have it.

2. The constructive trust is not "intent-enforcing". It is "fraud rectifying". See Bogert, pp. 287–290.

   NOTE—Compare the theory of a constructive trust with that of a resulting trust which enforces a presumption of intent. See *Resulting Trusts—General Principles*, Chapter X, above.

3. A constructive trust is created by the court's decree that a wrong-doer holds property as a constructive trustee.

   e.g. T by fraud induces C to convey C's Blackacre to T for no consideration at the time of the conveyance. T holds legal title to Blackacre and C has only a cause of action against T. T can cut off C's equity by selling and conveying Blackacre to a bona fide purchaser. If C sues T in equity prior to any such conveyance the equity court will enter a decree that T is holding title to Blackacre as a constructive trustee for C. The constructive trust comes into existence when the court of equity makes its decree. Because such a "construed" trust is always dry or passive, the court orders legal title transferred to the injured party.

4. A constructive trust may be decreed by a court having equitable jurisdiction in any situation where one person is holding title to property which rightfully belongs to another. Common instances are:

   (a) where title to property is obtained by fraud, duress, mistake or undue influence, see Case 24, above,

   (b) where a person murders another in order to inherit the victim's property.

   (c) where one takes property from a trustee with notice of the trust,

   (d) where a grantee obtains property by absolute deed on an oral promise he will hold in trust and the oral trust is voidable under the Statute of Frauds,

   (e) where a person obtains a gift by will or intestacy on oral promise to hold in trust for another, see number 10, below and

   (f) where one is holding property by reason of a breach of fiduciary duty.

5. Fraud or mistake may be the basis for a constructive trust.

   e.g. P agrees to sell and D agrees to buy Blackacre from P for $5,000. D pays the money and P executes a deed to D but by mistake describes both Whiteacre and Blackacre. Title to Whiteacre is then in D by mistake when it should have remained in P. Note three elements:

(a) title to Whiteacre is in D,

(b) if permitted to keep it, D will be unjustly enriched, and

(c) it is inequitable for D to retain title to Whiteacre.

On these facts P may have a decree in equity making D a constructive trustee of Whiteacre and ordering its reconveyance to P.

6. If a person murders his ancestor or testator and through such wrong receives title to property, the murderer holds the property in constructive trust for him who would otherwise take the property.

   e.g. S makes his will giving $10,000 U.S. Government bonds to T and the residue of his property to C. T murders S through which murder and the probate of S's will the title to the bonds comes to T. But T cannot profit by his own wrong. The legacy in favor of T will be treated as though it were revoked. T holds it in constructive trust for the residuary legatee. See Bogert, pp. 296–298.

   CAVEAT—There are many cases which hold to the contrary: e.g., that a murderer is not barred from inheriting from his victim except where by statute such limitation is imposed. See Bird v. Plunckett, 139 Conn. 491, 95 A.2d 71 (1953).

7. Where the trustee of an express trust wrongfully transfers the trust property to a third person who knows of the trust, such third person holds the property in constructive trust for the beneficiary of the express trust.

   e.g. T holds U.S. government bonds in trust for C and the terms of the trust prohibit T's disposing of such bonds. In breach of trust T transfers the bonds to X who knows about the trust but pays T full value for the bonds. C may in equity compel X to hold the bonds in constructive trust for C. The reason is that having taken with notice X is not a bona fide purchaser and it is inequitable for X to hold the bonds for himself as against C even though X paid full value for them. See *Tracing Trust Funds*, Chapter XIV, below.

8. Where property is conveyed to a person who orally promises to hold it in trust for a third person and later refuses to carry it out because the trust is voidable under the Statute of Frauds:

   (a) The *majority* rule is that a constructive trust will *not* be decreed either for the grantor or the intended beneficiary because to do so would circumvent the Statute of Frauds.

(b) Some jurisdictions hold *contra* and will enforce a constructive trust in favor of the intended beneficiary where the grantee would otherwise be unjustly enriched.   See Bogert, pp. 300–308.

9.   Exceptions are made to the traditional majority rule in number 8 above and a constructive trust will be decreed where:

(a) the grantee obtained the property by misrepresentation as to his intended performance of the trust, or

(b) if the grantee was in a confidential relationship with the grantor.   See Case 100, below.

NOTE—Many modern cases adopt the traditional minority view and do not require a showing of fraud or confidential relationship but only unjust enrichment.

10. Whenever a person obtains property by will or intestacy because the decedent in making a will or dying intestate relied upon his promise to hold the property in trust for another the heir holds it in constructive trust for the intended beneficiary.   The essential elements are:

(a) express or implied promise to hold in trust by the donee, and

(b) reliance by the decedent.

e.g.   D asks his brother T whether if he bequeaths Blackacre to him T will hold it in trust for their parents W and H and at the death of the survivor distribute it to all D's nephews and nieces, then living.   T agrees to do so.   A then executes a will and bequeaths Blackacre to T and dies.   T will be compelled to hold the property upon a constructive trust for W, H and nephews and nieces.   This is sometimes referred to as a secret trust.   See Rest. § 55.

CAVEAT—The above cites the position adopted by a majority of the cases and the Restatement, Second, Trusts.   Other courts have held it a violation of the Statute of Wills to raise a constructive trust in such cases.

11. If a fiduciary obtains property in a transaction with the person to whom he owes a fiduciary duty without full disclosure and utmost good faith he may be holding the property as a constructive trustee for such person.

e.g.   A director of a corporation purchases property from the corporation where he has knowledge it is to be appropriated for a highway which he does not disclose.   He will hold the property as a constructive trustee for the corporation.

12. A constructive trust cannot be based on a theft or a conversion for the reason that the thief or converter does not acquire title through his wrong.

> e.g.　D steals P's lumber.　P cannot sue D in equity to make him a constructive trustee because the theft cannot lodge the legal title to the property in D.　Such title is still in P and his remedy is in law in an action in replevin to get back the lumber in specie, or in trover for the value thereof.

> See genrally Bogert, pp. 287–318;　Clark, pp. 602, 607;　Palmer, pp. 481, 598–599;　Rest. §§ 44, 45, 55, 288, 291d, 320, 428, 438;　Ritchie, pp. 102, 529;　and Scott, §§ 44–45.4, 55–55.9, 461–552.

Parol evidence inadmissible to prove deed absolute intended as trust　　Case 99

P is the heir at law of D who died intestate.　Prior to his death D seriously wounded a man and fearing arrest and prosecution fled the country.　At the time he conveyed real property to his brother B who orally agreed to hold the property in trust for the use and benefit of D and his heirs.　Can P recover the property from B on a theory of constructive trust?

> ***Answer.***　*No.　In the absence of fraud or mistake parol evidence cannot be received to prove that a deed absolute on its face was given in trust for the benefit of the grantor or a third party.　The only fraud that can be shown in such circumstances is breach of the parol trust but the Statute of Frauds precludes establishment of the trust by parol.　A distinction must be made, "between fraud in the procuring of a conveyance and that which arises only from refusal to execute a parol trust or agreement, connected with a conveyance obtained without fraud".　In the latter circumstance the parol trust cannot be proven because of the provisions of the Statute of Frauds and therefore its breach cannot be shown.　In the former case one could show the fraud or the inducement for the conveyance.　In this case such fraud cannot be proved and P has no remedy.*

> See *Rasdall's Administrators v. Rasdall*, 9 Wis. 350 (1859);　*Rosen v. Rosen*, 384 Pa. 547, 121 A.2d 89 (1956).

Constructive trust imposed where parties in confidential relationship　　Case 100

D prior to her death placed title to Blackacre in the name of her eldest daughter C and the daugher's husband H.　It was orally understood that C and H were to hold the property for the benefit of all D's children.　After D's death her other children claim a part of the property by seeking to impose a constructive trust on C and H. Will they be able to do so?

Answer. Yes. The rule is well settled that an express oral trust cannot be engrafted on land conveyed by a deed absolute. The Statute of Frauds prevents the establishment of such trusts. Where, however, the owner of land transfers it to another inter vivos in trust for third parties but no writing is signed evidencing the trust, the grantee holds the property on a constructive trust for the third parties if the transferee procured the transfer by fraud or duress or the transferee was in a confidential relationship with the grantor. In the present case D and C were in a confidential relationship involving the confidence that grows out of a family member's trust of others in the family. Although C's promise to hold for the benefit of her brothers and sisters cannot be proved by oral evidence of her promise, equity will allow parol evidence of the trust to be offered—not to enforce the trust but to show the unjust enrichment arising out of the breach of confidence. Otherwise, C would be unjustly enriched by violating a confidence. The remedy of constructive trust is available whenever a person has procured title to property, real or personal under conditions which make it inequitable or unconscionable for him to keep such property and the circumstances giving rise to a constructive trust are always proved by parol or oral testimony. In this case, the oral evidence of W's promise is admissible to prevent the violation of her fiduciary relationship and unjust enrichment. W should be declared a constructive trustee of Blackacre and ordered to reconvey the property to H.

See *Masino v. Sechrest*, 268 Wis. 101, 66 N.W.2d 740 (1954).

PART THREE

PROBATE, ADMINISTRATION AND THE FIDUCIARY

XII PROBATE— DOMICILE AND JURISDICTION

Summary Outline

A. Jurisdiction in Probate Matters

   1. state in which decedent domiciled

   2. state in which decedent left property

B. Domicile in Probate Matters

   1. common law

   2. modern law

   3. types of domicile

C. Territorial Limitations on Powers of Personal Representatives

   1. primary or domicilary administration

   2. ancillary administration

D. Title of Personal Representatives

   1. personal property

   2. real property

E. Jurisdiction Over Trusts

   1. probate court

   2. court of general jurisdiction

   3. choice of law

1. An administrator may be appointed to administer a decedent's estate in any state in which:

   (a) the decedent was domiciled at the time of his death. See Domicile, below.

   (b) the decedent left any property, or

   (c) jurisdiction can be had over the person whose wrongful act caused the decedent's death, if such state has a statute permitting the administrator to sue such person in such state.

2. The will of a decedent may be proved and an executor appointed in the state of decedent's domicile at his death, *the domiciliary administrator*; or in any state where he left property, *the ancillary administrator* if the state is other than his domicile.

3. The duties of the administrator, domicilary or ancillary, are determined by the law of the place of his appointment.

4. Most states have special courts, usually called the probate courts, which have sole and exclusive jurisdiction over probate of wills, the granting of administration, appointment and supervision of the personal representative. Under the English law, various matters with respect to probate were vested in different courts, depending upon the type of property, nature of interest in the property, and status of the decedent. Probate courts were developed to consolidate all such matters in one court.

5. No probate court has jurisdiction to administer the estate of a person unless and until that person is actually dead and any proceeding which attempts to do so is a nullity and void.

   See generally Atkinson, pp. 29, 481–490; Clark, pp. 689–691; Palmer, p. 45; Ritchie, p. 284; and Stumberg, pp. 398–417.

1. Domicile is the place which is assigned to a person for certain legal purposes.

2. Domicile usually refers to a person's home if he has one, and if he has more than one residence it is usually the residence where he spends the most time.

3. At common law it was said that no person has more than one domicile—he always has one and never none.

4. Modern thinking recognizes that the term "domicile" is one that has a variety of functions. It may have as many meanings as it has fields of application.

   (a) In the famous *Dorrance* cases, two different states found that Dorrance, heir to the Campbell Soup fortune was domiciled there at his death for inheritance tax purposes, and thus each was able to impose an inheritance tax of approximately $17,000,000. These cases are seen by some as "irreconcilable," and as "holding" that Dorrance had two domiciles at the same time—one in New Jersey and one in Pennsylvania, thus exceeding the traditional rationale of "only one" domicile. More modern thinking, however, sees these cases as reconcilable for the reasons: (i) The facts in evidence were such that reasonable men could differ as to the conclusions to be drawn from them, (ii) The Standards applied in determining change of domicile were different in the two states, and this is constitutionally permissible, (iii) The first action was not res judicata in the second litigation because the parties were not the same, and (iv) Finally, some reconcile the cases on the "avarice or pig theory"—that is that both states wanted the $17,000,000. See In re Dorrance's Estate, 309 Pa. 151, 163 A. 303 (1932), and 115 N.J.Eq. 268, 170 A. 601 (1934).

(b) In Texas v. Florida, 306 U.S. 398, 59 S.Ct. 563, 83 L.Ed. 817 (1939) the U.S. Supreme Court *did* make a determination of domicile where four states had made tax claims based on domicile which *exceeded* the total of the $42 million estate.

5. There are three types of domicile:

(a) domicile of origin,

(b) domicile of choice, and

(c) domicile by operation of law.

6. Domicile of origin is that which is assigned by law to a person at birth.

7. Domicile of choice is a newly acquired domicile, acquired by one having capacity to make a selection of a new domicile. It is a change from one domicile to another.

8. Two essential elements must concur in point of time to establish a domicile of choice:

(a) the person exercising the choice must be physically present at the place selected as his new home, and

(b) he must have the intent to make that place his home presently.

e.g. D's domicile is New York. He moves to Arizona and takes up residence in a rented stationary house trailer with the intention either to live there indefinitely or without any present intention to live elsewhere. D is domiciled in Arizona. While D was enroute from New York to Arizona his domcile was still in New York. When he arrived within the borders of Arizona his domicile was still in New York. When he selected the physical trailer as his home and his intent to remain there concurred, at that instant his domicile was changed from New York to Arizona.

9. Domicile by operation of law occurs when the law assigns one a domicile by reason of legal status.

   (a) An illegitimate takes the domicile of its mother.

   (b) A wife's domicile is generally that of her husband. A wife living separate and apart from her husband has the power to establish her separate domicile regardless of whether she has a cause of action for divorce or is guilty of desertion.

10. The administration-in-chief of an estate should be in the county and state in which decedent was domiciled at his death.

11. A finding of domicile by the courts of one state is not binding upon courts of other states which may also find domicile and grant domiciliary letters. As a result each court administers the property within its own jurisdiction. See number 4, above.

   See generally Atkinson, pp. 594–602; Clark, pp. 651–652; and Rest. Conflict of Laws, 2d §§ 11–20, See also Smith's Review Conflict of Laws, Chapter II. Domicile.

Only actual death confers jurisdiction on probate court to issue letters of administration   Case 101

A statute in state X provided that one domiciled therein is deemed civilly dead if convicted of a felony and sentenced to a penitentiary in any state and is presumed to be dead if he absents himself and has not been heard from by relatives or friends for a period of seven years. T had been absent from state X for more than seven years and had not been heard from. In fact he had been sentenced to the penitentiary for life for murder in another state. D was granted letters of administration of T's estate in state X and completed proceedings in probate and distributed the property according to statute. Six months after his property was distributed T was pardoned and returned to his home in state X and sued D for trespass and conversion. May he recover?

   Answer. *Yes. Neither civil death nor presumption of death nor a finding by the probate court that a person is actually dead will confer jurisdiction on a probate court to issue letters of administration if, in fact, the person is alive. Actual death alone confers such jurisdiction. In this case T, in fact, was alive, the presumption of death notwithstanding. All probate proceedings involving T's prop-*

erty, therefore, were absolutely void for want of jurisdiction in the court. Every act which was done by D without lawful authority as to T's property made D a trespasser for which he is liable as a wrong-doer. Further, any statute which attempts to confer jurisdiction on a court to deal with property of a living person on the theory that he is dead when in fact he is alive and which gives no protection to the absentee, would take property without due process and is unconstitutional. However, such a statute drawn in the form of a statute of limitations would be valid.

See *Scott v. McNeal, 154 U.S. 34, 14 S.Ct. 1108, 38 L.Ed. 896 (1894).*

Case 102   *Proof of will condition precedent to title and right of possession*

T died testate bequeathing all of his personal property to X. Among the items of such personalty was a herd of sheep in the possession of D. Without probating the will X demanded the possession of the sheep from D which D refused whereupon X sued D in replevin and offered in evidence the unprobated will as evidence of his right to possession of the sheep. May X recover?

Answer. No. In the first place the unprobated will is not admissible in evidence for the reason that the probate court alone and exclusively has jurisdiction to determine the validity of the will. The courts of general jurisdiction, law and equity, will not receive in evidence as proof of title or right to possession an unprobated will. It is not always necessary that a will be probated in order for title to vest in a beneficiary but there can be no legal proof of that title without the will being first admitted to probate. In this case in order for X to prove his title and right of possession it is absolutely necessary that he first prove the will in the probate court. Even if he did prove the will and that he was a legatee thereunder, still he would have neither title nor right of possession to the sheep for the reason that an executor named in the will or an administrator with the will annexed would be appointed and qualify and would have both title and right of possession of the sheep as of the date of T's death. The rule therefore is this: probate of a will is absolutely necessary to prove title to personal property in a legatee under that will.

See *Champollion v. Corbin, 71 N.H. 78, 51 A. 674 (1901).*

NOTE—Likewise, for a devisee of real property under a will to prove his title he must first prove the will, See Atkinson, p. 505.

Case 103   *Appointment of administrator necessary to collect debts of intestate decedent*

T died intestate leaving two sons, X and Y, as his sole statutory heirs. D owed T on an open account the sum of $100 at T's death. There was no administration of T's estate.   X and Y joined as plaintiffs in a suit against D to collect the debt which D owed T.   They alleged that T had died intestate, that there had been no administration of his estate, that there were no unpaid debts of T and that X and Y were his sole statutory heirs and that they were entitled to the debt which remained unpaid after demand.   To this complaint D demurred on the ground that X and Y were not the proper parties to sue and that there were not sufficient facts stated to constitute a cause of action.   Should the court sustain the demurrer?

Answer.   Yes.   The reason is plain.   While facts well pleaded are taken to be true on demurrer, the facts here show that there is no administration in the probate court which has exclusive jurisdiction to appoint an administrator who is the only person in law entitled to own and collect a debt of a deceased person, and the only court having jurisdiction to determine heirship.   Hence, on the face of the complaint the facts pleaded are not legally true.   The real reason that these heirs cannot collect is that administration in the probate court is the only way by which the unpaid creditors of the deceased can be protected by assuring them that T's property will be used to pay their debts.   Furthermore, if D were to pay X and Y and later an administrator of T's estate were to be appointed, he could compel D to pay the debt again because the administrator would be the only person who could legally receive such payment and give a binding receipt therefor.   So administration is necessary to protect the debtors of the deceased against possible double payment.

See Brobst v. Brobst, 190 Mich. 63, 155 N.W. 734 (1916).   See also Atkinson, pp. 567–568.

Persons not parties to action in one state not bound by finding of   Case 104
domicile in another state

T died intestate leaving property in three states, Florida, New York, and Delaware.   In a proceeding to administer T's estate in Florida, it was found that T was domiciled in Florida and that under the laws of Florida T's property in that state should go to X who was a party to such Florida proceedings.   In a similar proceeding in the state of New York to which Y was a party, it was found that T was domiciled in New York and that Y was entitled to T's property.   Y was an administrator, appointed by the State of New York.   The property which T left in Delaware consisted of shares of stock in Z corporation which was a creature of Delaware laws and in which state the situs of the shares of Z corporation was in Delaware.   Both X and Y claimed the shares in the Delaware corporation whereupon Z corporation brought suit against both X and Y in Delaware and made personal service of process in interpleader on both X and Y in Del-

aware for the purpose of determining which of the two Z corporation should recognize as a stockholder. The Delaware court found that T was a domiciliary of New York and decided that the shares of stock in Z corporation belonged to Y under the laws of New York, and gave full faith and credit to the New York proceedings. It was then contended by X that Y was bound by the Florida judgment finding that T was domiciled in Florida. Is X's contention valid?

Answer. No. Since Y was not a party to the proceedings in Florida, he was neither bound thereby, nor was he entitled to any benefits thereunder. Neither is Y a privy of T or T's administrator in Florida. Conversely, X was not a party to the proceedings in New York, and was not bound thereby, nor was he entitled to any benefits thereunder. Consequently, as between X and Y, the contestants, the Delaware court was at liberty to determine independently the domicile of T. Having so decided, both X and Y who had participated in the contest in Delaware, were bound by its decision. Had Y appeared in the Florida proceedings, then of course he, as well as X, would have been bound by the determination of domicile in that state, and Delaware would have been required to give full faith and credit to such decision. Typically, an ancillary administrator is acting in conjunction with, and thus is regarded as being in privity with, the domiciliary administrator. However, on these facts, the position of the New York ancillary administrator was totally in opposition to the Florida administrator and, thus, was not bound by the Florida litigation.

See *Riley v. New York Trust Co.*, 315 U.S. 343, 62 S.Ct. 608, 86 L.Ed. 885 (1941). See also Goodrich, pp. 408–410.

TERRITORIAL LIMITATIONS ON POWERS OF PERSONAL REPRESENTATIVES

1. An executor or administrator as such can exercise no powers beyond the boundaries of the state wherein he is appointed.

2. If a personal representative is appointed in State X he can act as such in State Y only by virtue of a statute in State Y.

3. If a decedent dies domiciled in State X and leaves property in States X and Y, usually a separate administration is necessary in each state.

4. The administration in X the state of domicile is called *primary* or *domiciliary* administration and in Y is called *ancillary* administration.

5. Many states permit the domiciliary personal representative to act also as ancillary administrator. Other states require that the ancillary administrator be a resident; therefore, the domiciliary administrator is precluded from acting.

6. The principal purpose of ancillary administration is to assure the payment of the debts of the decedent to the local creditors.

7. The ancillary administrator's duties are to:

   (a) collect decedent's assets,

   (b) pay the local creditors, and

   (c) distribute the remaining assets to the domiciliary personal representative.

8. The state of ancillary administration usually defers to the state of domiciliary administration on matters pertaining to the personal estate of the decedent.

   e.g. If a will is admitted to probate at the decedent's last domicile the validity of the will is conclusive as to personalty in all jurisdictions. The validity of a will concerning realty is determined by the state in which the land is located.

   See gnerally Atkinson, pp. 585–593; Clark, pp. 659, 667–671; and Ritchie, pp. 1132–1136.

Title to decedent's personal property in one state does not pass to personal representative appointed in another state　　**Case 105**

T died domiciled in State X and E qualified as his executor in State X. At his death T owned an automobile in State Y. E conceived it to be his duty to gather together the assets of T wherever they were and demanded the car in State Y from D who had possession thereof for T. D refused and E brought action in replevin to get possession of the car in State Y. May he recover?

Answer. No. *The cloak of authority conferred on E by State X through its probate court is coextensive with the borders of State X. The order appointing E had no extraterritorial effect. To make his case E would have to say, "I am suing as executor". Hence, the rule that title to the decedent's personal property passed to his personal representative is limited in its application to the state wherein the personal representative is appointed. The real reason why E cannot recover the car in State Y, however, is not one of title or lack of it but the desire of State Y to protect local creditors of T who reside in State Y. If E could recover the car and take it to State X, then local creditors of State Y would have their claims subjected to the laws of State X. If it turned out that T's estate were insolvent, then T's creditors who lived in State Y would have their claims paid only after T's creditors residing in State X were paid their pro rata share of the estate in full. See Case 107, below. Compare, Case 106, below.*

Case 106 *Assets in state required for ancillary administration*

T died domiciled in State X and with property therein. E was appointed and qualified as T's executor in State X. Among T's assets were a Ford car in State X and a debt of $1000 owed to T by D who lived in State Y. T owed $500 to C who lived in State Y. K converted the Ford car in State X and drove it into State Y. On these facts C petitioned the probate court of State Y for letters of ancillary administration in State Y. E appeared and objected to C's petition on the ground that the probate court had no jurisdiction because there was no property left by T in State Y. Is the objection good?

Answer. No. There must be assets of the deceased in the state to invest the probate court with jurisdiction to appoint an ancillary administrator. Did T die with assets in State Y in the facts given? Surely the Ford car did not constitute assets of T in State Y for the reason that at T's death that car was in State X and became the property of E and he could replevy it from K in Y without suing in his representative capacity but as owner thereof. On the other hand the situs of the $1000 debt owed by D to T was in State Y. No collection of that debt could be made without service on D in State Y. On this ground the probate court in State Y would have jurisdiction to grant letters of ancillary administration to C. Upon C's being appointed and qualified he could collect the $1000 debt from D and give D a good discharge for the payment thereof. He could then deduct the expenses of administration and his own debt of $500 and distribute the balance to E in State X.

See In re Cornell's Will, 267 N.Y. 456, 196 N.E. 396 (1935).

Case 107 *Non-resident creditors participation in ancillary administration*

T died domiciled in Washington but owned property in Michigan as well. A domiciliary administration is pending in Washington and an ancillary administration in Michigan. The claims allowed in the domiciliary administration are in excess of the value of the assets located in Washington. Claims of Michigan creditors do not equal the whole of the assets in Michigan. The estate as a whole is insolvent. C, a creditor resident in Washington, seeks to have his claim allowed in Michigan. The probate court disallowed the non-resident claim. On appeal will C be entitled to have his claim allowed in Michigan.

Answer. Yes. But resident creditors will be paid their pro rata share of the total estate prior to any payment to non-residents from Michigan assets. The purpose for providing ancillary administration is to protect local creditors. Such protection, however, by the majority rule extends only to allowing local creditors to be paid their *pro rata share of an insolvent estate out of local assets before non-resident creditors will be allowed to participate in ancillary assets. "An attempt to provide by statute or to hold by judicial determination that local creditors of an insolvent were entitled to be paid in full while other creditors were not would clearly seem to violate the . . . Federal Constitution," which provides that a state may not give a preference to its citizens as against citizens of the other states or United States.*

See *In re Estate of Brauns*, 276 Mich. 598, 268 N.W. 890 (1936).

TITLE OF PERSONAL REPRESENTATIVES

1. When a person dies testate or intestate the title to his *personal* property vests in the personal representative when appointed and qualified and relates back to the instant of death. See *The Appointment of a Personal Representative*, Chapter XIII, below.

2. When the personal representative distributes the personal property, after payment of decedent's debts, to the legatees in case of testacy and to the next of kin or statutory heirs in case of intestacy, then title vests in the legatees and statutory heirs respectively.

3. When a person died *testate* the title to his *real property* vests in his devisees subject to the right and duty of the personal representative to take possession thereof and use for the purpose of paying debts.

4. When a person dies *intestate* the title to his *real property* vests in his heirs subject to the right and duty of the personal representative to take possession thereof and use for the purpose of paying debts.

   See generally Atkinson, pp. 664, 668; Clark, pp. 693–694; and Ritchie, pp. 1121–1122.

JURISDICTION OVER TRUSTS

1. The court having jurisdiction over matters pertaining to the establishment and enforcement of trusts varies from state to state depending upon local statutes or practice. In some jurisdictions the probate court will have jurisdiction over testamentary trusts. In others the court of general jurisdiction will have jurisdiction over all trusts.

2. In the absence of a statute to the contrary the court having equity jurisdiction has plenary jurisdiction of all questions relative to the establishment, construction, enforcement and preservation of trusts.

3. Equity's jurisdiction is not limited to express trusts but extends to resulting and constructive trusts.

4. In many states statutory provisions confer either concurrent or exclusive jurisdiction over testamentary trusts on the probate court.

5. The law of the place where land is situated determines the validity and effect of a trust concerning the land.

6. The validity of a testamentary trust of chattels (including movables, specialties and nonspecialties) is determined by the law of the domicile of the testator, the lex domicilii, unless to apply such rule would defeat the intent of the testator, in which case it may be determined by the law of the place where the chattels are situated.

   e.g. T has lived many years and has accumulated much property in the state of Washington and the chattel property is still there. T moves to California to retire and dies domiciled there. His will disposes of his chattels in Washington to B in trust, the trust to be administered in Washington. The trust is invalid under the California Rule Against Perpetuities, but is valid under the law of Washington. T's heirs sue in Washington to invalidate the trust. May they succeed? Ans. No. Under the general rule the answer would be in the affirmative, for the law of the testator's domicile at the time of his death usually governs the testamentary trust of chattels. But where, as here, the application of the general rule would run contrary to the testator's intent and make the trust invalid, that law will govern which will make the trust valid and will carry out the testator's intention. See Matter of Chappell, 124 Wash. 128, 213 P. 684 (1923).

7. The validity of an inter vivos trust of chattels is governed by the law of the place where the chattels are situated at the time of the creation of the trust.

   e.g. S, a resident of Louisiana, takes securities and cash worth $100,000 to the state of New York and delivers them to T to hold in trust for specific persons and purposes. Under the law of Louisiana, the domicile of the settlor, the trust is invalid, but by the law of New York the trust is valid and enforceable. Is the trust valid? Ans. Yes. The chattels being transferred to the trustee in New York and having their situs there at the time of the creation of the trust, the law of New York governs and the trust is valid. See Hutchison v. Ross, 262 N.Y. 381, 187 N.E. 65 (1933).

8. The administration of a trust of chattels is governed by the law of the place where the settlor designates that such trust shall be administered.

   e.g. S, a resident of Oregon, transfers securities to T in San Francisco, to hold in trust for C who is a resident of Kentucky, the trust instrument providing that T shall administer the trust in San

Francisco. What equity court may supervise T in the administration of the trust? Ans. The equity court in California. In this case the situs of the securities is in California, the trustee is in California and subject to the jurisdiction of the California courts, and the settlor's intention is that California shall be the seat of the administration. Therefore, the California court only has jurisdiction of the administration of the trust. See Rest., Second, Conflict of Laws §§ 271–272.

See generally, Rest., Second, Conflict of Laws §§ 267–282; Ritchie, pp. 1144–1146.

"Minimal contacts"—insufficient to sustain jurisdiction   **Case 108**

Mrs. D, who was domiciled in Pennsylvania, created a trust with a Delaware trust corporation as trustee. She reserved life income, a power of appointment, power to revoke or amend the trust, and other powers. Mrs. D then became domiciled in Florida, and there executed an instrument exercising the powers of appointment and her will. On her death litigation arose in both Delaware and Florida as to the distribution of her estate, involving the validity of her power of appointment and with it the question of what part of her estate passed under the residuary clause of her will. The beneficiaries under the power of appointment prevailed in the Delaware courts, and the residuary legatees prevailed in Florida. The Delaware Court refused to honor the Florida decree, on the basis that Florida has no jurisdiction to bind the absent Delaware trustee. The parties appealed to the United States Supreme Court contending that Delaware failed to give full faith and credit to the Florida decree. Were they correct?

Answer. *No. There was not sufficient "minimal" contact by the Delaware trustee with Florida to justify personal jurisdiction over it. The Delaware Trust Company had no office in Florida. It transacted no business in Florida. None of the trust assets was ever held or administered in Florida. There was no solicitation of business in Florida, in person or by mail. Since there was no personal jurisdiction in Florida over the Deleware Trustee, the Delaware Court was not bound to give the Florida Court's decree full faith and credit.*

See *Hanson v. Denckla,* 357 U.S. 235, 78 S.Ct. 1228, L.Ed.2d 1283 (1958). See also Stumberg, p. 397; Weintraub, pp. 121–125.

NOTE 1—The court rejected the argument that the *International Shoe* and *McGee* Cases, which had established the "minimal contacts" basis of jurisdiction sustained the jurisdiction of the Florida Court. See International Shoe Co. v. State of Washington, 326 U.S. 310, 66 S.Ct. 154, 90 L.Ed. 95 (1945) and McGee v. International Life Insurance Co., 355 U.S. 220, 78 S.Ct. 199, 2 L.Ed.2d 223 (1957). See also discussion of this line of cases in Smith's Review, Conflict of Laws, pp. 36–49.

NOTE 2—The "contacts" of the Delaware trustee with Florida are, arguably, greater than those of the insurance company with California in the *McGee* case. In the *McGee* case the "contacts" consisted of one insurance policy. From this it may be reasoned that the *McGee* case may be confined "to its facts" —that is, to the small individual suing the large insurance company defendant.

NOTE 3—The Court reiterated that the due process limitations on the exercise of jurisdiction are "more than a guarantee of immunity from inconvenient or distant litigation. They are a consequence of territorial limitations on the power of the respective States". Thus, by reference to "territorial" limitations, and "power", the traditional and classical foundations of the concept of jurisdiction, in the *McGee* case, the Court is said to have reached the "high water mark" in its extention of in personam jurisdiction.

NOTE 4—The Supreme Court also rejected the argument that Florida had jurisdiction "in rem" over the trust *assets* (in contrast to "in personam jurisdiction" over the trustee).

LIFE CYCLE OF ESTATE ADMINISTRATION

Summary Outline

A. Necessity for Probate of Will and Administration

B. Initial Steps in the Probate Process

C. The Hearing on Probate—Testimony of Witnesses

D. Will Contests

E. Proceedings After Probate

F. Conditions Against Will Contests

G. Agreement Not to Contest or to Settle Will Contest

H. The Appointment of the Personal Representative

I. Revocation of Administration and Effect Thereof

J. The Process of Administration—Claims Against the Estate

K. The Process of Administration—Inventory and Appraisal

L. The Process of Administration—Collection and Preservation of Assets

M. The Process of Administration—Management of the Estate

N. The Process of Administration—The Construction of Wills

O. The Process of Administration—Distribution and Accounting

P. Informal Administration

Q. The Uniform Probate Code

NECESSITY FOR PROBATE OF WILL AND ADMINISTRATION

1. The Probate proceeding consists of either:

    (a) In the case of *intestacy*, the appointment of a personal representative;

    (b) In the case of *testacy*, the probate of the will and the appointment of a personal representative.

2. Probate proceedings are necessary in order to achieve:

    (a) the orderly transfer of assets on the death of their owner,

    (b) protection of creditors, and

    (c) identification of successors.

3. Probate comes from the Latin word *probatio* which means "to prove" and thus the probate of a will means the proving thereof in the probate court.

4. Probate is the process whereby a document is judicially established as the duly executed last will of a competent testator.

5. The probate proceeding is not concerned with the construction of the will, but with the external validity, including:

    (a) genuineness;

    (b) due execution;

    (c) capacity of the testator; and

    (d) chronology, as the last formal expression of the testator's intent.

6. Every will must be admitted to probate in the probate court before it is admissible in evidence for any purpose in any other court.

7. The personal representative is the public official whose duty it is to wind up the affairs of the decedent.   See *The Appointment of a Personal Representative*, Chapter XIII, below.

    See generally Atkinson, pp. 503–505; Clark, pp. 691–692; Dukeminer, pp. 89–90; Rheinstein, pp. 477–483; and Ritchie, pp. 1121–1123, 1127–1128.

INITIAL STEPS IN THE PROBATE PROCESS

1. Probate cannot take place until after the testator's death.   In the majority of jurisdictions there is no time limit after testator's death within which a will may be probated.

2. The person having custody of a will is under a duty to produce it.   Many states have statutes imposing penalties for concealing or destroying a will, or for failing to produce it within a given time.

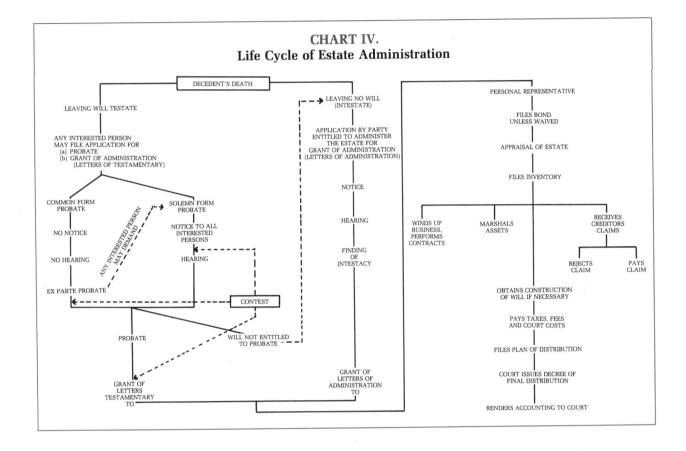

CHART IV.
Life Cycle of Estate Administration

3. The first step in the probate process is to file the will in the appropriate court with a petition to admit to probate and to grant letters testamentary to a fiduciary.

4. A petition to admit to probate may be filed by the executor named in the will, or by any interested person.

5. In early English law there were two kinds of probate:

    (a) common form—the proponent of the will was permitted to prove it by his oath and testimony of other witnesses without notice to other parties. If this procedure was used an interested party at any time within thirty years could question the grant of probate and require the solemn form procedure be followed.

    (b) solemn form or per testes (through witnesses)—the interested parties were given notice and an opportunity to be heard and testimony of witnesses was at greater length. Probate by this form might only be questioned on appeal.

6. Some states still allow probate without notice, but the majority require notice by service and/or publication on all interested persons prior to a hearing.

See generally Atkinson, pp. 484–495; Clark, pp. 698–700; Dukeminer, pp. 120–121; Rheinstein, pp. 487–488; Ritchie, pp. 285–286; and Scoles, pp. 468–469.

THE HEARING ON PROBATE— TESTIMONY OF WITNESSES

1. At the hearing on probate the proponent of the will must prove:

   (a) the death of the testator,

   (b) domicile,

   (c) genuineness of the will,

   (d) compliance with statutory requirements for the execution of wills, and

   (e) testamentary capacity.

2. Execution and mental capacity are usually shown by the attesting witnesses.

3. Some states permit probate on the testimony of less than all witnesses; others require all witnesses if they are available.

4. Where some or all the witnesses to a will are unavailable:

   (a) If the required witnesses are located outside the jurisdiction, a commission may be sent to the foreign jurisdiction to take their testimony under oath and return it to the court.

   (b) If the required witnesses have predeceased the testator, the proponent offers proof of such fact, plus evidence of the genuineness of the signature and any other proof of execution available.

   (c) If required witnesses cannot be located, proof must be offered of a diligent search with tracing to last known whereabouts, plus evidence of the genuineness of the signatures and other proof of due execution.

5. If the will of the testator is written in a foreign language in most states it may be admitted to probate, in the same way as had it been in English. A translation is usually required to accompany the will.

6. Lost or destroyed wills may be admitted to probate in the same manner as those extant upon full and satisfactory proof of contents and due execution.

   NOTE—Some states have special statutes relating to lost and destroyed wills.

7. If no objection is made at the time of the hearing the will, on a prima facie case of due execution, will be admitted to probate.

See generally Atkinson, pp. 495–497, 506–513; Clark, p. 697; Palmer, p. 97; Rheinstein, pp. 509–510; and Scoles, pp. 323–324, 469–470.

1. Statutory provisions in all states govern the methods by which either a will may be contested or a will denied probate may be established.   These generally are:

WILL CONTESTS

   (a) contest (or caveat) in the court having jurisdiction over probate.

   (b) appeal from the order granting or denying probate, and

   (c) separate actions to set aside the order granting or denying probate.

2. In states where wills may be probated ex parte without notice contest is usually after probate and is either:

   (a) in the probate court upon notice filed by the interested parties after probate, or

   (b) in a higher court on appeal with trial de novo or by separate action.

3. In jurisdictions which require notice prior to probate, the procedures vary.

   (a) In some states contest is permitted only prior to probate: *i.e.* the probate proceeding is the forum for the contest where objections have been filed by interested parties.

   (b) Some states allow contest both before and after probate, the one prior being carried on in the probate court the other in some higher court.

   (c) Some states allow contest only in a higher court after probate.

   (d) Some states allow contest prior to probate and an appeal to a higher court on a trial de novo.

4. There is no constitutional right to trial by jury in probate or will contest proceedings since these were not common law proceedings.   Most states, however, have statutes giving the right to trial by jury in a will contest.

5. Statutes usually set time limitations upon the bringing of will contests.

6. A will contest is usually considered a proceeding in rem, that is binding on all parties having interests in the property whether or not they are parties to the proceeding, the question being *will* *or no will,* but statutes usually require notice to interested parties.

7. Will contests are concerned only with *external* validity issues, such as failure of due execution, fraud, undue influence, mistake, lack of testamentary capacity, revocation, or lack of intent that instrument be a will. Issues of *internal* validity, such as violation of the Rule Against Perpetuities or Mortmain, must be raised in other proceedings at a later stage of administration.

8. The general rule is that only "persons interested" may contest a will, *i.e.* it is to such person's pecuniary advantage to have the will set aside. These may include:

   (a) next-of-kin who would receive property if the will is set aside and intestacy results,

   (b) beneficiaries under prior wills,

   (c) purchasers of property from heirs,

   (d) administrators or executors under prior wills, and

   (e) the state if there is a question of escheat.

9. A party may be estopped to contest a will if he has accepted benefits under the will, failed to object to probate proceedings or took action relative to the will relied on by a third party.

10. The same general rules of evidence relating to competency of witnesses and admissibility applied to other actions are also applied to will contests.

11. The general rules as to burden of proof in will contest cases are:

   (a) The person seeking to establish the validity of the will, the proponent, has the burden of proof on the issues of:

      (i) due execution, and

      (ii) mental capacity.

   (b) The contestants have the burden of proof on the issues of:

      (i) undue influence and fraud,

      (ii) revocation.

   CAVEAT—Some states have passed statutes placing the burden of proof on all issues on the contestant. See Atkinson, p. 543.

   See generally Atkinson, pp. 514–527, 535, 545–554; Clark, p. 703; Rheinstein, pp. 510–511; Ritchie, pp. 297–298, 300–301, 305–306; and Scoles, p. 472, 482–485.

PROCEEDINGS AFTER PROBATE

1. Collateral attack of a will will not be allowed on matters of external validity. See *Will Contests,* number 9, above.

2. A decree of probate may be set aside on grounds of fraud or collusion upon the court, failure to comply with the provisions of the Soldiers' and Sailors' Relief Act, new evidence or failure of notice.

3. If a later will is discovered after either an earlier will has been admitted to probate or a decree of intestacy entered, it is generally held that the later will may be probated in the same manner as if no other proceeding was had.

4. Where a decree of probate or intestacy is set aside, bona fide purchasers and others who relied on the earlier decree are usually protected.

   See generally Atkinson, pp. 500–503; Clark, p. 704; and Rheinstein, pp. 495–501.

1. The validity of a condition in a will that a gift shall be void if the beneficiary disputes or contests the will usually depends on the nature of the contest and the construction of the particular condition.

   CONDITIONS AGAINST WILL CONTESTS

2. If a beneficiary contests the will and the will is declared invalid, the forfeiture condition fails with the remaining parts of the will.

3. Courts will generally uphold the no contest condition if the contest is without probable cause.

4. If a will contest is based on probable cause, there is a disagreement among jurisdictions about the effect of a no contest clause.

   (a) Some courts uphold the forefeiture even though the will contest is based on probable cause.

   (b) Other courts refuse to enforce the no contest condition if there is probable cause, reasoning that public policy requires the protection of the family and the exposure of frauds.

5. Early cases distinguished between gifts of realty and personal property where there was a contest clause and no gift over.

   (a) If the no contest clause affected a gift of personalty, it was void.

   (b) If the no contest clause affected a gift of realty, it was valid even in the absence of a gift over.

6. Modern cases make no distinction based on either the nature of the property or the presence of a gift over.

7. Whether or not there is in fact a breach of a no contest clause depends upon the construction of the clause.

   e.g. A provision for forfeiture in case of contest may be construed as requiring a forfeiture against beneficiaries who do not as well as those who do participate in the will contest.

8. Where the provision requires forfeiture in the case of a contest, it must be decided whether a given action is a contest under the particular clause.

    e.g. Claiming title in property given to another is generally held to be a contest. Filing a creditor's claims is generally not a contest.

9. Courts generally construe contest provisions strictly on the grounds of disfavoring forfeitures.

Case 109   *Interest of beneficiary forfeited by filing will contest proceeding*

T died leaving a will which provided that B, her nephew, have a half interest in the rentals accruing during his lifetime from certain property. The will also provided for forfeiture of the interest of any person contesting the provisions of the will. In the event of such a contest the interest devised to any such person should be disposed of under the provisions of the will as though his name had not been mentioned therein. B, along with other relatives, contested the will on the grounds of lack of execution, mental incapacity, fraud, coercion and undue influence. At the hearing, no evidence was presented to justify the allegations with respect to proper execution, mental incapacity or fraud. The only evidence of undue influence was proof of T's attachment to a young man who during the last several years of her life showed her care and attention and aided her in her business affairs. The court found that such evidence supported contention that the young man had cultivated her friendship with the expectation of profit; however, the court concluded there was no evidence that he substituted his will for hers in the disposition of her property. The court, therefore, found the will valid and ordered probate. Thereafter, the exector brought an action to determine the right of B and other devisees under the will who had filed the contest. Is B entitled to the provisions made for him in the will?

Answer. *No. Under the circumstances in this case the interest of B under the will was forfeited by his filing a caveat. Since there was no evidence to support the grounds alleged for contest, the general rule is that such a clause discourages unmeritorious litigation and thus will be upheld. Even where probable cause does exist, many jurisdictions have upheld the validity of no contest clauses based on the reasoning that only a very small percentage of will contests made on the ground, of defective execution, mental incapacity or undue influence are successful and there is no public interest in freeing such contest from the restraining influence of conditions of forfeiture. A higher principle is served by enforcing the* *will of the testator that those who share in his property should not be a party to attempts to thwart his intention. A contest on the ground of forgery or subsequent revocation, neither of which were involved in the present case, may present different policies and arrive at another result.*

See *Barry v. American Securities & Trust Co.,* 135 F.2d 470 (D.C.Cir. 1943).

NOTE—In some jurisdictions where there is probable cause for contesting the will, the forfeiture clause will not be given effect. See *Conditions Against Contests,* above.

1. A testator may enter into a contract with his heir at law not to contest a will. If the contract is supported by good consideration and the agreement otherwise is valid, the heir will be estopped to contest the will.

AGREEMENT NOT TO CONTEST OR TO SETTLE WILL CONTEST

2. The beneficiaries under a will and the heirs at law may enter into a valid contract not to contest a will.

3. States vary as to the remedies a party to an agreement not to contest a will may have on its breach. These include:

(a) injunction against the prosecution of the contest,

(b) action at law for damages, or

(c) defense to contest.

4. In order to support an agreement not to contest it is usually held that the heir must have either:

(a) a reasonable ground for contest, or

(b) good faith intention to contest.

5. The settlement of a will contest action is valid if all interested parties agree even though it may defeat the intention of the testator.

6. The states vary as to the effect which a probate court will give to a settlement of a contest action:

(a) Some states will admit or reject a will and order distribution in accordance with the stipulation.

(b) Some states require that the settlement be carried out among the parties and that any remedy be sought on the contract in courts of general jurisdiction.

See generally Atkinson, pp. 527–530; Rheinstein, pp. 512–515; Ritchie, pp. 512–515; and Scoles, p. 478.

THE APPOINTMENT OF THE PERSONAL REPRESENTATIVE

1. One who is authorized by the probate court to administer the estate of a deceased person is called a personal representative.

2. The personal representative:

    (a) if nominated by the decedent's will is called an *executor*;

    (b) if appointed by the court when the decedent died intestate is called an *administrator*,

    (c) if appointed by the court to administer the estate according to the terms of the will of the decedent is called an *administrator with the will annexed* (in Latin, cum testamento annexo, or c.t.a.),

    (d) if appointed by the court to administer an estate which a prior executor or administrator has not completed is called an *administrator de bonis non* or d. b. n., which means administrators of goods not administered.

3. A *special administrator* is one appointed by the court to preserve the estate while regular proceedings get under way. *E.g.* to sell perishables in the grocery store of the deceased. The proceeding of appointment is usually ex parte and his authority ceases automatically when a regular personal representative is appointed and qualifies.

4. In an intestate estate the administration is usually initiated by filing a petition for the grant of letters of administration by the person entitled to appointment under the applicable statute. Non-residence, lack of mental capacity, infancy, conviction of crime or other causes are usually statutory disqualifications to act as a personal representative. See *Appointment and Qualification*, Chapter XIV, below.

5. If there is a will the petition for probate is usually accompanied by an application for the court appointment of the executor named in the will.

6. The majority of states require notice, usually by publication, and a hearing with respect to the application for appointment of the personal representative. Some jurisdictions allow appointment without notice and anyone who desires to object must bring a motion to set the appointment aside.

7. The executor or administrator of an estate must file a bond for the protection of those interested in the estate. Statutes prescribe the sureties, terms and amount usually conditioned upon the lawful administration of the estate in twice the amount of the personalty in the estate. The value of real estate is, generally, not included for purposes of setting a bond because of the comparative difficulty in dissipating the realty, and because title passes directly to the heirs.

8. Many states allow the testator to waive bond from the executor(s) named in the will, but the court still has authority to require a bond if it finds it necessary for protection of the estate.

9. When a bond satisfactory to the court is filed, the court under its seal issues a certificate of appointment to the personal representative, called:

(a) in the case of a will, letters testamentary,

(b) in the case of intestacy, letters of administration.

These letters are evidence that the personal representative has been made an officer of the court authorized to carry out the administration of the estate as prescribed by law.

See generally Atkinson, pp. 576–581; Clark, pp. 710–711; 715–716; Dukeminer, p. 80; Rheinstein, pp. 517–520; and Richie, p. 1154.

REVOCATION OF ADMINISTRATION AND EFFECT THEREOF

1. The probate court has original and exclusive jurisdiction:

(a) to determine whether a decedent died testate or intestate, and

(b) to appoint a personal representative, whether executor, administrator, or administrator with the will annexed.

2. Once being properly appointed and qualified as such, the acts of a personal representative within the scope of his authority are valid and binding until his letters are revoked.

3. The court may revoke the letters of appointment of the personal representative on the grounds that, at the time of appointment, the letters should not have been granted in that:

(a) the supposed decedent is not dead,

(b) a will is found naming an executor after an administrator is appointed,

(c) a later will is found,

(d) the appointment was obtained by fraud,

(e) decedent was not domiciled in the state nor had any property there,

(f) another person had priority for appointment, or

(g) lack of qualification at the time of appointment.

4. The court may remove or revoke the letters of the personal representative on the grounds that, subsequent to his appointment:

(a) he becomes incapacitated, or

(b) he fails to properly administer the estate.

5. If such personal representative sells property of the estate to a purchaser the purchaser is protected in his purchase.

6. If one who owed a debt to the decedent pays the debt to such personal representative, such debtor is protected in such payment.

7. If the letters testamentary or of an administration of the personal representative are revoked and a new one is appointed and qualifies, such new one cannot undo the acts of his predecessor either as to sales or as to the collection of debts owed the decedent.

8. The newly qualified personal representative, however, can compel return of property of the estate which the former personal representative has distributed to the next of kin or legatees who are, of course, mere volunteers, provided such next of kin or legatees have not changed their positions.

9. A personal representative is usually allowed to resign, either by the terms of applicable statutes or of the will. To be effective, however, such resignation must be accepted by the court.

See generally Atkinson, pp. 624–628; UPC 3–608—3–612; Clark, pp. 716–717; Rheinstein, pp. 519–520; and Ritchie, p. 1151.

Case 110 *Rights of executor under newly found will after appointment of administrator—prior acts of administrator sustained*

T died and A was appointed and qualified as his administrator. In performing his duties A collected a debt of $100 which K owed to T and sold to R a herd of sheep which was part of T's estate. A paid T's debts and distributed the remaining property to T's statutory heir, J. Thereafter, E found and proved a will which T had executed and within the allowed statutory period asked that A's letters of administration be revoked, and that letters testamentary be issued to E. This the court did. T's will gave all his property to H. E then demanded that K pay to E the $100 debt which he owed T and that R return the sheep to E as part of T's estate and demanded possession of all the assets which had been distributed to J. All refused E's demands. May E enforce his demands against any of the three?

Answer. *He may not enforce his demands against K or R, but he may do so in equity against J provided J has not changed his position. First, on this set of facts the court had jurisdiction to determine whether there was no will and to appoint A. A was then the legal personal representative of T and had power to act as such. He performed his duty when he collected from K the $100. It being his duty and he having authority to collect he could and did discharge K from further liability when he accepted payment from K of the debt he owed T. Hence, K need not pay a second time. Also A being the qualified administrator had title to and could pass title to the sheep* *and did so to R, assuming of course that R had no knowledge of the will. Hence, R may keep the sheep. But the case of J is different. As statutory heir he is a mere volunteer in the sense that he has given no value for the goods distributed to him. Hence, he must hold in trust for E such goods as were distributed to him and which he still possesses. If, however, he has sold the goods and spent the proceeds he would have a good defense to that extent on the ground that he had changed his position. Were these holdings not correct then there would be a constant cloud on the titles of property purchased or received through a decedent and the value of estates would be quite unprotected. Hence, the rule is that if the probate court has jurisdiction and determines that there is a will or no will and appoints a personal representative, finding no will such appointment is effective until revoked and the acts of the personal representative in the interim are valid and binding.*

See Harrison v. Carter, 226 N.C. 36, 36 S.E.2d 700 (1946). See also Atkinson, pp. 627–628.

1. Immediately following appointment, the personal representative must publish notice of his appointment for a stated period of time in a newspaper of general circulation in the area. The notice serves to notify creditors that claims against the estate must be presented within a statutory period of limitation.

THE PROCESS OF ADMINISTRATION— CLAIMS AGAINST THE ESTATE

2. At common law generally contract claims survived the death of the debtor and could be enforced against and by the personal representative. Tort claims did not. Most jurisdictions have extended survival to various tort claims. Statutes dealing with this problem are of several types. They provide:

   (a) enumerated causes of action survive in addition to those which survived at common law;

   (b) all causes of action survive except enumerated actions; or

   (c) all causes of action survive.

3. Statutes usually provide that all claims whether matured or not must be presented to the personal representative or filed with the probate court by a certain time or be "forever barred".

4. Debts are matured if they are due at the time of decedent's death, and perhaps, if due before the time expires for presenting them to the personal representative.

   (a) Debts are unmatured if they are certain to become due but are not due by the time the creditor is required to present them to the personal representative.

(b) Debts are contingent if it cannot be ascertained at decedent's death whether they will ever become due.

5. States vary with respect to the treatment of contingent claims.

(a) Some require that they be presented, or else be barred, and that the personal representative either save out assets to pay or take a bond from the distributees requiring them to pay if the claim becomes absolute.

(b) Others do not require any action by the contingent creditor and if his claim becomes absolute allow him to proceed against the distributees.

6. Statutes barring claims not presented are called statutes of "nonclaim" and a claim which is not presented within the period provided is not only barred procedurally, but it ceases to exist legally.

7. Neither the personal representative nor the court has the power to allow such a claim after the nonclaim statutory period has elapsed.

8. If the general statute of limitations has run on a debt of the decedent before his death the personal representative should not pay such claim. If he does he cannot charge the estate therewith.

9. A secured creditor may collect the value of the security without presenting his claim to the personal representative but will lose the excess of the claim, if any, over the value of the security if he does not do so within the period of nonclaim.

10. An heir, legatee or devisee who receives mortgaged property is entitled to have the personal representative pay the debt, out of the general assets, if the deceased owed it and have the property free of the mortgage, unless the will or statute indicates otherwise.

NOTE—Number 10, above, states the general rule of exoneration, but the provisions vary from state to state and the result depends upon: (a) the source of mortgage, (b) the nature of property out of which exoneration would come, and (c) the particular statute. Some states provide that exoneration must be expressly provided for in the will.

11. Various statutes establish special procedures and priorities for the payment of claims in insolvent estates. The usual order of priority is:

(a) family allowances,

(b) funeral expenses,

(c) costs of administration,

(d) federal taxes,

(e) state taxes,

(f) wages, rents and judgment debts, and

(g) all other debts.

12. Under modern statutes the personal representative pays debts only on court order after the period for proving claims is over. In this way he receives protection against personal liability if it turns out that the estate is insolvent.

13. Statutes usually fix a period within which the personal representative can reject claims. Rejection must usually be in writing.

14. Statutes usually require a creditor to file suit upon any rejected claim within a certain time after rejection or be forever barred.

15. Overpayment made to creditors, legatees or distributees may be recovered by the personal representative on the ground of mistake of fact.

> See generally Atkinson, pp. 687–715, 764–766; Clark, pp. 722–724, 731–733; Dukemener, pp. 85–86; Rheinstein; pp. 501–503; and Ritchie, pp. 1257–1260.

Conduct of attorney for the estate will not estop the executrix   **CASE 111**
from raising nonclaim statute to bar claim

Prior to his death D owed P $1000. which was evidenced by a promissory note. Shortly after D's death, P went to the office of B, the attorney for the estate, which office was designated in the notice to creditors as the place for the presentation of claims against the estate. P advised B of her claim but also told him that she had mislaid the note and could not find it at the time. B as a matter of accommodation to her prepared a claim which did not refer to the note which P verified and left with him. Shortly thereafter P was notified that her claim had been disallowed and rejected. P then informed B that she had found the note. He came to her house, secured the note and after keeping it a day or two returned it to her with the assurance that she would have no trouble getting her money. P's claim was rejected, and she subsequently sued on the note. The jurisdiction at the time had in effect the following statutes: "No holder of any claim against an estate shall maintain any action thereon unless the claim is first presented to the executor or its administrator. . . . All claims arising upon contract whether the same be due, not due or contingent, must be presented within the time limited in the notice,

*and any claim not so presented is barred forever." May P maintain
her action against D's estate?*

> ***Answer.*** *No. The claim filed by plaintiff did not purport to be
> founded on a promissory note, and therefore, she cannot maintain
> the claim under the specific terms of the statute. Nor is the estate
> estopped by the actions of its attorney with respect to plaintiff's
> claim. Compliance with the statutes of nonclaim is essential to any
> right of action against an estate. The executor or administrator is
> in effect the trustee of the funds of the estate for the benefit of the
> creditors and heirs and cannot waive any substantial right which
> materially affects their interests. Nor can the executor be affected
> by the attorney's action. Equitable estoppel might be invoked
> against an executor so far as an individual interest in the estate is
> concerned, but it cannot operate to the prejudice of heirs or other
> creditors. Even misleading statements, assurances or conduct which
> induces the creditor to omit compliance with the statutes will not
> operate as an estoppel to prevent his contesting the claim upon the
> grounds of noncompliance. In failing to present her claim in the
> correct form, P suffered the penalty of the nonclaim statute and can-
> not assert her cause of action against the estate.*

See Vanderpool v. Vanderpool, 48 Mont. 448, 138 P. 772 (1914).

**THE PROCESS OF
ADMINISTRATION—
INVENTORY AND
APPRAISAL**

1. The personal representative is required to prepare and file with
   the court an inventory of the assets of the estate.

2. The inventory usually contains an itemization and description of
   all property in the estate. This serves as prima facie evidence of
   the extent of the assets of the estate.

3. The court appoints, either prior to or after the filing of the inventory, appraisers who are disinterested persons who value the items
   in the inventory. The appraisers valuations are presumptively
   correct but not binding on anyone.

4. Some states have procedures whereby an interested party's objections to the inventory may be heard and determined by the court.

   See generally Atkinson, pp. 629–634; Clark, p. 721; and Dukeminer, pp. 81–82.

**THE PROCESS OF
ADMINISTRATION—
COLLECTION AND
PRESERVATION
OF ASSETS**

1. The principal duty of the personal representative is to marshal
   all of the assets of the estate into his own hands, then to pay the
   creditors and hold the remainder for distribution.

2. The personal representative may commence actions and compromise claims. Some jurisdictions, however, require court approval of compromises.

3. The personal representative must have himself substituted as a party with respect to all pending actions to which the decedent was a party during his lifetime.

4. The personal representative is personally liable for his torts committed in the course of administering the estate.

5. The personal representative is personally liable on his contracts in the course of administration although made to benefit the estate. He may, however, attempt to protect himself by express stipulation.

    e.g. Such a stipulation may provide: 'This note is given by X, executor of the estate of D, and not individually; it constitutes a promise to pay only to the extent that the assets of the estate are sufficient for such purpose and it is expressly agreed that any judgment will only be satisfied out of the assets of the estate and not out of X's individual assets."

    CAVEAT—To obtain limited liability, it is *not* sufficient to sign "X Executor of Estate of D."

6. The personal representative is entitled to reimburse himself from the assets of the estate for reasonable expenditures made for the estate. See *Trustee's Compensation and Right of Indemnity*, Chapter XIV, below.

7. Debts of the estate are debts owed by the decedent while he lived. By contrast, expenses off administration are obligations undertaken by the personal representative for the estate after the decedent died. In most jurisdictions expenses of administration are paid out of the estate's assets prior to the satisfaction of decedent's debts.

8. The reasonableness of expenditures by the personal representative for the estate is determined by the discretion of the probate court.

9. Reasonable amounts for decedent's funeral, for preservation of estate assets, for attorney's fees and other costs of administration may be deducted from the estate by the personal representative.

10. The personal representative has a duty to file all appropriate federal and state returns relative to taxes on the estate and to pay the taxes due thereon.

    See generally Atkinson, pp. 645–656; Rheinstein, pp. 534–536; and Ritchie, pp. 1225–1228.

THE PROCESS OF ADMINISTRATION— MANAGEMENT OF THE ESTATE

1. The personal representative is bound to perform an impersonal contract of the decedent, such as a promissory note to pay money, but need not perform a purely personal contract, such as to try a lawsuit or paint a portrait.

2. The personal representative must wind up a business conducted by decedent at his death unless he is given authority to continue its operation by:

   (a) the court,

   (b) the testator's will, or

   (c) consent of all interested parties.

3. If it is necessary to sell personal property to satisfy obligations of the estate the personal representative may do so:

   (a) without court authority if:

      (i) there is no statute providing otherwise, or

      (ii) the testator has given him a power of sale in the will;

   (b) by court order. Some jurisdictions absolutely require court authority or the sale is invalid.

4. Although the general rule is that real property passes directly to the heirs or devisees, the personal representative may have authority to sell realty if:

   (a) he is given authority by the will to do so, or

   (b) the personal assets are insufficient to pay the debts and the court orders the sale.

5. In most jurisdictions where either realty or personalty is sold by court order the personal representative is required to report the sale to the court and obtain a confirmation of the sale.

   NOTE—In the process of managing an estate the personal representative is a fiduciary and owes duties to the creditors and beneficiary of the trust in its administration. See Chapter XIV, The Fiduciary. The scope of such duties is limited, however, by the function of the personal representative as a liquidator and the temporary nature of his service.

   See generally Atkinson, pp. 657–676; Dukeminer, p. 82; Rheinstein, pp. 539–543; and Ritchie, p. 45.

Case 112   *Bank appointed both executor and trustee has executor's duty only during probate of estate*

D died leaving the bulk of his estate in a testamentary trust for the benefit of his four children. In his will he named T Bank as both executor and trustee.   D's estate included 30,000 shares of oil and gas stock.   During the administration of the estate the executor sold 3,000 shares of the stock for approximately $16.00 a share, to raise funds towards the payment of claims, taxes and expenses administration.   By the time that the remaining shares were distributed to the trustee a year later, their value had declined to $6.00 per share. The residuary beneficiary filed an objection to the executor's account claiming that the estate was entitled to damages for the executor's alleged negligence in not selling the stock while its market value was above its appraised value at the date of death.   The contestants claimed that the bank acted during probate administration in a dual capacity as executor and trustee, and therefore its capacity as trustee subjected the bank's decisions concerning the retention or disposition of the oil and gas stock to rules of investment imposed on trustee which would require that investments be diversified and that the retention of the unsold shares of oil and gas stock violated the diversification requirement.   Was there a difference between the bank's duties as executor and its duties as trustee?

Answer.   Yes.   The powers and duties as executor are different and distinct from powers and duties as trustee, even though the same bank may be named by the will in both capacities.   Moreover, the anticipation that the bulk of the state is to be tranferred to itself as testamentary trustee does not require the executor to manage the estate assets as if they were already being held under the terms of the trust.   The executor has numerous functions and obligations not normally imposed upon a testamentary trustee such as presenting the will for probate, locating assets, locating beneficiaries, handling creditors claims, paying and providing for the payment of taxes and distributing the remaining assets to the beneficiary.   The executor manages the estate incidental to the performance of these various duties in contrast to a trustee whose primary mission is to serve the trust beneficiaries under the terms of the trust.   The management by the executor concerns the interests of the trust beneficiaries only through its effect on the nature and value of the property distributed to the trustee and the timing of the distribution or distributions.   In handling the oil and gas stock in the probate estate, the executor had the duty to take reasonable steps to preserve the assets.   However, an executor is not liable for any decreases in the value of estate assets on account of his acts or omissions done in good faith and without negligence.   The fact that the banks did not anticipate fluctuations in the price of a publicly traded stock arising from general market conditions where the executor used reasonable care to become informed about any special circumstances that might affect the value of the stock will not subject it to liability.   The executor also has a responsibility to exercise due care in deciding which trust assets to sell and which to retain for distribution to the trust when it is necessary to raise money for expenses of administration.   To do this it *must take into account the suitability of the various investments, the circumstances and resources of the beneficiaries and the income produced by the various assets. An executor also has the responsibility to consider the potential effect on the trust beneficiaries as to the timing of the distribution of particular assets from the probate estate into the trust, and to avoid unreasonable delay in distribution. In order to show that the bank failed in its duties, the beneficiaries would have to have presented evidence that an earlier distribution of the oil and gas stock would have resulted in its being sold by the trustee at a higher price than its market value at the time it was in fact distributed.*

See Estate of Beach, 15 Cal.3d 623, 125 Cal.Rptr. 570, 542 P.2d 994 (1975).

THE PROCESS OF ADMINISTRATION— THE CONSTRUCTION OF WILLS

1. The jurisdiction of probate courts to construe wills is usually limited to matters necessary to the administration process. i.e., matters relating to whom the executor should pay funds.

2. Will construction proceedings other than those ancillary to the administration process are usually conducted in the courts of general jurisdiction.

3. Testamentary provisions giving the executor power to make a binding interpretation of the instrument are usually upheld.

4. Construction proceedings are usually brought after the will has been admitted to probate:

    (a) upon the initiative of the personal representative in order to carry out his duties without incurring personal liability,

    (b) by parties to an action at law such as ejectment or trespass where the outcome may be affected by the interpretation of the will, or

    (c) at the time the personal representative files his plan of distribution by persons who oppose it.

5. Construction proceedings usually are necessary to:

    (a) clear up ambiguities in the will,

    (b) provide for situations which the testator did not foresee,

    (c) determine meaning of words used by testator, or

    (d) determine which is controlling where two or more terms of a will are contradictory.

6. For cases in which the court is unable to ascertain the testator's intention from the language of the will and surrounding circum-

stances, but the will is not such as to fail for indefiniteness, the courts have developed a series of *maxims of construction* which will be applied. These have developed from what it is thought most testators would desire if they had considered the matter. See *Wills—Miscellaneous Rules of Construction*, Chapter IV, above.

7. In any construction proceeding all interested parties must have notice of the preceding and an opportunity to participate.

See generally Atkinson, pp. 804–817; Clark, pp. 709–710; Rheinstein, p. 471; Ritchie, pp. 367–372; and Scoles, pp. 130–131.

Case 113

Trust interest of unborn contingent remainderman may be adjudicated where the unborn's interest is adequately represented.

H transferred property to T Trust Company in trust for the benefit of H and W, and their four minor children. The trust was to terminate on the death of the last survivor of the six beneficiaries and the corpus was then to go to H and W's then living issue and in default of issue then to the living spouses of the four children if any and otherwise to H's heirs. A number of years later H brought suit to set aside the trust alleging fraud and undue influence. H and W agreed upon a compromise of the litigation which effected substantial changes in the terms of the trust. With the exception of the trustee, all parties personally or by guardians ad litem, joined in a petition to the court to authorize and approve the compromise. The trustee argued, however, that the judgment approving the compromise deprived unborn remainderman of property without due process of law in that their interests were impaired by the reduction of corpus and the elimination of certain contingent rights to income. Is the trustee's contention correct?

Answer. No. The general rule is that where litigation seeks to fix the interest of a share of one beneficiary in a trust and where the judgment in his favor would inevitably determine the amount available for others, all beneficiaries are indispensable parties and without their presence the trial court has no jurisdiction to proceed. Where, however, there are remainderman not in being, and when it is apparent that it is essential in the interest of justice to adjudicate the rights of living persons, there is an exception to the rule which allows the court to adjudicate the rights of living persons in the interest of justice. The rule is that a judicial proceeding has binding effect as against the future interest limited in favor of an unborn beneficiary at the time of the commencement of the proceeding when (a) the person is duly represented in such proceeding either by virtual representation or by representation by a trustee; or (b) such person is duly represented by a guardian ad litem appointed to protect the interest limited in favor of unborn persons. As one court has said: "The reason behind the exception is a simple one of human relationship implicit in the principle that human laws, and all other temporal things, are for the living; not for the dead or for those not yet in being, if to hold otherwise would result in injustice to living persons. Because parties are not in being, and therefore cannot be brought before the tribunal, it is not sufficient reason for a court to stand by, helpless and impotent, when rights of living persons, in ordinary common sense ought to be adjudicated." In the present proceedings the unborn contingent remainderman were adequately represented in the litigation. Under the doctrine of virtual representation, they were represented by the living children if the computations showed that neither the income nor corpus would be depleted to the disadvantage of the remaindermen. Nor was there any incentive on the part of living children not to protect or preserve the rights of their issue. Moreover, the interests of the unborn were protected by the court and to aid it in its exercise of jurisdiction the court appointed guardians ad litem to represent and protect the interests of the contingent remaindermen. The trustee also ably presented to the court opposition to the judgment so that all sides of the case were heard.

See *Mabry v. Scott,* 51 Cal.App.2d 245, 124 P.2d 659 (Dist.Ct.App.1942), cert. denied 317 U.S. 670, 63 S.Ct. 75, 87 L.Ed. 538 (1949).

NOTE—The Uniform Probate Code has developed elaborate provisions for virtual representation in appropriate cases and for appointment of guardians ad litem. See UPC § 1–403 and 1–401.

THE PROCESS OF ADMINISTRATION— DISTRIBUTION AND ACCOUNTING

1. Statutes generally require that the personal representative render an accounting (showing the receipts and expenditures of the administration) to the court at stated intervals and upon the completion of the administration.

2. Statutory penalties for failure to render accounts include: an action on the personal representative's bond, revocation of letters, attachment or imprisonment.

3. Where notice is given to interested parties with an opportunity for them to object to the accounts, acceptance by the court after such notice and a hearing on the objections, if any constitutes a conclusive adjudication of the correctness and propriety of the accounts.

4. Upon final settlement of the estate, the court gives a decree of final distribution finding the persons entitled to share in the estate

and their respective shares under the will, or the statutes of descent and distribution, if an intestate estate.

5. The decree of final distribution is a judgment and is conclusive of the rights of the legatees, devisees and heirs, subject only to the right of appeal or relief for fraud.

6. The decree is res judicata both as to persons to take and the shares of each even if there is obvious error.

7. The decree is not subject to collateral attack.

8. The manner of distribution is:

   (a) specific legacies—delivery of chattel to legatee,

   (b) pecuniary legacies—payment in cash,

   (c) residuary legacies and intestate distributions—personal representative may have duty to convert personalty to cash, but statutes in many states provide that the court may order distribution in kind in whole or in part.

   NOTE—The order of distribution, in contrast to the *manner*, is governed by the rules as to abatement.   See *Abatement*, Chapter IV, above.   See generally, Atkinson, pp. 796–799; Clark, pp. 807–808; Dukeminer, p. 86; and Ritchie, pp. 1356–1360.

1. In response to widespread criticism regarding the expense and time involved in formal estate administration, a number of states have adopted provisions for administering estates of certain maximum sizes which qualify under the statute with a minimum of court supervision and a minimum of formality.

INFORMAL ADMINISTRATION

2. A few states permit non-intervention administration which allows the executor to administer the estate without court supervision if

   (a) the testator so provides in the will, or

   (b) the residuary legatees and the executor consent to such administration.

3. Many states have statutes which provide a summary procedure for releasing the small estate from formal administration.   Such statutes usually are based on the estate's having an amount of assets less than a statutory maximum, such as $5000, or on the fact that assets are not in excess of statutory exemptions and allowances.

4. Such statutes vary in detail, but in general contemplate:

   (a) the filing of an application with the court setting forth the assets of the estate as being less than the statutory amount,

(b) notice (usually by publication) after which the court enters an order relieving the estate from administration and directing delivery of the assets to the persons entitled thereto, and

(c) *no personal representative is appointed.*

5. Some states have statutory provisions allowing (in limited amounts) the payment of bank accounts, wage claims, and insurance without administration.

e.g. The Uniform Probate Code provides that if it appears from the inventory and appraisal that the value of the entire estate, less liens and encumbrances, does not exceed homestead allowance, exempt property, family allowance, cost and expenses of administration, reasonable funeral expenses, and reasonable and necessary medical and hospital expenses of the last illness of the decedent, the personal representative, without giving notice to creditors, may immediately disburse and distribute the estate to the persons entitled thereto and file a closing statement with the court.   See UPC 3–1203, 3–1204.

See generally Clark, p. 699, Rheinstein, p. 506;   and Ritchie, pp. 1127–1128.

Case 114   *Purpose and effect of nonclaim statute*

T died July 1, 1947 owing two notes to P, one for $100 due June 1, 1947 and the other for $200 due Feb. 1, 1948.   A was made administrator and published notice to creditors for the first time on Sept. 1, 1947.   The statute of nonclaim provided that "all claims" against the estate of a decedent must be in writing and verified and presented to the personal representative within four months of the date of the first publication of notice to creditors.   Shortly after A qualified as administrator P spoke to A about the notes which T owed to P and A said, "We'll take care of all of the claims in due time".   On January 15, 1948 P presented written verified claims for the amounts on the two notes to A which claims A rejected as being too late.   P brought suit immediately to establish the validity of his claims against the estate of T.   May he recover?

Answer.   No.   The purpose of the non-claim statute is to enable the personal representative to settle the decedent's estate within a reasonable time.   It requires "all claims" against the estate to be presented within the four months period after first publication of notice to creditors.   "All claims" includes both matured and unmatured claims.   Such statutes compel creditors to act in some instances when they would have no right to proceed were the decedent living.   Furthermore, the effect of such statutes is not only to bar the *claims not presented but actually to eliminate all claims. Hence, the personal representative cannot waive the effect of failure to make proper presentation of the claims under the statute. In this case the oral statement of A to P is immaterial even though it may have had the effect of causing P to fail to act in reliance thereon. The statute required that the claims be presented in writing and verified. Under such statute an oral claim is ineffective. Furthermore, the time for presentation of claims expired four months from Sept. 1, 1947 which would make Jan. 1, 1948 the last day for presenting claims unless each day be a holiday in which case Jan. 2, 1948 would be the last day. The fact that one note was due before T's death and the other was not due until Feb. 1, 1948 is immaterial. Under the statute requiring "all claims" to be presented within four months both the claim which was due and the one which would become due must be presented within the period or both are lost forever to the creditor. P has failed to comply with a mandatory statute and he is without redress by virtue of the nonclaim statute.*

See *Halloran-Judge Trust Co. v. Heath,* 70 Utah 124, 258 P. 342 (1927). See also *Latham v. McClenny,* 36 Ariz. 337, 285 P. 684 (1930).

Personal representative has duty to pay debts of decedent—   **Case 115**
including debt secured by mortgage on real property

T purchased Blackacre from G for $10,000 and paid for same by giving $5000 in cash and executing to G his note and mortgage on same for $5000. He died testate devising Blackacre to X and the residue of his estate to Y. A qualified as administrator, paid all the debts except the $5000 note to G, and had $15,000 cash left in his hands as residue. Y insisted that the entire residue of $15,000 be paid to him. X insisted that $5000 of the residue be used with which to pay the note to G which would exonerate Blackacre from the mortgage. Who should prevail, X or Y?

Answer. X. *It is the duty of the personal representative to pay the debts of the decedent. The note which T made to G was a debt and should be paid like any other debt unless T's will or a statute provides otherwise. The mortgage is only an incident to the debt which is the principal thing. Of course, the effect of paying the debt will be that Blackacre is exonerated and the devisee X will have $5000 more in value whereas Y, the residuary beneficiary, will have $5000 less in value. But the rule of the common law was that the heir, devisee or legatee of mortgaged property has the right to have such property exonerated from the burden of the mortgage debt. Such debt must be paid by the personal representative out of the residuary property in the estate. The result is that X takes Blackacre, free and clear of all liabilities. The doctrine is not a favored one and leads* some courts to hold that property available for general legacies should not be used to exonerate mortgaged property.

See Hill v. Hill, 95 N.J.Eq. 233, 122 A. 818 (1923).

Case 116   *Legatees bound by decree after passage of appeal period*

T died testate and in his will was this provision: "I give to my son, A, an undivided one third of my property, to my son, B, an undivided one third of my property, to my grandson, X, an undivided one sixth of my property and to my grandson, Y, an undivided one sixth of my property". There were no debts, no other legatees or devisees and no pretermitted heirs. M was appointed and qualified as administrator with the will annexed and gave proper notice of final settlement of account of the estate which provided for distribution of the assets which consisted of $8000 in cash as follows: "an undivided one fourth of such $8000 to each of following persons, to wit: A, B, X and Y". A hearing was had and an order settling the account was made in accordance with such provision. A decree of final distribution was made which provided that $2000 was distributed to each of the legatees, A, B, X and Y. The administrator made out his check to each of such persons for $2000 and each being sui juris endorsed and cashed his check. There was no fraud and the time for appeal for such decree was six months. One year after the date of the final decree of distribution A discovered that his check should have been for one third of $8000 or $2666.67 instead of $2000 and brought suit against M, X and Y seeking relief. The defendants set up res judicata as a defense. Is the defense good?

Answer. Yes. The final decree of distribution discloses manifest error. Both A and B should have had $666.67 more than each received and both X and Y received $666.67 more than each should have received. But proper notice of the final settlement was given to A and B and they made no objection. Further, after the final decree of distribution was entered each had six months in which to appeal. Neither did so. There being no fraud, when the time for appeal expired the final decree of distribution became res judicata as to the rights of all of these parties even though there was manifest error therein. The reasons for such holding are clear. Litigation must be brought to an end and the estates of deceased persons must be finally settled sometime. Furthermore, when the court has jurisdiction to enter the decree and the parties are given their day in court, the decree is and must be binding on the parties. In this case there is obvious conflict between the provisions of the will and the provisions of the final decree of distribution. When the decree is entered the provisions of the will are merged in the provisions of the final decree of distribution and the will exists no more as an effective instrument and the decree becomes the source of all the rights of the *parties. Thus, the final decree of distribution is absolutely binding on the legatees, devisees and heirs of T and there can be no relief for A and B who had proper notice and had their day in the probate court which had jurisdiction to enter such decree.*

See Shattuck v. Shattuck, 67 Ariz. 122, 192 P.2d 229 (1948).

NOTE—In 1962, the American Bar Association and The National Conference of Commissioners on Uniform State Laws began a study of the various probate laws. This study resulted in the promulgation of the Uniform Probate Code in 1969 as amended in 1975. The Uniform Code seeks to effect modernization and uniformity among the states with respect to probate law and procedures. Its most significant suggested changes from the traditional rules of probate law are in the procedures for the administration of estates. See number 1, below. At this date the Uniform Probate Code has been adopted in fourteen states. It is presently under study and consideration by state legislatures and bar associations elsewhere throughout the country. It has been a major influence on Probate law revision even in States where it has not been adopted. Other states are likely to adopt it in the near future. It is certain to be influential with respect to all probate law revision undertaken in any state in the forseeable future.

1. The Uniform Probate Code adopts a "flexible system" of administrative of decedent's estates. In general, it provides procedures whereby:

   (a) the amount of procedural and adjudicative safeguards is adapted to the particular circumstances, and

   (b) the court's role in the administration of the estate remains passive until an interested party invokes its power to secure resolution of the problem, and then the role is limited to only the relief sought. See UPC, Article 3, General Comment.

2. The Uniform Probate Code contemplates that:

   (a) some form of probate must occur to make a will effective to transfer property, and

   (b) court appointment of a personal representative is necessary in order to create the powers and duties of such office. See UPC 3–102, 3–103.

3. The Uniform Probate Code does not require any type of probate or administration proceeding. It is within the discretion of persons claiming an interest in the estate to ask either for probate of a will or the appointment of an administrator. If no proceeding is brought within a three year period, informal distributions of the decedent's property become final.

THE UNIFORM PROBATE CODE

4. The Uniform Probate Code provides two methods for probating wills:

   (a) informal—non-adjudicative (much like common form probate), see UPC 3–301;

   (b) formal—adjudication after notice to all interested persons (much like solemn form probate).   See UPC 3–401.

5. The Uniform Probate Code provides two methods of appointment of a personal representative:

   (a) informal—appointment by a non-judicial officer without notice or final adjudication of matters with respect to priority of appointment, see UPC 3–301;

   (b) formal—appointment by judicial officer with notice to interested persons.   See UPC 3–402, 3–414.

6. Probate of a will may be had without having a personal representative appointed.

7. The Uniform Probate Code contemplates two schemes of estate settlement:

   (a) fully supervised administration, and

   (b) "in and out" supervision.

8. Fully supervised administration is little different from the administration scheme in effect in most states.   It requires:

   (a) formal probate of a will or a judicial finding of intestacy,

   (b) court appointment of a personal representative, and

   (c) settlement of the estate under the continuing supervision of the court.

9. The "in and out" type of administration allows persons interested in the estate to obtain an adjudication on a particular matter without subjecting the whole administration process to supervision.

   e.g.   It is possible under this system to determine the status of a decedent as testate or intestate without subjecting the estate to court supervised administration.

10. Personal representatives whether informally or formally appointed are given statutory powers to collect and manage the assets of the estate and to distribute the estate.   See UPC 3–704.

11. Special Uniform Probate Review provisions protect:

    (a) purchasers from personal representatives and distributees without adjudication of the property of the sale, and

    (b) personal representatives who distribute the estate without a formal adjudication.

See UPC 3–910.

12. Statutes of limitation:

    (a) make informal probate final if no formal proceeding is begun within three years after death, see UPC 3–108;

    (b) make intestate status final if no probate within three years, see UPC 3–108;

    (c) bar all claims of creditors not presented within four months after publication of administration, if such claims are not waived by the personal representative and successors, see UPC 3–802; and

    (d) bar all unsecured claims not presented within three years from death, see UPC 3–803.

See generally, Clark, pp. 700–703; Dukeminer, pp. 118–125; Rheinstein, pp. 736–796; Ritchie, pp. 50–52, 285; and Scoles, pp. 433–434, 443–444.

XIV THE FIDUCIARY

SUMMARY OUTLINE

INTRODUCTORY NOTE—While the major emphasis in the material that follows is on the trustee as fiduciary, the term "fiduciary" includes many other relationships which have relevance to estates and trusts, in particular executors and administrators. Although the functions and powers may vary depending upon the respective capacity in which he is serving, the basic fiduciary duties and responsibilities are the same wherever one person has control of property in which others have rights of enjoyment.

APPOINTMENT AND QUALIFICATION

1. The trustee of an inter vivos trust derives his authority from the trust instrument, and he administers the trust without supervision of the court.

2. Executors, administors and testamentary trustees derive their authority from court appointments. The court usually appoints the executor or the trustee named in the will. He is responsible to the court and must account to it at specified periods.

3. State statutes usually provide a list of priorities among individuals for the appointment of administrators of intestate estates. Such statutes are subject to the Equal Protection Clause of the U.S. Constitution. See Case 92, below.

4. Special rules and limitations may apply with respect to the appointment of nonresidents or aliens.

5. A bond is usually required before a person may qualify as administrator, executor or testamentary trustee. Wills often waive such requirement with respect to the executors or trustee nominated therein.

   See generally Atkinson, pp. 612–616; Clark, pp. 711–712, 715–716; Dukeminer, p. 80; Palmer, p. 611; Rheinstein, pp. 517–520; Ritchie, pp. 1151–1155; and Scoles, pp. 501–505.

Case 117   *State statute preferring males over females in administration of estate violative of equal protection clause of U.S. Constitution.*

D died intestate in the State of Idaho. His parents H and W had separated prior to his death. Shortly after D's death W, his mother, filed a petition in the probate court seeking appointment as administratix of his estate. Prior to the hearing on the petition the father also filed a petition to be appointed administrator. The probate court held a joint hearing on the petitions and ordered letters to be issued to the father on the ground that the state statute required the result. The Idaho statute governing the preference of persons to be appointed as administrator designated eleven classes entitled to administer an intestate's estate, one of which was "the father or mother," of decedent. Another section provided; ". . . of several persons claiming and equally entitled to administer, males must be preferred to females . . .". The state supreme court held this provision of the Idaho Code mandatory leaving no discretion in the court for determining who is better qualifed. W appeals to the United States Supreme Court claiming the Idaho statute is unconstitutional. Is she correct?

Answer. Yes. The Idaho statute violates the Equal Protection clause of the Fourteenth Amendment of the U.S. Constitution. The state statute provides that different treatment be accorded to applicants on the basis of their sex. It, therefore, establishes a classification subject to the Equal Protection requirement. To be valid any such classification must be reasonable, not arbitrary, and be related to the objective of the statute. The state court concluded that the purpose of the statute was to eliminate controversy between two or more persons equally entitled. "Clearly the objective of reducing the workload on probate courts by eliminating one class of contests is not without some legitimacy . . . [but] to give a mandatory preference to members of either sex over members of the other merely to accomplish the elimination of hearings on the merits is to make the very kind of arbitrary legislative choice forbidden by the Equal Protection Clause of the Fourteenth Amendment and whatever may be said as to the positive values of avoiding intra family controversy the choice in this context may not lawfully be mandated solely on the basis of sex."

See Reed v. Reed, 404 U.S. 71, 92 S.Ct. 251, 30 L.Ed.2d 225 (1971).

1. It is the duty of the trustee to take possession without delay and maintain control of the trust property; he must use every reasonable means including the resort to litigation to recover trust property in the hands of a third party.

   e.g. T holds in trust for C a $1000 promissory note signed by the maker, D. The note becomes due and is collectible. T negligently permits the statute of limitations to run thereon. T sues D who sets up the statute of limitations in defense. The defense is good and the trust estate loses the note and the interest due thereon. T is liable to C for the loss.

2. The fiduciary owes an absolute duty of loyalty to the beneficiary to administer the property solely in the interest of the beneficiary. He may not:

   (a) sell to or buy from himself personally on behalf of the trust without the approval of a court regardless of the fairness and good faith of the transaction,

DUTIES OF THE FIDUCIARY

(b) sell trust property to a third party with the understanding that he will convey to the trustee individually or hold it for him; what he may not do directly he may not do indirectly.

(c) purchase for himself trust property or a claim against the trust at a private or judicial sales. See Estate of Rothko, 84 Misc.2d 830, 379 N.Y.S.2d 923 (1975).

(d) purchase for himself individually property which it is his duty to purchase for the trust,

(e) use trust property for his own purposes,

(f) enter into competition with the beneficiary, or

(g) disclose information detrimental to the trust to third persons.

> e.g. T holds $20,000 and Blackacre worth $10,000 in trust for C. T personally owns 10,000 shares of stock in X corporation which are worth $4,000. T transfers these shares of stock to himself as trustee and pays himself $10,000 from the trust money for same, thus causing a loss to the trust estate of $6,000. He then buys Blackacre from himself as trustee for $8,000 and sells it for $12,000, thus making $4,000 profit for himself. Both of these transactions constitute breaches of T's fiduciary duty to use the trust property wholly and solely for the benefit of the cestui. T is liable to C to account for the $4,000 profit made on Blackacre and for the $6,000 loss caused by the stock transaction. In no event has a trustee any right to deal with himself respecting the trust property unless he discloses all the facts to the beneficiary and the beneficiary is sui juris and consents thereto.

3. It is the duty of the trustee to use due care to preserve the trust property.

> e.g. T holds Blackacre consisting of a dwelling house and lot in trust for C. T negligently permits the roof to deteriorate and leak so that the water from the rains causes the plaster to fall from the ceilings and the hardwood floors to warp, and the house to become unrentable. T is liable to C for the loss and damage to the trust property.

4. Although a trustee may deal with the beneficiary in his individual capacity, if the transaction concerns the interest of the beneficiary under the trust he must disclose to the beneficiary all relevant facts including a statement as to the legal rights of the beneficiary and deal fairly in the matter. See Rest. § 170(2).

5. Except as otherwise permitted by the terms of the trust, the trustee cannot delegate his duties to personally administer the trust. He cannot delegate to another the performance of which

a person of ordinary prudence, in the management of his own affairs, would not employ an agent to do.

6. A trustee can, however, delegate the performance of purely ministerial acts. In determining the acts which a trustee may properly delegate certain circumstances may be important:

    (a) the amount of discretion involved,

    (b) value of the property,

    (c) whether the act is related to principal or income,

    (d) the remoteness of the subject matter of the trust, and

    (e) whether the act involves professional skill or facilities possessed by the trustee himself. See Rest. § 171.

7. A trustee may take advice from others as to matters concerning the trust which he could not delegate, but he must personally decide the matter based on the advice.

8. A trustee generally must supervise acts and conduct of agents and co-trustees to whom he has properly delegated duties in connection with trust matters. See Rest. § 171K.

9. The trustee has the duty to keep clear and accurate accounts with respect to the trust. He may be compelled to render an account of his administration.

10. In many states testamentary trustees, executors and administrators must submit accounts to the court at regular intervals for approval.

11. At the reasonable demand of the beneficiary the trustee is under a duty to furnish complete information as to the trust property and to permit him to inspect the property and records of the trust.

12. The trustee has a duty to take reasonable action to enforce claims which are held in trust and to defend to the extent reasonable actions which may result in a loss to the trust estate.

13. The trustee may not commingle the trust property with his own or with other property not subject to the trust. When he makes deposits of trust property in a bank he must use reasonable care to select a bank in sound condition and have the deposit earmarked as a deposit by him as trustee.

    e.g. T has $20,000 in trust for C. T has an account in B bank entitled merely "T". T deposits the $20,000 trust money in that account. B bank has a claim against T and sets off the money in the account on such claim. T has committed a breach of trust when he intermingled the trust funds with his own and is liable to C for breach of trust. See Case 93, below.

See generally Bogert, pp. 343–365; Clark, pp. 740–741, 753, 772–773; Palmer, pp. 624–625, 629–631, 636, 639–641; Rest. §§ 170–172; Rheinstein, pp. 530–534; Ritchie, pp. 1167–1175, Scoles, pp. 513–519, 524–526, 544–546; and Scott §§ 170–172.

Case 118 *Trustee not liable for loss on securities registered in his own name where loss due to general income conditions*

T a trustee of a trust for the benefit of B took securities purchased for the trust in his own name. He did, however, keep the certificates separate from his own and made notations of income and remittances on separate slips of paper from which the accountant could prepare trust accounts and learn the condition of the trust. The stock depreciated in value by $7,500 through no fault of the trustee. B brings an action to recover that amount from the trustee. Will the trustee be surcharged?

Answer. No. The general rule is that it is the duty of a trustee to earmark and segregate the trust assets. A trustee who fails to earmark is liable for any loss that is the "direct and natural" consequence of the breach. In this case, however, where the loss is caused by general economic conditions and the securities have the same value they would have had if earmarked, the trustee is not liable, where he acted in good faith.

See *Miller v. Pender,* 93 N.H. 1, 34 A.2d 663 (1943).

NOTE—The Case above states the majority rule. However, some jurisdictions take the position that the trustee must suffer the *loss* as a penalty for breach of the trust duty to earmark.

Case 119 *Restrictions in trust which militate against the interests of beneficiaries and the public welfare are invalid as against public policy*

D died leaving a will which established a trust consisting of two parcels of land. The will restricted the height of the buildings to three stories and limited all leases to periods of one year. The trustee was instructed to pay long term annuities and then to distribute the remainder among the heirs of the blood of D's father per stirpes. Subsequently, the trustee brought an action to determine whether the restrictions placed by D with respect to the property are binding upon the trustee. It was agreed that the effect of the restrictions was to retard the normal development of the property as well as other property in the neighborhood in its use and value. But that the effect of such restrictions was apparent to D when he executed his will and thereafter until his death was known to him. May the trustee be relieved from D's restrictions in managing the trust property?

Answer. Yes. The general rule is that a testator may impose such restrictions and conditions as he pleases with respect to the management of property which he places in trust. Such directions are obligatory upon a trustee unless they are uncertain, unlawful or opposed to public policy. In the instant case the only purpose which can be attributed to testator in establishing the restrictions is to compel the trustee to follow his own peculiar ideas as to the proper and advantageous way to manage properties. The restrictions which he imposed are damaging to the interests of the beneficiaries of the trust, imprudent and unwise. Their effect is not confined just to the beneficiaries. Since the property is located in the heart of a financial and retail business district, its lack of development disadvantages neighboring properties, as well. To continue the restrictions as D intended for a long period of time would carry a serious threat against the proper growth and development of certain areas of the city in which the lands are situated. Since the restrictions militate against the interests of both the beneficiaries and the public welfare and benefit no one, they are invalid as against public policy and the trustee may disregard them in managing the trust estate.

See *Colonial Trust Co. v. Brown,* 105 Conn. 261, 135 A. 555 (1926).

1. The trustee has a duty to invest trust property and make it productive.

2. In making investments the trustee may be bound by:

   (a) directions by the settlor with respect to the investments to be made,

   (b) statutes governing investments by trustees, and

   (c) the standards which would govern a prudent man in making investments of his own property having in mind the preservation of the estate and income to be earned.

3. The settlor often specifies in the will or trust instrument the types of investments the trustee is to make. The trustee is obligated to follow such directions and is protected against liability in doing so. See number 7, below.

4. States which have statutes governing investments by trustees are divided into:

   (a) "Prudent man" states, which require the trustee only to invest as, "men of prudence, discretion and intelligence manage their own affairs not in regard to speculation but in regard to the permanent disposition of their funds considering the probable income, as well as the probable safety of the capital to be invested." *Harvard College v. Amory,* 26 Mass. 446,

THE INVESTMENT OF TRUST PROPERTY

(1831). This is also the standard where there is no statute governing investments.

(b) "Legal list" states, which by statute prescribe investments (usually non-equity) in which a trustee is to invest. These statutes are of two types:

    (i) "Permissive" where the trustee may invest outside the list but if so he has the burden of justifying any investments not on the list.

    (ii) "Mandatory" where the trustee is liable for any investment not on the list.

5. The settlor will often grant to the trustee discretion in making investments. In such cases he does not have to select from the legal list; however, he does not have the right to exercise his discretion recklessly. He must use good faith and prudence.

NOTE—In some legal list states such clauses in wills and trusts as "invest as he deems proper" may be narrowly construed to mean "within the legal list."

6. Because of the rule against commingling, until recent years it was held that investments in participating mortgages, common trust funds and investment trusts were improper. The modern trend, however, is to allow such investments usually by way of specific legislation subject to restrictions which vary from state to state.

7. If the settlor directs the trustee to make or retain certain investments and because of changes in circumstances not known to or anticipated by the settlor compliance will result in loss to the trust or defeat of the trust purposes, the trustee may petition the court for permission to deviate from the terms of the trust. The court, however, will not authorize a deviation merely for convenience or to produce greater income. See *Enforcement and Duration of Charitable Trust*, numbers 5 and 6, Chapter VIII, above.

8. Except as the terms of the trust may otherwise provide, the trustee has a duty to dispose of investments which are included in the trust property when the trust is created which are not proper investments for trustees.

9. If investments, although proper when acquired subsequently become improper, the trustee has a duty to dispose of them as soon as reasonably possible.

See generally Bogert, pp. 366–396; Clark, pp. 781–783, 787–789; Rest. §§ 227–231; Rheinstein, pp. 543–544; Ritchie, pp. 1179–1182; and Scott, §§ 227–231.

Court will order administration of trust pursuant to requirements   **Case 120**
of Federal Tax Reform Act as testator intended

The Federal Tax Reform Act of 1969 set up certain requirements for
a trust having a charitable remainder if it is to qualify for estate and
income tax deductions.   Shortly after the effective date of the Act
D executed a will attempting to establish a remainder which would
qualify under the Act.   Both at the time of the execution of the will
and at the time of D's death no regulations had been published by
the Internal Revenue Service with respect to the new Act.   Subsequently regulations were promulgated requiring that the governing
instrument must bar the trustees from engaging in certain prohibited
acts in order for the remainder to qualify for an estate tax deduction.
D's will did not include language expressly prohibiting the trustee
from exercising all the prohibited powers.   Two were so prohibited.
All others were forbidden by the general trust law of the state.   D's
executor and trustee bring an action asking the court for instructions.
What relief will the court give?

Answer.   The court will direct the trustees to administer the trust
fund within the requirements of the Act and prohibit by its decree
the trustees from exercising the prohibited powers.   Since the clear
intent of the testator was to comply with the Act and have the trust
administered in keeping with that purpose and in addition the state
law would prevent the trustees from exercising the prohibited acts,
the court will order the trustees to refrain from any exercise of such
power.

See In re Estate of Klosk, 65 Misc.2d 1005, 319 N.Y.S.2d 685 (1971).

A court may permit a deviation from the terms of a trust only   **Case 121**
when the settlor's main purpose will otherwise fail

A testamentary trust was created by T's will.   The terms of the will
provided that the trustees: "shall have full power and authority to
invest and reinvest the trust property as the trustee shall deem fit and
proper", subject, however, to the limitation that: "investments by
the trustee shall be made only in bonds of the United States government, in bonds of the State of the United States, and municipalities
thereof, and in such other bonds as shall be rated at least 'AA' by
Moody's Investor Service."   The income of the trust was given to
certain beneficiaries for life with a general testamentary power of
appointment in them over the remainders following their respective
life estates, with issue of the life tenants designated as takers in
default.

The trust was established in 1936.   In 1951 the life beneficiaries
petitioned that the trustee be authorized to deviate from the terms of

the trust concerning investments and invest in accordance with the "prudent man rule". The evidence before the Probate Court showed that the trustees received assets in 1936 of the value of $2,323,000. Eighteen years later, these assets were worth $2,860,000. The distributable annual income had also increased from $89,000 to $110,000. No evidence was presented that any beneficiary was in want or that the distributable income was not sufficient to supply the reasonable needs of all beneficiaries. No emergency existed threatening the trust. The contention of the beneficiaries was that the intent of the settlor was to secure an income to the life beneficiaries in as large an amount as possible commensurate with reasonable safety, that the sole purpose of the restrictions on investment was to protect the corpus and that because of changes in the general economy, the purpose of the trust was being defeated and thwarted, a result the testator could not have foreseen prior to his death. The beneficiaries argued that all of the interested beneficiaries had consented to the deviation and all would benefit by the proposed modification. The evidence showed a marked decline in the purchasing power of the dollar and that the return on bonds as compared to the return on stocks was very low. Should the beneficiaries have a decree enabling the trustees to deviate from the terms of the trust governing investments?

Answer. No. The power to permit deviation from the terms of private trusts is analogous to the cy pres doctrine applicable to charitable trusts. The general rule is that the trust instrument constitutes the measure of the trustee's powers. Except in unusual or emergency situations, courts will limit the trustees to the power conferred. The courts, however, will not permit the main purpose of a trust to fail by adherence to administrative limitations of the trust instrument and in such cases will grant permission to deviate from the restrictive administrative provisions. A court, however, will not permit a deviation simply because the beneficiaries request it when the main purpose of the trust is not threatened and when no emergency exists or is threatened. The theory of the rule of deviation is that, by the exercise of this power, the court is furthering the intent of the testator in that it is doing what the testator would have done had he anticipated changed conditions, i.e., the specific intent of the testator is disregarded in order to enforce his general intent. In ascertaining that general intent the court may take into account factors such as the consent of all persons interested in the trust and the fact that the preferred modification concerns only the administrator of the trust rather than the rights of any beneficiaries. The court must also consider expressed opinions of the testator regarding what should constitute appropriate investments. This is particularly so where the testator had accumulated a large fortune and during the depression stock had seen investments wiped out over night if therefore, he wanted to provide safety of the investment. Although there has been a continued inflationary cycle for a number of years, there is no guarantee that a recession will not follow. While the testator may not have been omniscient, neither are the beneficiaries nor the courts, and the court should not try to guess what economic conditions may be in a few years by permitting deviations when no real emergency exists or is threatened. In the present case, the clear proof necessary to show that a deviation must be granted in order to preserve the trust or carry out the intention of the testator is missing. Therefore, no deviation can be allowed.

See *Stanton v. Wells Fargo Bank & Union Trust Co.,* 150 Cal.App.2d 763, 310 P.2d 1010 (D.C.App.1957).

Court may not order trust deviation where future beneficiaries will be prejudiced thereby

Case 122

D by her will left the residuary to T in trust to pay the net income, one-third each to her children, Margaret, Ethel and William during their lives. On the death of Margaret one-third of the corpus is to be paid to her issue per stirpes; if she dies without issue, to her husband; if she dies survived by neither issue nor husband, one-half is to be added to the shares of Ethel and one-half to be added to the share of William. At the time of D's will Margaret's husband was earning sufficient income to support him and his wife in comfort. He died shortly after D leaving no estate. Margaret developed epilepsy and is in a nursing home. The trust income is not sufficient to take care of her needs, and she will be placed in a public institution if she is unable to obtain additional funds. D suffered a stroke shortly after executing her will and never realized Margaret's condition and need. Margaret asks that the court direct the trustee to pay out of the corpus sufficient monies to keep her in the private home. Margaret has no children. Ethel and William and a niece who is sui juris have consented to the invasion. Other possible remaindermen are infants and there is a possibility of after borns who would be entitled to share. Will the court allow the invasion of corpus?

Answer. No. To grant Margaret's request would be to give her property which belongs to others. The infants cannot consent and afterborns may take an interest. Since the life beneficiary is not the only person interested in the trust the rights of the other residuary beneficiaries must be protected. ". . . in an emergency and for the preservation of the estate and for the benefit of the cestui que trust [chancery] may direct the trustee to deviate from the express provisions of the trust instrument . . . But the court cannot order the trustee to pay to one cestui part of a fund which the testator has established for the benefit of others." Despite the fact that the court may be convinced that were D alive she would devote her estate *to caring for her needy child she gave her only a life interest and the courts cannot rewrite her will.*

See *Hughes v. Federal Trust Co.,* 119 N.J.Eq. 502, 183 A. 299 (1936); *Estate of Van Deusen,* 30 Cal.2d 285, 182 P.2d 565 (1947).

NOTE—Pennsylvania recently passed the following statute: "(a) Failure of original purpose. The court having jurisdiction of a trust, heretofore or hereafter created, regardless of any spendthrift or similar provision therein, in its discretion may terminate such trust in whole or in part, or make an allowance from principal to a conveyor, his spouse, issue, parents, or any of them, who is an income beneficiary, provided the court after hearing is satisfied that the original purpose of the conveyor cannot be carried out or is impractical of fulfillment and that the termination, partial termination or allowance more nearly approximates the intention of the conveyor, and notice is given to all parties in interest or to their duly appointed fiduciaries. But, distributions of principal under this section whether by termination, partial termination, or allowance, shall not exceed an aggregate value of twenty-five thousand dollars from all trusts created by the same conveyor." Pa.Stat.Ann.tit. 20, § 301.2(a)(Purdon).

TRUSTS—PRINCIPAL AND INCOME

1. The trustee has a duty where there are successive beneficiaries to act impartially and with due regard for their respective interests.

   e.g. A trustee may not invest in unproductive property which will produce no income for the life beneficiary although it is probable that the property will increase in value and thus unduly benefit the remainder.

2. It is the duty of the trustee to distribute income and principal in accordance with the terms of the trust. A settlor may specifically provide for the allocation of receipts and expenses to principal and income.

3. Where the trust documents are silent as to allocation of principal and income the general rule is that income is the return derived from the principal and principal is the property received as a substitute for or change in form of the original corpus of the trust.

   e.g. In the case of a business, the net profits are income while increase in good will or the value of assets is principal.

4. There are a number of views as to proper allocation of dividends:

   (a) The Kentucky Rule—all dividends regardless of form or source are income. In jurisdictions accepting this view the Rule has been modified to regard stock dividends from the declaring corporation as principal.

   (b) The Pennsylvania Rule—ordinary cash dividends are income. Extraordinary cash and stock dividends are examined to determine source and allocated to keep book value of stock at the date of creating the trust.

(c) The Massachusetts Rule—cash dividends of whatever kind are income, as are dividends paid in the stock of a company other than the one declaring the dividend. Stock dividends in the declaring corporation are principal. This is the most widely used rule and has been adopted by the Uniform Principal and Income Act which is in effect in a majority of states.

See Uniform Principal and Income Act, § 5.

5. Where the trustee is under a duty to sell unproductive property and the sale is delayed, a portion of the proceeds is to be allocated to income equal to the amount it would have earned had it been sold at the time the duty to dispose of it arose.

6. If a wasting asset is part of the trust property, the general rule is that the trustee is under a duty either to make provision for amortization to the beneficiary of the corpus or to sell the property.

7. Where the trust instrument does not provide for allocation of expenses between income and principal, ordinary expenses are to be satisfied out of income (e.g. recurring taxes, accountant's fees, repairs, maintenance, utility charges) and other expenses from principal. See Uniform Principal and Income Act, § 6.

NOTE—A trustee is now generally held to be able to establish depreciation reserves and charge them against income.

8. Where the instrument does not specifically provide, income usually begins:

(a) in the case of a testamentary trust, on the date of death;

(b) in the case of an inter vivos trust, on the effective date of the trust.

9. Where property is held in trust to pay income to a life beneficiary and then to pay principal to others, income accruing but not paid out prior to death of the life beneficiary is paid to his personal representative.

See generally Bogert, pp. 418–428, 435–440, 450–453; Clark, pp. 795–797, 799, 804–807; Palmer, pp. 681–687; 692–693; Rest. §§ 232–239; Ritchie, pp. 1193–1194, 1205, 1210–1215; and Scott, §§ 232–239.1.

By the majority view, stock dividends in the declaring corporation are attributable to principal rather than to income

Case 123

D died leaving to B a life estate in certain real estate and "during her natural life all dividends accruing and payable on the capital stock I own in X Corporation as well as all dividends on my 17 shares of capital stock in Y Corporation." During the life estate Y Corporation declared successive common stock dividends of 50%, 33⅓% and 25%. Who is the owner of the shares issued as a result of the several stock dividends?

Answer. The remainderman rather than the life tenant. There is a wide divergence of opinion among the various jurisdictions as to the proper allocation of stock dividends as between the life tenant and a remainderman. The Kentucky rule awards all dividends, regardless of form, to the life tenant. The Massachusetts rule awards stock dividends to remaindermen and the Pennsylvania rule occupies a middle position and inquires as to the time covered by the accumulation of earnings embraced by the extraordinary distribution. The majority of jurisdictions have adopted the Massachusetts rule, and it is the rule set forth in the Uniform Principal and Income Act. The Massachusetts rule is the sounder rule in that a stock dividend is not a true dividend at all since it involves no division or severance from the corporate assets of the subject of the dividend. A stock dividend does not distribute property but simply dilutes the shares as they existed before. In addition, the Massachusetts rule is direct, simple and easy of application.

See *Bowles v. Stilley's Ex'r*, 267 S.W.2d 707 (Ky.App.1954).

Case 124   *Capital gains distributions of registered investment companies are to be treated as principal rather than income*

S established an inter vivos trust naming W as life beneficiary with remainder over to C. S transferred to the trustees 100 shares of a mutual investment trust stating that if the trust were liquidated, the trustees were to receive the distributive share in the assets "properly allocable to them" to pay over the net income therefrom monthly to W. S died subsequently and thereafter all the assets of the mutual investment trust were sold to BS Investment Corporation, a mutual investment trust subject to the Investment Company Act of 1940. The original trust was liquidated following this sale. The trustees of S's trust receive 55,434 shares of BS Trust in exchange for their shares. Thereafter, BS paid the trustees two cash dividends from income and then delivered to the trustees, 1,463 additional shares of BS as "distributions of gains" as distinguished from "dividends from income" on the shares the trustees then held. Under the Internal Revenue Code, the trustees pay a capital gains tax on the shares received. The trustees paid to W the dividends from the income paid by BS, but refuse to transfer to her the 1,463 shares. These shares were paid to the trustees at their request and at their option they could have received these shares in cash. Nothing in the terms of the inter vivos trust showed what the settlor's intent was with respect to capital gains dividends. The life beneficiary now seeks *a declaratory decree that the distribution of capital gains be treated as income of the trust. Is she entitled to the decree?*

Answer. No. The general rule is to regard cash dividends as income and stock dividends as capital. This rule, however, is based in some degree upon the substance, rather than the form, of the transaction as carried out by the entity declaring the dividend. Dividends in cash paid out of capital or in liquidation have been treated as belonging to principal. The substance of a transaction, therefore, must be examined to determine whether it is equivalent to a stock dividend. Where the trustee, as shareholder, is given an option to receive a dividend in stock or in cash, the cases often treat the dividend as a cash dividend and as income. It is necessary, therefore, to look at the substance of a capital gain distribution made by BS in order to determine whether or not the distribution should be treated as capital or income. On the one hand, it is argued that dividends from gains on the sales of securities held in a mutual fund's portfolio are income from the ordinary conduct of the fund's business, bought or sold like inventory, and thus should be treated as income. The contrary view is that the sale of a security in an investment company portfolio involves the sale of a capital item, so that, if the gain therefrom is distributed, the capital is necessarily reduced. It is said that a trustee's investment in an investment company is in substance nothing more than a fractional ownership in the securities of a diversified portfolio as to which the trustee should account as if he held the portfolio securities directly. The special character of regulated investment companies and a specialized tax treatment under the Internal Revenue Code also have some tendency to give capital gains distribution the aspect of principal. The dividends and distributions of a regulated investment company may be more nearly analogized to those of a common trust fund than to that of an ordinary industrial company. To say that the realized gains of a common trust fund are not distributed to the participating trust, whereas those of an investment company are distributed to fiduciaries who are shareholders, is merely to state the obvious fact that a common trust is administered by the trustee itself, whereas the regulated investment company is a separate entity from the trustee who invests in its shares. If a trustee elects to take shares of the investment company in payment of any distribution made to him of capital gains, he will be able to achieve the same substantive result as that achieved by the common trust fund. The method of determining the purchase and sale prices of investment company shares in relation to the net asset value of shares is consistent with the concept that the trustee is obtaining diversification by an indirect participation in the investment company's portfolio. Since the trustee could redeem his shares at a profit just before the capital gain distribution and necessarily allocate that gain to principal, the capital gain distribution, when made in any different way, should be treated as a part of the principal of the trust. *This view is the view adopted by the Commissioners on Uniform State Laws after full deliberation and, therefore, seems to be the better view. As a result, it may be concluded that from the standpoint of a trustee investing in its shares, the regulated company is merely a conduit to the trust fund of its realized gains and that in the hands of the trustee, the gains should retain their character as principal.*

  See Tait v. Peck, 346 Mass. 521, 194 N.E.2d 707, 98 A.L.R.2d 503 (1963).

POWERS OF THE FIDUCIARY

1. The trustee has such powers as are expressly given to him in the trust instrument and such implied powers as are necessary to the accomplishment of the trust purpose and which are not prohibited in the terms of the trust.

2. The trustee must do the things which the trust instrument commands and he may do the things which are left to his discretion provided he does not abuse such discretion.

  e.g. S conveys Blackacre to T in trust for C and directs T to sell Blackacre and invest the proceeds in U.S. Government bonds bearing 4 percent interest. S reserves no power to revoke the trust. T takes possession of Blackacre and is about to sell it for a very good price for such land, $50,000. S changes his mind and tells T not to sell Blackacre. T advises S that he is directed in the trust deed to sell Blackacre and feels he must obey such command. S sues T to enjoin such sale. S will fail in his suit. Unless the settlor reserves some power over the trust in the trust instrument, he has no right, power or authority over the trust or the trust property. The rights, duties and powers of the trustee are determined by the trust instrument or terms of the trust at the time of its creation. Therefore, T is bound to sell Blackacre and invest the proceeds in U.S. bonds and the fact that S has changed his mind is quite immaterial.

3. Unless forbidden to do so by the trust instrument a trustee may incur reasonable expenses to carry out the trust purposes.

  e.g. S conveys Blackacre, a house and lot to T to hold in trust for C and to pay the income therefrom to C. The house is in a good location and in good repair, but is old and does not have a modern kitchen. The house is either not rentable at all or must be rented at a very low rent. With a modern kitchen it would be readily rentable for $350.00 per month. T makes a contract to have a new kitchen installed for $2,500. The remodeling is done and he rents the house for a year at $350 per month. T personally pays for the improvements. T is entitled to reimbursement from the trust. Ordinarily a trustee does not have power to expend trust funds for the improvement of the trust property unless the trust instrument so provides; however if such improvements are reasonable in amount and are necessary to carry out the trust purpose or to make the property reasonably productive the trustee is empowered to make such improvements and to reimburse himself for the expenses incurred in making such. In this case it might be said that the trust instrument impliedly authorized T to improve the property because he was to pay C the income therefrom and that could not be done if the property could not be rented. Be that as it may the trust purpose requires an income, the improvements are necessary to make the property reasonably productive and the expenditure of $2500 is reasonable under the circumstances when the property is made to rent for $350 per month. Hence, the expenses incurred for the improvements are proper and T is entitled to reimbursement.

4. Unless expressly so provided in the terms of the trust instrument the trustee has no power to mortgage or pledge the trust property or to borrow money on the credit of the trust.

5. Unless forbidden to do so by the trust instrument the trustee has the power to lease trust property for such periods and on such terms as are reasonable.

6. The trustee has a power to sell trust property if:

   (a) the trust instrument expressly confers such power, or

   (b) the sale is necessary or proper to carry out the purposes of the trust.

   NOTE—Courts almost always find the power of sale implied as to personal property. By contrast many jurisdictions are likely to find no such implied power with respect to real estate.

7. The trustee may if appropriate to the trust purpose, compromise, abandon or submit to arbitration claims affecting the trust property.

   e.g. S bequeaths to T all of his property in trust for C. Among the assets T receives is a promissory note for $1,000 signed by X who is honest but insolvent and judgment proof and his other creditors are threatening to force him into involuntary bankruptcy. As a compromise T accepts $500 from X and returns the note to X marked paid in full. This is within T's power as trustee.

8. The trustee holding securities has the power to vote the shares and exercise any rights of ordinary shareholders.

9. In a private trust if there are several trustees they must act jointly

to be binding unless the terms of the trust provide otherwise. A majority may act in a charitable trust.

10. A successor trustee or surviving trustee may exercise the powers conferred upon his predecessor unless it is otherwise provided in the terms of the trust.

See generally Palmer pp, 697–699; Rest. §§ 186–196; Ritchie, pp. 1231–1232; and Scott, §§ 185–196.

Case 125   *Court will not override good faith discretion of trustee*

Testatrix by will left money to trustees to hold for the benefit of her daughter, Lucy, during her life with power in the trustee, "should they in their discretion think it is wise to do, at any time to pay over and transfer to my said daughter the property or any part thereof held by them in trust for the benefit of my said daughter." At the time of the will Lucy was confined to a hospital for the insane. About one year after the testatrix' death, she was released and adjudged sane. At that time she demanded the trust property be delivered to her. The trustee refused to do so. Is Lucy entitled to the trust property?

Answer. No. The power granted to the trustees under the will is neither one which the trustees were compelled to exercise on the finding that the beneficiary was sane nor was it a power to be exercised on the whim of the trustees without being subject to the control of the courts. The power in the trustees was to be exercised upon making a judgment that it is wise to do so. In making such judgment the trustees may consider all circumstances surrounding the beneficiary such as her health, and ability to manage her affairs. It is the duty of the trustees to exercise an honest discretion and so long as the trustees do exercise discretion in good faith a court will not overrule that discretion.

See *Watling v. Watling,* 27 F.2d 193 (6th Cir. 1928).

LIABILITIES OF THE TRUSTEE

1. The trustee is personally liable on all contracts made by him in the administration of the trust unless it is expressly agreed that the creditor shall look only to the trust property for his compensation.

   (a) T holds Blackacre in trust for C with express authority to sell the land and invest the proceeds in securities. T lists Blackacre for sale with broker, B, who sells it and earns the agreed commission of $2000. T refuses to pay B's commission. B sues T for such. T insists that he should be sued in his representative capacity as "T, trustee for C". Is T's contention valid? Ans. No. Of course T's contention is immaterial for a suit against "T" as defendant has the same legal effect as a suit against "T, trustee for C". In both cases T is personally liable and a judgment against him can be satisfied out of T's individual property. Furthermore, there is no right on the part of the judgment creditor to satisfy such judgment out of the trust property in the absence of an equity decree permitting such. In this case when T listed Blackacre for sale with B and agreed to pay the commission for B's sale of the property, it was T's promise to pay and he alone is liable personally on the obligation. If it is an expense properly incurred in the administration of the trust, as this one is, then the trustee may reimburse himself out of the trust property. If it is not a proper expense then the trustee has no right to reimburse himself for such out of the trust property.

(b) Had T when he made the listing with B told B that he, T, would not be personally liable on the contract for B's commission but that B would have to look to the trust fund solely for his pay, and B had agreed to such, then of course, B's sole remedy would have been against the trust property. See Rest. §§ 262–263.

2. A trustee is personally liable for all torts committed in the course of the administration of the trust assets to the same extent that he would be had he held them free of trust.

   e.g. A is trustee of an apartment house. B, a business visitor falls in the lobby due to the negligence of A's employee. A is personally liable to B for any injuries B sustains. See Rest. § 264.

3. The remedies of the beneficiary for breach of trust are in equity except that the beneficiary may sue at law for money or a chattel presently and unconditionally due from the trustee. In equity the question of the fiduciary's conduct of the trust may be raised in the following proceedings:

   (a) a request by fiduciary for instructions,

   (b) an injunction action by beneficiaries against a threatened breach of trust,

   (c) an action by beneficiaries for specific performance of trust obligation,

   (d) objections filed to fiduciary's accounts with request to surcharge,

   (e) an action to remove fiduciary,

   (f) an action to appoint receiver, or

(g) an action to waive fiduciary's compensation. See Rest. §§ 197–198.

4. In addition a beneficiary may maintain an action:

(a) to compel the trustee to perform his duties,

(b) to enjoin a breach of trust,

(c) to compel trustee to redress a breach of trust, or

(d) to appoint a receiver to administer the trust. See Rest. § 199.

5. The trustee is liable to the beneficiary for any injury caused by a breach of trust. This means the breach of any duty owed to the beneficiary.

6. The trustee is not liable to the beneficiary for loss or decrease in value of the trust property unless there is a breach of trust.

(a) T holds money in trust for C and deposits it in B bank using due care in the selection of the depositary. The B bank becomes insolvent and pays only 10 percent to the depositors. T being free from negligence is not liable.

(b) T holds negotiable securities in trust for C and has them in the safe deposit box in B bank. Burglars break into the bank and steal the securities. There being no negligence or breach of duty on T's party, he is not liable for the loss to C.

See In re Bank of New York, 35 N.Y.2d 512, 364 N.Y.S.2d 164, 323 N.E.2d 700 (1974).

7. The trustee is liable to the beneficiary for loss of interest if he holds trust money an unreasonable time without investing when such investments are readily available.

e.g. T has $10,000.00 which he holds in trust for C. T deposits the money in a commercial bank which does not pay any interest on deposits. Reasonable diligence on T's part would disclose many sound investments for the money at 6% interest within 90 days from the time T receives the money. T leaves the $10,000.00 in the bank for more than a year without investing it. T is liable to C for interest on the money after the 90 day period.

8. The trustee is liable to the beneficiary for loss caused by a breach of trust by a co-trustee if he participates in such breach or delegates the administration of the trust to a co-trustee improperly.

e.g. T and X are trustees of a $100,000 trust estate for C which is in the form of negotiable securities and readily reduced to cash. T tells X to make such investments and do with the trust property as he wishes without consulting T about such because T does not know anything about investments anyway. T makes no inspection of the trust accounts nor does he even so much as inquire of X about the trust property on hand or the form in which it exists. He simply trusts X to administer the trust entirely. This goes on for several years and X dies insolvent and having embezzled $60,000 of the trust property. T is liable to C for the loss, he having breached his duty to exercise due and constant diligence concerning the administration of the trust property and the investments made thereof. A trustee is appointed for the purpose of administering the trust property and when he qualifies as such it becomes his personal duty to supervise the administration by and with his co-trustee. He has no right to delegate or divide the powers of administration. See Rest. § 224.

9. The trustee is liable for payment of trust funds or income to anyone other than the beneficiary.

   e.g. T is trustee of $60,000 for C for life and then for D, which T has invested at 5% interest. For many years T who lives in Chicago has been sending a regular monthly check for $200 to C who lives in Seattle. C dies and T learns nothing about it. T continues to send the checks which are returned in T's regular monthly vouchers, having been paid out of the trust estate. T does not examine the monthly vouchers or he would easily have discovered that the endorsements thereon were forgeries. This continues for 2 years after C's death. T is liable to D for the loss of $200 per month for 2 years, or $4800. See Rest. § 226.

10. The trustee is liable to the beneficiary in the event of a breach of trust for:

    (a) any loss resulting from the breach of trust,

    (b) any profit resulting from the breach of trust,

    (c) any profit the trust would have made in the absence of the breach of trust.

11. The trustee is *not* able to offset gains against losses.

    e.g. The trust corpus is $200,000. The trustee invests $100,000 in speculative gold stocks on which he realizes a profit of $9,000. He also invests $100,000 in speculative oil stock on which he realizes a loss of $50,000. He is liable for $209,000. The trustee may not charge off the $9,000 profit against the $50,000 loss. See Rest. § 205.

12. The trustee is liable to the beneficiary for any profit arising out of a transaction involving the trust property even though he has not committed a breach of trust.

    e.g. A devises Blackacre to T in trust for C. Blackacre is subject to a first mortgage for $10,000, and a second mortgage for $5,000.

In order to prevent the foreclosure of the second mortgage T purchases it with his own funds for $3,000. Later the full amount of the second mortgage is realized. T is only entitled to $3,000. See Rest. § 203.

13. No one, including the settlor, except the beneficiary has a right to enforce the trust or to maintain an action for breach of trust, unless the settlor has retained an interest which would be affected by the breach such as the power to revoke. See Rest. 200.

See generally Clark, pp. 793–795; Palmer, pp. 646–647, 653–657; Rest. §§ 197, 221, 223–226, 262–264; Ritchie, pp. 1248–1249, 1256–1257; Scoles, pp. 554–555; Scott, §§ 197–221, 223–226, 261–265.

Case 126   *A successor fiduciary has obligation to redress breach of duty committed by predecessor fiduciary*

D died leaving a will which created a trust for the benefit of his widow and daughter. The will named T as both executor and trustee. During the administration of the estate a mistake was made by counsel for the executor in preparing the state inheritance tax return which involved a substantial overpayment which was not refundable. The account of B as executor was nevertheless approved. Thereafter, the beneficiaries of the trust filed an objection to the account of T as trustee on account of the overpayment. Is T as trustee chargeable with the overpayment of the state inheritance tax?

Answer. *Yes. A trustee of a testamentary trust owes to the trust beneficiaries a duty to collect and preserve the assets of the trust estate, and is liable for breach of trust if it neglects to take proper steps to compel the predecesor to deliver all of the trust property to it. These general principles of trust law make it clear that upon the assumption of administration of the trust, T as trustee had an obligation to redress the breach of duty which occurred when the executor overpaid the inheritance tax. Failure to discharge that obligation constituted a breach of trust on the part of the bank in its capacity as trustee. The fact that the beneficiaries did not assert a claim against the executor when the executor's account was filed does not bar them from asserting the breach of trust against the bank in its capacity as trustee. The bank as trustee was under an unqualified duty to take action to recover for the benefit of the beneficiaries that portion of the trust property which had been wrongfully disbursed by the bank while acting as executor. Since this liability is based upon its failure to discharge its responsibilities as trustee, the failure of the beneficiary to file exceptions to the final account of the executor does not preclude exceptions to the account of T in its capacity as trustee.*

See *In re First Nat'l Bank of Mansfield,* 37 Ohio St.2d 60, 307 N.E.2d 23 (1974).

A corporate trust may not retain its own shares in a trust portfolio without express approval of settlor   **Case 127**

S transferred property in trust to Farmers Bank as trustee. Included in the property transferred were securities of City Bank. Under the terms of the trust the settlor, who was also the life beneficiary, had the power to revoke the trust or to amend it so as to remove the trustee or to require the trustee to sell the stock of City Bank. Subsequently, Farmers Bank became affiliated with City Bank and City Bank was substituted as trustee for Farmers Bank. The result was that City Bank as trustee became the beneficial owner of its own stock. The settlor approved the investment and asked that as long as she lived the shares be retained by the trustees. There was subsequently a loss on the investment in City Bank. Thereafter an action is brought by the trustee for judicial approval and settlement of its accounts. The guardian ad litem of certain infant defendant beneficiaries seeks to have the trustee surcharged for loss in the value of the bank's stocks contending that the loss occurred while the trustee was in a position of divided loyalty. (a) Did the trustee commit a breach of trust by continuing to hold the investments in its stock after it became a trustee? (b) Even if there was a breach of trust, are the beneficiaries estopped to claim a surcharge against the trust?

Answer. (a) Yes. (b) Yes. The standard of loyalty required of a trustee does not permit the trustee to occupy a position in which he has interests to serve other than that of the trust estate. A trustee must preserve undivided loyalty in all of its transactions. Here undivided loyalty did not exist after City Bank became the trustee of the trust which owned shares in City Bank. The officers of the trustee responsible for the administration of the trust also had a duty of loyalty to serve the interests of the bank. These were conflicting interests insofar as the trust investment in City Bank required a decision whether to hold or sell shares in a falling market. Even if the trustee acted in the utmost good faith the trustee would still have been in breach of trust. It is not enough to act in good faith for when the trustee has selfish interests which may be served, the law stops the inquiry when the relation is disclosed and sets aside the transaction or refuses to enforce it and in a proper case surcharges the trustee for an unauthorized investment. "It is only the rigid adherrence to these principles that all temptation can be removed from one acting as a fiduciary to serve his own interest when in conflict with the obligations of his trust. The rule is designed to obliterate all divided loyalties which may creep into a fiduciary relationship and utterly to destroy their effect by making voidable any transactions

*in which they appear.'' On the other hand, here the donor approved
the investment and in so doing has estopped the guardian ad litem
from objecting to the investment since the settlor had reserved absolute power of modification and revocation and insisted on the trust
investment.   Her action in approving the retention of the shares and
opposing the sale of the shares effectively estopped her and the remaindermen from surcharging the trustee from the loss in investments.*

*See City Bank Farmers Trust Co. v. Cannon, 291 N.Y. 125, 51 N.E.2d
674 (1943).*

Case 128   *Executor is liable for torts committed by employees of business
conducted by the executor as part of estate*

*P, a delivery man, was injured when a door fell on him as he was
entering a garage of an automobile agency operated as part of D's
estate by E, D's executor.   The door fell as a result of the negligence
of the agency's employees.   E had continued to operate the business
as part of the estate pursuant to the terms of D's will and a state
statute which provides,   ''. . .   the court may authorize the executor or administrator to continue the operation of the business to
such an extent and subject to such restrictions as may seem to the
court to be for the best interest of the estate and those interested
therein.''   P brought an action for personal injuries sustained by him
against E individually.   The action was brought subsequent to the
closing of D's estate, the distribution of its assets and the discharge
of the executors.   Is E personally liable to P?*

> **Answer.**   Yes.   The rule is that an executor is liable for torts
> committed by employees in the administration of the estate.   The
> personal liability of an executor for torts committed during the course
> of his administration is not confined to actions that are outside the
> scope of his authority.   The statute has no effect on this rule of
> liability.   Its principal effect is to provide authority for the executor
> to carry on the decedent's business if the will does not authorize him
> to do so.   Prior to the statute, an executor who carried on decedent's
> business with an authorization in the will did so at his own risk and
> anything that occurred in the course of conducting the business was
> personal without any right of reimbursement from the estate.   As
> executor of the estate the employees of the business were his em-
> ployees and he is liable for their actions the same as any other em-
> ployer.   See Johnston v. Long, 30 Cal.2d 54, 181 P.2d 645 (1947).

**EFFECT OF
EXCULPATORY
CLAUSES**

1. A settlor, by the express provisions of the trust, may relieve the
    trustee from liability for breach of trust.

2. Such provisions are strictly construed by the courts and are generally limited to cases of errors in judgment and mistakes committed in good faith.

3. An exculpatory provision which attempts to relieve the trustee from liability for wilful wrongdoing or gross negligence is against public policy and void.

4. An exculpatory provision is ineffective if it is made part of a trust agreement by reason of the trustee's breach of a fiduciary or confidential relationship.

   e.g.   The trustee, an attorney, draws the trust document for his client who is not a person of business experience and inserts the clause without discussing it with the client or the client's obtaining independent advice.   The exculpatory provision would be held to be of no effect.

   See generally Bogert, 339–343;   Clark, p. 795;   Rest. §§ 222; Scoles, p. 555;   and Scott, § 222.

1. A trustee is entitled to reasonable compensation for his services. The amount may be:

   (a) stipulated in the trust agreement;

   (b) fixed by the court after considering the value of the trust assets, cost of comparable services, amount of responsibility, time consumed, skill of the trustee and other relevant factors; or

   (c) fixed by state statute or court rule, usually on the basis of capital or income and capital.

2. A trustee may waive compensation by paying out all net income to beneficiary or making an accounting without asserting the right to compensation.

3. The trustee has a lien on the trust property to the extent of any amount properly due him for services.

4. The court may reduce or deny compensation to a trustee guilty of a breach of trust.

5. The trustee is entitled to indemnity out of the trust property for:

   (a) expenses properly incurred in the administration of the trust;

   (b) expenses not properly incurred in the administration of the trust if such expenses were incurred;

      (i)   conferring a benefit on the trust to the extent of the benefit incurred, or

TRUSTEE'S COMPENSATION AND RIGHT OF INDEMNITY

(ii) where the beneficiary accepts the transaction out of which the expenses are incurred.

See *Liabilities of the Trustee*, above.

6. The trustee is entitled to exoneration for liabilities incurred by him either on contracts or in tort if such liabilities were incurred by him in the proper administration of the trust. See *Powers of the Fiduciary*, number 3, above.

See generally Bogert, pp. 509–517; Clark, pp. 717–721; Dukeminer, pp. 104–109; Rest. §§ 242–249; Ritchie, pp. 1158–1159, 1165–1167; Scoles, pp. 511–513; and Scott, §§ 242–249.

TRACING TRUST FUNDS

1. If a trustee wrongfully disposes of trust property, the beneficiary may trace either the property or its product into the hands of third parties or the trustee and secure its return to the trust.

2. The beneficiary in each instance must elect whether to trace the original trust property or the product. If the product is more valuable than the trust property used in its acquisition, the beneficiary may, by tracing, obtain any profit involved from the disposition.

3. Tracing of trust property or product of wrongful disposition places the beneficiary in a position of priority over general creditors if the trustee is bankrupt or insolvent.

4. In order to trace trust property the beneficiary must be able to identify the trust property, or the product as the product of the disposition of trust property.

5. In making identification of the trust property the beneficiary is entitled to the benefit of certain presumptions:

(a) If the trustee mingles trust property with his own property and exchanges the mingled property for other property the beneficiary may enforce a constructive trust on the property for which it is exchanged proportionate to his share of the mingled fund.

(b) If the trustee mingles trust funds with his own funds in an account or fund, it is presumed that any withdrawals from the fund were of trust moneys proportionate to the total of the fund.

e.g. A is trustee for T of $5,000 which he deposits in his bank account where he has personal funds of $5,000. T withdraws $5,000 and purchases stock which increases in value to $50,000. B is entitled to one-half of the stock as well as one-half of the money remaining in the bank.

6. If the trustee mingles trust funds with his own personal funds, then withdraws and dissipates the withdrawn commingled funds, subsequent additions from his personal funds to the commingled deposit may not be claimed by the beneficiary unless:

(a) the amounts withdrawn were not dissipated and are redeposited, or

(b) the trustee makes subsequent deposits *intending* restitution.

7. In any case where a beneficiary may trace the trust funds or product of wrongful disposition, he may elect instead to enforce an equitable lien upon the product in the hands of the trustee to secure payment of damages for breach of trust.

8. The beneficiary may not enforce a constructive trust against a bona fide purchaser for value who takes without actual or constructive notice of the trust.

See generally Bogert, pp. 509–517; Rest. § 202; and Scott, § 202.

TABLE OF CASES

TABLE OF STATUTES

INDEX

†